THE WORLD

AND

THE BO TREE

THE WORLD

AND

THE BO TREE

HELEN BEVINGTON

Duke University Press   Durham & London

The author's book review of Annie Dillard's
Teaching a Stone to Talk ("Tranquility &
Trembling") originally appeared in *The New York
Times Book Review,* November 28, 1982, © 1982
by The New York Times Company; reprinted by
permission. The poem "Childhood" originally
appeared in the *Kentucky Poetry Review.*
"The Snow Man," from *The Collected Poems of
Wallace Stevens* by Wallace Stevens, © 1923 and
renewed 1951 by Wallace Stevens; reprinted by
permission of Alfred A. Knopf, Inc., and Faber &
Faber Ltd. "Afterthought," from *Notebook, 1967–
1968* by Robert Lowell (New York: Farrar, Straus
& Giroux, 1969), © 1969 by Robert Lowell;
reprinted by permission of Farrar, Straus & Giroux.
© 1991 Duke University Press
Printed in the United States of America
on acid-free paper ∞
Library of Congress Cataloging-in-Publication data
appear on the last printed page of this book.

It is not a chronicle or almanac;
many events turn
up, many others of equal or
greater reality do not.
This is not my diary.
—Robert Lowell, "Afterthought"

But why not say what happened?
—Robert Lowell, "Epilogue"

to Joanne Ferguson,
editor and friend

C O N T E N T S

liam Golding, *Lord of the Flies*   St. Jude oil   The day after
"Encounters"   Journey to Spain

FOREWORD

According to the writer Jan Morris, who has traveled over the world for half her life, there is nothing necessarily commendable in travel. No more, you might say, than there is in staying at home. You don't inevitably gain a better understanding of the world by either pursuit, or a larger vision of world peace. And yet either way there are certain benefits. Each time I leave home I seem to go in search of something—call it a bo tree, or Shangri-La, or earthly paradise— which is only another name for peace itself and these days decidedly a fool's errand. The wonder is that it does turn up in the most unlikely places, visible, say, in Tibet or on the road to Mandalay, in the look of the midnight sun or in the silence of Africa.

This discovery I made lately during the unsteady decade of the 1980s, when an alarming amount of chaos—a threatened world versus a desire for peace—is what you had to expect. In such a world as this where is the place to look? Under a bo tree?

1 9 8 0

"What is this world? What asketh men to have?"—Chaucer

In the *New Yorker* cartoon a couple is sitting before the television screen on New Year's Eve. He says, "You know something? I'm already tired of the eighties." The following week the wife in the cartoon says, "Then what about the *nineties?*"

James Reston writes in the *New York Times:* "Let me fill you in: it is clearly not going to be a Happy New Year"—not with inflation, soaring prices, more unemployment, more crime, the fuel crisis, a presidential election, revolution in Islam, and threat of war with Russia. Reston gives his newborn grandson some advice about becoming a member of the human race: "Stick with the optimists, Niftie; it's going to be tough enough even if they're right."

President Carter says in his State of the Union message: "We must face the world as it is." Edward Teller, father of the hydrogen bomb, predicts war in the Persian Gulf, with Russia's goal world domination: "The Russians are on the march toward the oil spigot. We are facing today the most serious crisis the world has ever faced."

There are the Creationists and there are the Survivalists. The one defines the beginning of the world and the other the end, which is said to be near.

The Creationists, in growing numbers in the South, call it Scientific Creationism, or pro-Creator as opposed to no-Creator. They agree with Dr. John Lightfoot who in 1642 published his observations on Genesis that heaven and earth were created "all together in the same instant" on October 23, 4004 B.C. at 9:00 A.M. The Archbishop of Armagh disputed this claim, said it happened the day before at 6:00 P.M., but at the Scopes trial of 1925 William Jennings Bryan affirmed October 23 to be the right date. The Creationists reject Darwin, seeking to assure schoolchildren God did the entire work in six days and made man in his image. They deny that God resembles an ape.

The Survivalists or Catastrophists build fallout shelters and survival homes, storing food and weapons against the coming of the apocalypse or doomsday. This movement of the 1980s differs from the making of bomb shelters in the 1950s after World War II, when people dug their own little holes in the backyard and furnished them with canned goods and bottled water. Now bands of citizens prepare secret hideouts like fortresses in the mountains, build underground concrete bunkers, and dig foxholes to China. They say we're headed for annihilation, not only from nuclear war but from economic collapse. Any outsiders who beg for admittance will be shot.

Meanwhile, spring returns to North Carolina:
Monday headline: "Time is ripe to fertilize"
Tuesday: Performance-tested Bull Sale
Wednesday: Trellised Tomato Growers Annual Meeting
Thursday: Regional Swine Conference
Friday: Beekeepers Meeting to discuss "Packaged Bees"
Saturday: Weed Control Workshop. Blueberry Council. Potato meeting

When we moved to Durham, N.C., in the 1940s, it was a sociable world with an extraordinary number of club activities: garden clubs, book, travel, dining, bridge, newcomers clubs, League of Women Voters, and the Needlework Guild. Impressed by the happy bustle and stir, I wrote a verse, "Faculty Wife," to say, "She joins a club to read a book . . . "

Presently we have the pick of Overeaters Anonymous, Alcoholics Anonymous (Brown Bag Group), Narcotics Anonymous, Parents Anonymous (who abuse their children), Parents of Gays and Lesbians, Mothers of Twins, Mothers Against Drunk Driving, Abused Wives, Coalition for Battered Women, Women for Sobriety, Women in Action for Prevention of Violence, Parents without Partners, Singles Unlimited, Impotence Support Group, Survivors Group, ToughLove, Mended Hearts Inc., Compassionate Friends of Wake County, La Leche League (breastfeeders), and the Triangle Area Lesbian Feminists.

We moved here from New York, not having been south of Virginia before. On arrival we found the man next door was named Love. Mr. Love quickly presented himself to offer whatever we might be in need of.
"I'm Love," he said, holding out his hand.
"It's love," I said, "we're looking for."
"Yes, ma'am," he said.
Today I read in the paper of the death of Love.

The towhee cries, "Drink your tea-ee!" of a summer afternoon. I've found two other ways to survive the July heat and melancholy hoopla of the Republican convention in Detroit, where the reigning Reagan conducts a crusade to be president and "make America great again." George Bush calls him an aged ham.
    One way is to read Dr. Lewis Thomas, who in *The Lives of a Cell* reminds me I'm lucky to be alive. "Never kiss a buzzsaw," he says, if you want to go on living since by chance you happen to exist:

> Statistically, the probability of any one of us being here is so small that you'd think the mere fact of existing would keep us all in a contented dazzlement of surprise. We are alive against the stupendous odds of genetics, infinitely outnumbered by all the alternates who might, except for luck, be in our places.

It's a pleasure to violate statistical probability. Of a million million spermatozoa, said Aldous Huxley, one of them might have been another Shakespeare, Newton, or John Donne. "But the one was me."
    The other way is to thank God I wasn't Captain Cook's wife.
    Poor lady. She was Elizabeth Batts of Shadwell, wife for seventeen years to one of the greatest navigators and circumnavigators the world has known, Captain James Cook, whom she saw at rare intervals because he was more or less continuously at sea. On his last expedition, when he discovered the Sandwich Islands, 1779, and was murdered by the natives, Captain Cook was fifty-one. Nothing in his well-kept logs

under sail revealed he had a family, a private life, joys or griefs or a longing for home.

They had six children, who in their brief existence hardly saw their father. Mrs. Cook, a dutiful wife, bore them and buried them. Two boys died in infancy, one whom Cook never saw; Elizabeth died age four. Nathaniel at sixteen went down with all hands aboard the frigate *Thunderer* in a hurricane in 1780. Hugh at seventeen died of a fever at Christ's College, Cambridge. A few months later James Jr., commander in the Royal Navy, was drowned.

Boswell mentioned meeting Captain Cook's wife with her husband at dinner at Sir John Pringle's in London: "It was curious to see Cook, a grave steady man and his wife, a decent plump Englishwoman, and think he was preparing to sail around the world." With his loss and the loss of all six children, Mrs. Cook retired at thirty-seven to mourn in Clapham, where she lived in a house full of mementos from his voyages. "I remember her as a handsome and venerable lady," Canon Bennett described her in old age, a sea captain's widow dressed in black satin, wearing a ring with her husband's hair in it. She said she couldn't sleep on stormy nights thinking of men at sea.

When she died at ninety-three, keeping her faculties to the end, she had outlived Captain Cook by fifty-six years. Unaware of his greatness and extraordinary accomplishments, she had destroyed his letters. The truth is she didn't know him very well.

This November the country was thrown into hysteria over having to choose between Reagan and Carter for president, between a second-rate actor turned seventy and a smalltime Georgian found guilty of inconsequentiality. During their one public debate, Carter spoke of his daughter Amy as his consultant on nuclear missiles. Reagan said when he was a boy there was no race problem! The National Council of Teachers of English named Reagan the winner of the Doublespeak Award for deceptive assertions during the campaign. Carter won second prize. Reagan claimed Alaska has more oil than Saudi Arabia. He said he had serious doubts about the theory of evolution. Carter claimed the failure to rescue the American hostages in Iran an "incomplete success."

James Reston wrote: "In the twenty years since 1960 we have had five presidents. Kennedy was murdered. Johnson was destroyed by the

Vietnam War. Nixon was run out of Washington. Ford was rejected in the election of 1976. And now we are savaging Jimmy Carter, who has the lowest popularity rating in the history of the polls, and mocking his potential successor, Ronald Reagan."

Disenchanted or not, the country voted for Reagan, unwilling to endorse Carter who wept when he was told. Losing no time, Reagan came to Washington bringing Nancy and a jar of jelly beans. She said the White House needed instant redecoration and new china. He said he felt humility and humbleness.

I am by habit an end-of-year list-maker, inventory-taker, lover of categories. It's a vain search for order, to itemize the goods on hand, survey one's waning resources.

What extravagance this tidy habit can lead to is revealed by Irving Wallace's *Book of Lists,* a collection of orts and sweepings. He collects the nine breeds of dogs that bite the most, the ten birds that can't fly, the names of people who never went to college, never married, are left-handed, red-haired, one-eyed, have hemorrhoids, syphilis, vasectomies, or snore. He lists the shoe size of twenty famous men (Warren G. Harding, size 14), and the degree of flatulence caused by beans.

My list consists of eight men I admire and the reason why:

Memling for purity of his blues and purples
Vermeer for placidity
Thoreau for simplicity
Chaucer for *gentilesse*
Monet for waterlilies
John Donne for defining love
Wallace Stevens for defining a necessary order
Montaigne for knowing how to live and how to die
    of having been alive

On December 8 John Lennon was shot in New York at the entrance to the Hotel Dakota where he lived. Like the death of Elvis Presley, it shook the world. A policeman said, "It's as important as the death of John F. Kennedy." When Presley died in August 1977, to the wild grief of millions, President Carter said, "He was unique and irreplacable. He burst on the scene with an impact that was unprecedented and will probably never be equalled." Billy Graham said, "I believe I will see him in heaven." The press called him a Culture Hero who made the American dream a reality, Elvis the Pelvis who affected history by changing hair styles, popularizing rock and roll, and, the claim is, bringing on the sex revolution.

Yoko Ono, Lennon's wife, asked for a ten-minute silence around the globe on Sunday "to pray for John's soul."

1 9 8 1

From the Chicago *Sun-Times:* "Had 1980 been a play, most of it would have been a tragedy. 1981 looks even worse." It was a year of failure to keep up with inflation, invasion by Russia of Afghanistan, war between Iran and Iraq, international terrorism, a year when Mount Saint Helens blew up, and revolution erupted in San Salvador.

But what cheer? On January 20 two extraordinary events happened within minutes of each other, when Ronald Reagan was sworn in as our fortieth president "so help me God," and the fifty-two hostages in Iran were freed, ending 444 days of captivity that began when Iranian students raided the U.S. Embassy in Tehran.

It was a melodrama with a cast of fifty-two survivors and Reagan as leading man, an extravaganza out of Hollywood. The inauguration ceremonies began with a gala masterminded by Frank Sinatra, with Marie and Donny Osmond singing "Ronny Be Good," Ben Vereen, a black man, doing the cakewalk in oldtime minstrel blackface. The ten inaugural balls cost a record $15 million, the most expensive blowout in American history, the opposite of the Carters' modesty and restraint. Called putting on the dog.

With the flowering of spring, two months later, came the attempted murder of Ronald Reagan. Young John Hinckley, with the face of a schoolboy, fired six shots outside the Hilton in Washington, one piercing Reagan's left lung an inch from his heart, another all but fatally injuring his press secretary Jim Brady. Badly hurt, fast losing blood, Reagan walked into the hospital and said to his wife, "Honey, I forgot to duck." The country said in horror "Not again?" Hinckley said he did it for love of the actress Jodie Foster, who said "I never met the guy."

Walker Percy, in his novel *The Second Coming,* writes of the demented and farcical times we live in. Here we are, growing nuttier by the hour in North Carolina where everyone, Percy says, is a Christian and finds unbelief unbelievable. Will Barrett of N.C., a widower of fifty-five living a death-in-life, goes into the Lost Cave to await a sign of the existence of God. Putting the matter to the test, he prepares to die from an overdose of sleeping pills if no sign is forthcoming. Instead he gets a fearful toothache, stumbles out of the cave, and falls into a greenhouse where Allie, a young girl escaped from a mental institution, is holed up waiting for answers herself. Naturally they fall in love, a fine pair of loony innocents. What the Second Coming is, for them or for me, Percy must know—he calls it a happy ending.

Modesty in our authors:

Gore Vidal: "I've just finished reading *Henry Esmond* for the first time and much as I like the unfashionable Thackeray I couldn't help but think how much better I do that sort of book than he does."

Truman Capote: "I'm an alcoholic. I'm a drug addict. I'm homosexual. I'm a genius." (Verlaine, announcing himself a while ago on a visit to England: "Paul Verlaine, alcoholic, syphilitic, pederast, and poet.")

Cyril Connolly declaring the books he didn't write were better than the ones other people did.

B. F. Skinner, behaviorist, when asked why he wrote his autobiography: "In order to make people love me."

"I haven't been everywhere, but it's on my list."—Susan Sontag

JOURNEY TO SOUTH AMERICA   Mr. Utley, my yard man, the only yard man I know who owns a Lincoln Continental, drove me to the airport, saying "Are you going by boat?" Inside the terminal a breathless boy rushed up to ask "Is this a hospital?" On the plane the pilot strolled down the aisle to the cockpit, telling the hostess, "You're beautiful in a C bra." Undeterred by these omens, my friends Betty and Ted and I checked our luggage to Rio de Janeiro and flew nonstop to Miami.

The Cranfords, Lois and H. C., who are conducting us to South

America, arrived with twenty Carolinians and a stray couple from Bangladesh—a group of seasoned travelers, most of whom have followed the Cranfords around the world in past years. They know what to expect: the delays, the mishaps, the unquestioned pleasure that outweighs the rest—just as Peter Fleming learned such accommodation in *Brazilian Adventure:* "I learnt the necessity of resignation, the value of resignation, the psychology of resignation, everything except resignation itself."

At Rio's international airport, Betty's luggage was missing. We were driven to the Othon Palace, a thirty-story hotel on the Copacabana. My room has a view of encircling mountains and a store of Brazil nuts beside a refrigerator stocked with mineral water, Brahms beer, Coca Cola, vodka, Scotch, rum, and gin, which since we are told not to drink the water I would like to think the hotel hospitably provides free of charge (this is not the case).

On a lemon-bright day, June at home but December in Brazil, the temperature is 70°. There is no winter in Rio. We three walked on the beach, its curving length lined with an unbroken wall of hotels and four lanes of traffic to cross in one's bikini. We strolled alone except for the pigeons, though why not seagulls you wonder. It's said to be bad manners to drown in front of your hotel, but no swimmers attempted it today in the crashing surf. Nor were the muggers out after us, despite the warnings to beware of thieves who snatch purses, wrench earrings from ears, tear necklaces from throats, and are never caught. Don't drink the water. Don't wear any jewelry. Don't walk alone. They want you to feel right at home.

At dinner Lois introduced us: the Rotarians and their wives on their way to an international meeting in São Paulo, like Dr. Kahn and his wife Buri from Bangladesh; the retired executives; May Babson, a peripatetic widow; Doris Bouse, an art critic. Ted was identified as a distinguished professor of history, Betty as a teacher of music, I as writer-in-residence, a charge I'll have to live down.

Lovely Rio, startlingly lovely. It may be the most gorgeous city in the world, a playground like Honolulu with palm and jacaranda trees, twenty-three beaches, blinding sunshine. The conical rock of Sugar Loaf guards the harbor, but the spectacular mountain is Corcovado, where at the peak an immense Christ the Redeemer stands like a crucifix with arms outspread. In the morning we rode through tropical forest to the top of the mountain and the shrine emerging from mist and cloud. Twice Darwin climbed Corcovado to the summit and concluded, "It is wearisome to be in a fresh rapture at every turn of the road." Elizabeth Bishop found too many waterfalls and nature too gaudy. "Oh tourist," she wrote,

> is this how this country is going to answer you
> and your immodest demands for a different world,
> and a better life?

The long ride into the city brought us nearer the realities, hunger and survival, the inequalities between the rich and the others who live in a squalor of huts. Fear grows of Communist revolution. "Everywhere is hunger," our guide said, "every day is bad news. I mean *bad* news." In downtown Rio were conspicuous signs of American infiltration if not takeover: the Sears and the supermarkets, the posters of Elizabeth Taylor, a bookshop display of *The Power of Positive Thinking* by Norman Vincent Peale, a boy wearing a yellow T-shirt labeled "Harvard Yard." Ted, a Harvard man, laughed. "Doesn't he know it should be crimson?"

After a late dinner of gull's eggs and Brazilian beef at a bistro on the Avenida Rio Branco, we stayed for the floor show that began at midnight. Nearly naked showgirls with a diamond at each nipple swayed down the runway to deafening samba music. But since on their beautiful bodies they wore pantyhose under the diamonded G string, it was clear they weren't bare so much as overdressed. Instead of dancing to the savage Afro-Brazilian rhythms, they posed and postured the night through.

While we waited this morning in the hotel lobby for a flight to São Paulo, someone handed an English newspaper to Dr. Kahn. He stared at the headlines, cried out in horror and turned to his wife. President Zia of Bangladesh was murdered yesterday with seven of his aides in a coup to take over the government. Instantly we were caught up in the tragedy as if it had happened to us. Kahn's face was stricken, in Buri's eyes we saw the stunned grief. President Zia was their close friend as was his murderer. The Kahns' two sons, military aides, might already be dead. Dr. Kahn ran distractedly to the desk pleading for help in sending a cable to Bangladesh, but there all communication was closed with the outside world. The embassy at Brasilia was shut on Sunday. As we boarded the plane, the two in tears accompanied us.

São Paulo looked familiar, another New York or Chicago, a vertical city of skyscrapers and streets like tunnels. Riding downtown along the Pracada Bandeira, I noticed a skyscraper hotel so elegant in brown stone I wondered what millionaire could afford to stay the night. It was the Hilton, our hotel. This time the bar in my room was equipped with champagne. (Sydney Smith: "I hope it can be managed that I shall have soft beds, good dinners, fine linen for the rest of my life.")

The city was invaded by Rotarians, who wore funny hats and badges saying "I speak English." Ted, who had no intention of attending any convention, steered us through the crowds, where again we were cautioned—women must not walk alone, no one is safe in broad daylight. Martha stuffed her passport, money, jewels, and traveler's checks into her bra, which made her look like a caged bird. Thieves work in companies. It's a strange and terrible world where you may live in casual safety inside your hotel yet by stepping to the sidewalk be mugged, even murdered. Yesterday in front of the Hilton a man was slashed with a knife before the thief fled. You may cry "Help! Police!" but no police respond. You must go to police headquarters and wait in line to complain, taking along an interpreter.

On a tour of the fastest growing city on earth we rode from riches to slums and shanty towns. Gasoline is $3.50 a gallon. To have a telephone you pay $1,000 and become a shareholder. "We have everything you have in the States," said the guide, "but Brazil has more. Except for terrorists, inflation, threat of revolution, it is paradise!"

For three days and nights I found life at the Hilton very habit-forming. Dr. Kahn and Buri were comforted by cables their sons were alive in Bangladesh; Zia's murderer had been killed by angry soldiers. Betty's suitcase was permanently lost, obliging her to wear day and night the suit she came in, a disaster she faced with serenity. The women sought H. Stern's for sapphires, amethysts, emeralds, rubies, topazes, since Brazil is the place for gems and H. Stern's the place to buy them. We were told not to wear jewelry but at dinner each night the sparkling dinner rings covered half the finger. (Not mine. I'm no good at buying souvenirs.)

When Eleanor Roosevelt saw the Iguassú Falls of Brazil, she cried out "Poor Niagara." A noon flight took us west to the border of Brazil, Paraguay, and Argentina. At the mightiest waterfall on this planet we settled in at the Hotel das Cataratas, a pink colonial inn of mahogany interiors directly across the road from the falls. The view from my room was so close to them, roar and all, I hardly needed to cross the lawn and walk along forest paths beside the white raging torrents—a series of falls in places fifty feet higher than Niagara and twice as wide. With rainbows. In raincoats and ponchos, deafened by the roar, drenched by mist, we leaned on the railing to stare. "This is it," we said, "the end of the rainbow, the absolute and final wonder."

On our return to the hotel, an emu was stalking about in the grass. "What in God's name is that?" cried May in alarm. "A llama," Ted replied, and she believed him. "Isn't the llama a big bird," she said.

After dinner when someone suggested a journey to Paraguay, a few of us jumped into a car and in complete dark, unable to tell one country from another, crossed the border at the end of Friendship Bridge. In the town of Porte Presidente Posner, lit with shops, we wandered about exchanging smiles with the populace, who spoke Spanish not Portuguese and made heartening gestures of hospitality.

Paraguay is said to be one of the least-known countries in the world, poverty-stricken, so backward as to seem medieval. But we found even a poor border town had its night life. Across the street was a barnlike restaurant whose floor show I admired more than Rio's professional entertainment and gorgeous showgirls. While a couple of men with great amiability sang native songs, two young girls in cotton dresses came out to dance, the prettier one with three tall wine bottles balanced one above the other on top her head. Amazing! For refreshment I was served a quart bottle of beer and sat happy in Paraguay opposite a stray Rotarian whose teetotal wife glared at me.

If São Paulo reminds you of New York, Buenos Aires is Paris, with a gracious air of thinking so. The weather was wintry, women wore fur coats with leather boots accompanied by gentlemen in black overcoats. No skyscrapers hid a view of the spacious city on our way to the Claridge, an old hotel quietly elegant. In my bathroom was a pink telephone. A sign on the door said "No moleste!"

"Buenos Aires is perfectly safe," they assure us. It's hard to imagine the streets filled with howling masses from miserable slums crying "Evita! Evita!" (It's hard in Paris to imagine the French Revolution.) The Peróns were a disaster Argentina would obliterate from memory. But with the inflation rate the highest in the world, the country is reeling. On the streets are scrawled the graffiti, "Viva comunismo," "Castro y cubano," "Yoko y Lennon." They bring to mind Che Guevara, born in Argentina, Castro's chief lieutenant who in 1967 was captured in a terrorist movement in Bolivia and executed. You remember too Jorge Luis Borges, born in Buenos Aires, now at eighty-two the foremost writer of South America, who lives aloof from Argentina's woes:

> This, here, is Buenos Aires. Time which brings
> to men either love or money, now leaves to me
> no more than this withered rose . . .

A happy day. It took us seventy miles north of Buenos Aires on the Argentine pampas to an *estancia*, an Argentine ranch run by gauchos. Across the flat grassy plains where cattle and horses grazed without fences, such distances exist between houses that the cock crows only twice because it hears no answer (like Eliot's cock in the *Waste Land* that crows twice for the same reason, "co co rico co co rico"). We came at last to San Antonio de Areco, a large ranch with barns, cook house, and eight dogs. There handsome Mario, young Ricardo, and three other Argentine cowboys, dressed in tight shirts and baggy pants with knives in their belts, greeted us with "Buen provecho!"—good appetite, may it benefit you—and fed us Argentine beef grilled over an open fire, which we hastily agreed was the best on earth, eaten to the accompaniment of gaucho songs performed by the management. Then the gauchos mounted their horses and in the paddock put on a show of expert horsemanship, tearing hellbent down the stretch past us lined up along the fence.

Darwin loved the gauchos, whom he found extremely courteous: "They looked as if they would cut your throat and make a bow at the same time." W. H. Hudson recalled with longing the gauchos of his youth, lawless, violent, cruel men who loved their freedom "as much as a wild bird." They had no home but as vagrants roamed the pampas, captured with lasso or lariat what food they wanted or what horse they chose among the thousands of wild horses on the plains. But that gaucho and his way of life no longer exist, only in his songs, only in his machismo among vaqueros like Mario who easily won my heart.

An American scientist, Bryan Brady, having made a study of rocks under pressure, predicts that Peru will be wiped out this summer by a devastating earthquake. Brady wouldn't go to Lima on a bet, but we're on our way. From Buenos Aires in a four-hour flight to Lima, we crossed the continent from the Atlantic to the Pacific and made a short stop in Santiago, where I got out and stood squarely on the ground, in Chile for twenty minutes. The ultimate tourist.

Lima was founded in 1515 by the Spanish adventurer Pizarro, who called it the City of the Three Kings. Now a poor town "plundered and bankrupt," with some thirty thousand street vendors and thieves working in bands, it has its grand spectacles—the Gold Museum, the old Spanish palaces, the hand-carved cedar balconies, the monumental squares (one square of eight tall white buildings architecturally identical). In the Gold Museum, our Rotarian, wise-cracking Henry, after studying the hideous mummies among the collection of gold crowns and jewels, asked the guide "And where are the poppies?" He was silenced by a glance of incredulity mixed with scorn. Henry calls the Peruvians Lima beans—less funny than he thinks since lima beans came from Lima.

The shoppers among us went to work to acquire llama rugs, stuffed llamas, and alpaca sweaters. Outside the shops the vendors clung to our sides, pleading their shoddy wares. On this expedition Buri from Bangladesh, seeing my apathy and wanting nothing herself, drew me aside to ask the questions she apparently had saved up for days.

"How old are you?" she began. "How many servants do you have? Do you own a motor car? Who drives it for you? Do you live with your children? No? Why do you live alone in your house? Don't your children love you?"

Buri is homesick after two months away, worried to exhaustion over her sons and her country while obediently she follows at her husband's heels. In this first trip outside Dhaka where she was born, protected till she was married to a stranger she had never before seen, she finds the American woman a baffling puzzle. In her slow English she tried to measure the difference between us.

"You are so free, so—hm—independent. Is it good to be independent? I have nothing at all, you see, only my children. When my husband dies they will look after me. Nobody looks after you. I do not understand. I think you are lonely."

My impression was that, given the choice, Buri would not change places with me. As we entered our hotel, she turned and embraced me. She was plump and pretty with black hair and warm brown skin, diamonds in her ears and gold bracelets on her arms, a richly flowered sari for every day of the week. "I have nothing," she said, shaking her head gently to comfort me. "I have only my children."

At the Lima airport while we waited to board the plane to Cuzco, the announcement came: all flights were canceled. What was wrong, an earthquake in the Andes? Then they told us: a military plane had crashed at Cuzco, effectually closing the airport till the wreckage could be cleared. So we returned to the Hotel Sheridan, not a bad fate compared to the pilot's misadventure, but what to do on Sunday in Lima? The infamous Court of the Inquisition was closed, in case anyone cared to relive the terrors of the Spanish Inquisition, where in Lima's Plaza de Armas thousands of Jews, Muslims, and other heretics were tortured and burned at the stake. Instead, we rode out to the shining Pacific and a pre-Incan ruin called Pachácamac. Once a walled city, after that an Incan temple to the sun, plundered in due time by Pizarro and his conquistadors, it was a pyramid mountain in the sand with dirt terraces leading to a sweeping view of the ocean. At the summit Anita murmured, "Where are the rest rooms?" but I doubt the Incas had them, since they possessed neither the wheel nor the vaulted arch.

Because Lima is at sea level and Cuzco a Peruvian town in the Andes, we climbed two and one-half miles to the Incan world. This invited *soroche* or altitude sickness, and we were urged to move slowly, eat lightly, and do without alcohol, cigarettes, and sex till the body adjusted to being deprived of oxygen. Three of our group succumbed at once with nausea and violent headache. On arrival at the Hotel Picoaga we were served coca tea and told to take a nap. From coca leaves, chewed habitually by the natives like the Incas before them, is derived cocaine, Peru's biggest export. After drinking two steaming cups, I slept so soundly I planned to drink coca tea whenever I could get it. Our Coca Cola, first sold in 1886 as "The Ideal Brain Tonic," had as its principal ingredient the coca leaf.

Cuzco, the capital of the Incas, is a walled city that Pizarro and his men came upon in 1533 and with their cannon quickly conquered. Pizarro was one of a handful of Spaniards who marched with Balboa across the Isthmus of Panama to the Pacific. In Darien he heard rumors of a vast empire in Peru of gold palaces and streets paved with gold, and twenty years later he found in Cuzco the gold palaces of Inca emperors, the gold streets, the gold temple of the sun, and a highly developed Incan civilization. All this Pizarro, a crude, ruthless ex-swineherd, destroyed. He strangled their ruler. He and his 182 conquistadors melted down the gold and enslaved the inhabitants, while the Jesuits came and built churches on the foundations of the Incan temples, turning the temple of the sun into a Dominican monastery.

The Incas claimed divine descent from the sun. It was their god. Each ruler, the son of the sun, married his sister and built a palace that after his death remained staffed with his servants, presided over by his mummy. In death he wore fine garments, had a table of choice meats, and kept a harem of Chosen Women. On one occasion a mummy was married to a former mistress that his son might be declared legitimate.

Cuzco is smaller now, a terracotta city of narrow streets, llamas, and brown-faced Indians, descendants of Incas whose blood is mixed with Spanish. A statue of Christ overlooks the town, the hippie capital of the world, sought for cheap lodging and the available drugs. From 5:00 A.M. each day the marketplace is mobbed, a black market with everything for sale from cocaine to contraband cigarettes.

As if we weren't high enough in altitude, we went this afternoon up the mountain to the ruins of Sacsahuamán, a fortress built of giant stones by the Incas. Buri sat beside me in the bus, holding her head, moaning softly but making no complaint. On the way we passed Indian hovels with their pen of guinea pigs and waved to dirty ragged Indian children leading llamas. The native guinea pigs are prized as food; the llamas are beasts of burden, whose disposition is haughty—a regal llama with banana-shaped ears appears on the Peruvian coat of arms. With a look of perpetual surprise, they will spit a jet of saliva in the face of anyone who annoys them. The wooly alpacas and the vicuñas, valued for their silky fleece, graze high in the Andes. They too have bad manners and will spit in your eye.

As the day wore on, our guide became as captivating as the sights he showed us—a dark Peruvian who said his name was Herbert (for Herbert Hoover). Herbert was born in Cuzco forty years ago and has never been outside Peru, yet he speaks fluent English and knows enough about America, its history and current slang, to have come from there. The only oddity in his pronunciation is that he sounds the *ed* in words like *inspired*. Besides being a tour guide, he teaches history at the University of St. Anthony.

It was constantly entertaining to be with Herbert, to visit the cathedral in the square, the Plaza de Armas where Inca palaces once glistened, where Pizarro erected a scaffold. As we entered the church door the lights promptly went out. In total darkness we were led stumbling among what Herbert described as riches beyond measure. Stopping to astonish us before an immense wall painting of the Last Supper, with soaring voice he pointed out the food and drink on the table, all of it Peruvian. When we complained we couldn't see a thing, he kept going, enraptured by the glories around him. Then the lights came on and we were blinded by the gleaming gold altar, the spangled silver Virgin weighing a ton that will be carried through the streets on Corpus Christi.

That night H. C., who arranges these events, made the mistake of providing a bountiful dinner at El Truco, where we sat listless and wan. When the sixteen steak and four fish dinners we ordered became sixteen fish and four steaks smothered in an aromatic sauce, several guests hurriedly left the table, and in the confusion maybe a couple of waiters were fired.

At 7:00 A.M. we boarded the train for Machu Picchu, a trip of seventy-five miles north to the Lost City of the Incas. For four hours the narrow-gage railway cars proceeded by a frightening series of switchbacks, forward a mile, backward another, straining through formidable snow-capped mountains where landslides are common and passengers must wait till the rocks are removed. Bandits wait for the passengers. [In June 1986 this train was blown up by terrorists, killing seven people.] We made it in record time, while Herbert strolled up and down the aisle playing the kind of reed flute the Incas played by blowing across the top. "My other name is Pan," Herbert said, but Pan was no troubadour who knew "Dixie" and "Old Man River." We rode as far as the train could go, to the jungle gorge of the Urubamba River, where at the Putucusi Bridge several buses waited to take us the harrowing rest of the way. Stepping gingerly into one, I could see a bus halfway up the face of the mountain zigzaging beside the precipices. For the next thirty minutes I held my breath while we climbed, closing my eyes each time we met a bus on a hairpin curve and our driver backed up to the brink to let it pass. No one spoke till the bus stopped to unload us in front of a small hotel at the entrance to Machu Picchu.

I used to think the ruins at Delphi were reserved for my final journey, providing all I wanted to see of ancient ruins and lost worlds. Now the final mystery was at Machu Picchu, the Lost City that Pizarro never found or knew existed. It was lost for four hundred years, not discovered till 1911 by an American, Hiram Bingham, a Yale professor who became governor of Connecticut. When Bingham climbed the sheer rock surface and found the hidden city intact but roofless since the roofs had been thatched, choked as it was by jungle vines, alive with deadly snakes, he was moved to say of the portentous spectacle, "Emotions came thick and fast."

In pictures that never catch its majesty, Machu Picchu appears to lie on a flat plateau with hundreds of stone houses, streets, and terraces. This is far from true. Instead, on the edge of a precipice that plunges headlong to the Urubamba River far below, the city ascends in a series of shelves straight up the mountain. The shelves are connected by terraces, the terraces by steps, three thousand stone steps in all. Paul Theroux said Machu Picchu sprawls across the peak "a vast broken skeleton picked clean by condors," but I think he was carried away or at a loss for a metaphor, like the rest of us wordless and shaken. The sight is paralyzing.

Hiram Bingham believed he knew why the Incas had built this city in the wilderness, piling stone on stone without the use of mortar, at unimaginable cost of manpower. It was, he thought, a sanctuary for the worship of the sun, inhabited by the Virgins of the Sun who in white robes and gold crowns were elected to serve their god, and claimed the sun made love to them. Of the 173 skeletons found in burial caves, 150 of them were women. Here they lived and died in lifelong virginity, and when they were gone the city died too in the fading of the sun.

This is at best conjecture, since the Incas had no written language and left no records. Other explorers say it was more likely a fortress, citadel, or royal residence for Inca rulers, their last refuge. Fifty years after Bingham, Gene Savoy argued that Machu Picchu is not the Lost City but Espíritu Pampa is, deep in the jungle and so far not excavated. Herbert stayed to the tale of the Virgins of the Sun. With him we were up to our ears in Incas.

For hours we clambered over the ruins with him, Herbert the Pied Piper of the Andes, Herbert the mountain goat Pan. To the sweet sound of the Panpipe he led us like a troop of hamadryads from the cliff's edge up the perpendicular heights to the perched temple of the sun, to the huge stone slabs like Stonehenge, the burial caves, the ceremonial field, above that to the sun dial, and at the very top the watchtower. Over our heads loomed two mountain peaks between which Machu Picchu rises on a narrow saddleback. Herbert has climbed one of these peaks to watch the sunrise at the roof of the world where, Prescott wrote, the Incas gathered to greet their god with shouts of joy.

Beyond in the jungle, Herbert said, are Indians who still worship the sun. I didn't ask "Do you worship the sun?" but he would have told me, yes or no. He answered every question, so confident of his knowledge that Ted and I began to tease him by ranging afield, asking farfetched questions, laughing with him when almost unfailingly he had the answer. Three times during the day we increased his fund of information—"What are Hoovervilles?" named for the original Herbert. "Where is Patagonia?" Surprisingly he hadn't heard of it. "According to Ovid, how many reeds were there in Pan's pipe?" Each time he listened astonished, glad to learn for one thing there were seven reeds.

On the irresolute train back to Cuzco, Herbert, weary as we were, only intermittently played his pipe or chased a pretty girl guide in the next car. I sat with H. C. and we talked of our guide's appeal, marveling that a man of his intelligence should willingly undergo a bone-shaking trip to Machu Picchu four times a week. But he appeared to find the place satisfying to his soul. H. C. remarked he had kept for years a list of wholly admirable people he had met in his life, a list with no women in it (H. C. admires all women without qualification). He said he was seriously considering adding Herbert to the list.

On our last day in South America, we returned to Lima. And what had been apparent before was the same paradox of a city whose elegance is bygone, whose slums are the worst in the continent, whose luxury hotels are the finest. We were grand once more at the Gran Hotel Bolívar on the Plaza San Martín, near a theater where John Travolta in "Urban Cowboy" was flashily advertised as "macho."

Outside in the street in late afternoon, Doris and I found ourselves caught in a different world that scared us. Our intention was to slip out and visit the Cathedral where the skeletal remains of Pizarro are displayed under glass (possibly not the real Pizarro but an imposter, though he was buried in there somewhere after being murdered by his men). Equipped with a sketchy map drawn by the doorman, we immediately got lost.

"Let's take a cab," Doris said, hailing the first one that came along, a beat-up ruin with ragged upholstery whose driver knew no English but nodded his head at the three words at our command, *iglesia, catedral, Pizarro.* Soon we were stalled in heavy traffic circling the Plaza San Martín, which for the next half hour we continued to circle before I said to Doris, "I don't think he got the message." I leaned over and tapped him on the shoulder, and when he looked around I made the sign of the cross. "Pizarro!" I cried in his ear. That did it. Without a word he drew over to the curb, opened the door, and in a kind of paroxysm motioned us out of his cab, refusing to take a single centavo.

On our own we started to hike the eight long blocks to the cathedral, stopping to ask the way of each traffic cop we saw. He would study our map and, apparently not having heard of a church with Pizarro in it, would point in the opposite direction to the one we were taking. When we reached the Plaza de Armas, it was six o'clock and the cathedral was closed. Suddenly in the huge square things began to happen. At the president's palace, on the site of Pizarro's palace where he was slain, a mob had collected at the gate and were pounding and clamoring, making a noisy demonstration. In no time the smartly dressed military police gathered in watchful groups dotted round the square, beside the archbishop's palace and on the cathedral steps. One of them motioned to us to leave.

"I think a revolution is about to start," I said.

"Maybe it's only an uprising," Doris said. "Let's get out of here."

We ran across the square and darted single file through the narrow streets that by now were crowded with excited people shoving and pushing. Among them were more military police, several to a block, moving as if ready to handle trouble. Was this an ordinary evening in Lima? Were the people subjected every night to surveillance by the military? We ran faster, weaving in and out through the crowds, shouted at several times but not stopped.

At the hotel, breathless and panting, we got no information from the doorman. "Street vendors," said the desk clerk with a conciliatory smile. "The police try to chase them off the streets." But that wasn't the way it was at all.

"It was trouble," we told our friends at dinner. "And we were in it."

[Less than two months later a string of bombings occurred in downtown Lima, with threats of more violence by a terrorist group known as Shining Path, formed in 1980.]

The farewell party was at the Carlin on Avenue La Paz in the Miraflores district beside the Pacific. We toasted each other in Pisco sours, made of a Peruvian grape liqueur, lemon juice, sugar, egg whites, cinnamon on top. You could become addicted in no time to Pisco sours in Lima, and to the good life as well—that is, if you could find it and afford it.

I brought home no souvenirs of the journey except these passing moments—no stuffed llama, no maté gourd for sucking bitter yerba tea through a bombilla as the gauchos do. On the plane to Miami I wrote in my notebook, "I like guided tours, staying in comfortable hotels, going first class (since I can't change the world by wearing a sarape and carrying a backpack). I like eating well, having arrangements made for me, being personally conducted. I like tourists, who are people looking for pleasure, peace, postcards, even enlightenment and a better world, who will take a journey however circuitous to affirm the majesty of Machu Picchu or count the cats in Zanzibar. Tourists are investigators who make a temporary invasion and buy the souvenirs. They seldom offend, at least on purpose."

Especially I liked this tour and its friendly participants, among whom there were few complaints and no catastrophes. One or two disliked Brazilian coffee, called Argentine beef tough, objected to brushing their teeth in carbonated mineral water, caught colds, and ran out of film. But they didn't fume about it. I'd go to the top of the world with them any day. As we parted I was sorry to give up for the time being what I love to do—set out with travelers like these, neither spies nor missionaries, the wandering kind. Somebody has to bring back word of the sights and wonders. Somebody has to count the cats.

Across the aisle on the plane to Miami a small fretful baby cried all night.

There have been other years different from this one—and at home in the August heat I'm reminded of them—when B. and I went only to England, usually on sabbatical leave. I think of those cool rainy days in Hampstead where we lived just off the Heath and there wasn't a day I didn't walk on the Heath or lie in the grass and stare at the sky, weather permitting. As a result I fell in love with Constable and Turner—Constable who lived in Hampstead and painted the landscape of the Heath, the trees, woodland paths, glints of water from the Vale of

Health, especially the sky piled with turbulent clouds that sooner or later would open and drench me with rain. (Ruskin: "If you want to feel as if you were in a shower, cannot you go and get wet without help from Constable?")

"I have done a good deal of skying," Constable wrote in 1821 of his studies of cloud effects in the Hampstead sky—scudding clouds, black, gathering, hovering, scattering, windblown clouds and thunderheads. No one ever painted clouds so well. The older he grew the more he preferred tempestuous skies full of rain, till one critic wore a raincoat and raised his umbrella at an exhibition of Constable's paintings. After his wife's death in 1828, he wrote, "Every gleam of sunshine is blighted to me. . . . Can it therefore be wondered at that I paint continual storms?"

Occasionally Constable let a streak of sunshine steal through, but he never depicted the sun itself as Turner did. In a London winter when one needed reminders of the sun, I went to the Tate and blinded myself with Turner's sky. Constable, his contemporary, said Turner had golden visions. At first he was devoted to yellow mists and haze (*The Sun rising through Vapour, The Sun rising in a Mist*), obsessed by sunrises and sunsets that steamed a little. Then he took on the naked sun like a flame that lighted the world. "He must paint the sun in its strength," said Ruskin, "*not* rising above it." To Ruskin, who thought Constable honest but unteachable, Turner was the greatest man of the age, who caught the sublimity of the sun and made us gaze into it. He liked to stand next to a Turner in the Academy listening to dazed spectators: "I declare I can't look at it!" "Don't it hurt your eyes?" As he died, Turner is supposed to have said "The sun is God."

Thackeray likened the golden works to "huge slimy poached eggs."

In Hampstead, too, it was a dose of serenity to walk across the Heath to Ken Wood and look at the Vermeer. Kenwood House, built for the Earl of Mansfield, is a mansion designed by Adam about 1769 where one is free to step inside and gaze at the pictures, a Frans Hals or a self-portrait of Rembrandt as an old man in a white cap.

The Vermeer is over the grand piano in the drawing room, the *Girl with a Guitar*, wearing a string of pearls and yellow silk gown trimmed in ermine, her brown hair in ringlets. She looks familiar like the others—the girl with a flute or the girl playing a lute, the woman standing at the virginals or sitting at a spinet, the woman pouring milk, the woman in blue reading a letter or in yellow writing a letter, the woman putting on pearls or one weighing gold, the girl with a water jug, the girl in a red hat, the girl asleep at a table—all persons of Delft, young and reposeful with an inner peace, two of them pregnant. The room is the same room, presumably in Vermeer's house in the marketplace, where sunlight streams through an open window. Often they wear the same dress, same string of pearls, a figure standing or sitting alone, a placid Dutch housewife or maiden unperplexed, sheltered in a world where nothing untoward happens.

It is easy to love Vermeer of Delft, who thought well of women and had daughters.

The Snow Man

One must have a mind of winter
To regard the frost and the boughs
Of the pinetrees crusted with snow;

And have been cold a long time
To behold the junipers shagged with ice,
The spruces rough in the distant glitter

Of the January sun; and not to think
Of any misery in the sound of the wind,
In the sound of a few leaves,

Which is the sound of the land
Full of the same wind
That is blowing in the same bare place

For the listener, who listens in the snow,
And, nothing himself, beholds
Nothing that is not there, and the nothing that is.
—Wallace Stevens

It is accommodation one needs. To survive a wintry world one must have the mind of a snow man, a winter mind and a winter heart. One must have been cold for a long time, have grown accustomed to cold (the older one grows) and adapted oneself to it to take pleasure in beauty that is unaware, indifferent to man's desires—the beauty of icy junipers, the spruces glittering in the January sun.

It is a matter of self-preservation *not* to interpret the scene in terms of human misery, *not* to hear loneliness in the sound of the winter wind that is the same sound over the world; *not* to feel self-pity when winter comes. A final adjustment to life is to face the cold alone, ask no more when there is no more, reduce the ego to become nothing oneself—a snow man—imagining nothing that is not there, seeing, hearing, accepting *the nothing that is.*

1 9 8 2

For 1982 the gods predict a cold and stormy winter ahead. Life will be unaffordable: unemployment up, yacht sales down. Harvard will hold a conference on the decline of the presidency.

I could become a Taoist, like Lao-tzu, the Chinese philosopher whose mother carried him in her womb sixty-two years and he emerged white-haired, benevolent, and wise. Cyril Connolly wrote, "Taoists believe that devotion to anything but nature ages them and therefore they live simply on hillsides or near forests."

Resolutions for a private world (a sea of don'ts):

1. Never say "Have a nice day." Someone may be on his way to a hanging. Better say like Poo-Bah "Long life to you."
2. Never report last night's dream (unless it's irresistible. Last night I dreamed I was reading "Ash Wednesday" to T. S. Eliot. And he said, "I am not worthy").
3. Never use forced images and mixed metaphors (Shirley Hazzard in *The Transit of Venus:* "There was the glacial flow of Tertia's moiré on the carpet as she sailed away from her mother, a pinnace from the flagship").
4. Never use a triple negative (George Will: "not unmeaningless").
5. Never forget the Peter Principle, "Quit while you're behind."
6. Never clean a window with a soft-boiled egg (from *Dictionary of Catch Phrases*). Or let pigs eat the geraniums.

On March 22 a redbird, the cardinal, like a red flame launched itself from the roof of my car, while another bird, the shuttle, flew enveloped in flame into outer space. Before liftoff at Cape Canaveral, a seagull swooped down to inspect the strange bird poised for flight. It ascended, leaving us stunned by its beauty, and a week later flew back to land on the sands of the Mohave desert. "How about that?" said a bystander. "They make it look so easy."

Spring intelligence:
A lady interviewed on television says she has lost her rocker. She means she has lost her marbles and a few tailfeathers.
At Mt. Herman Baptist Church the sermon topic is, "Do Heart Transplants Pose Theological Problems?"
Sign in supermarket: "If you can't find what you want, ask the perishable manager."

Jonathan Schell has written *The Fate of the Earth,* a lucid, blood-freezing argument that nuclear war means annihilation of the human race, not only ourselves but generations yet unborn, the wiping out of the species. The world will be destroyed by its inhabitants—the only species ever to destroy itself—and it's unlikely we can stop it: "We the human race will cease to be."

Leo Szillard, one of the physicists who created the nuclear bomb in New Mexico in 1945, told a colleague he was going to write down the facts, not for publication, "just for the information of God." When a colleague said God might know the facts, Szillard replied, "not *this* version of the facts." Unable to reach God's ear, he published *His Version of the Facts.* It is not optimistic: "What the existence of these bombs will mean we all know."

Remember, say the fundamentalists, we *told* you the world is coming to an end. A nuclear war represents the fulfillment of the Book of Revelation, the war willed by God against Satan and forecast by the prophets. August 11, 1988 is confidently given as the date of Armageddon.

Endgame

If all things were to vanish from the earth
Or from my life (a likelier disaster)
Not to return, how greatly would I care?

What would I wish, once mine, were mine again?
A countryside, a book and a love affair.

Archibald MacLeish died the other day at eighty-nine. I remember him with particular clarity because he was the first poet I heard read his poems aloud. He came one evening to the President's House at New York University, and in the intimacy of the small drawing room hypnotized us by his vibrant voice and piercing eyes, glints of light penetrating my own. That's what I was—hypnotized; I didn't hear a word he said. It sounded like poetry, the song of lutes and angels. I haven't trusted a poetry reading since.

Years later in my course in modern poetry, I singled out his poem "Ars Poetica" because it recalled that extraordinary evening. "A poem should not mean / But be," MacLeish said flatly. In imitation of Horace's *Ars Poetica* he gave his definition of the art of poetry: a poem should be mute, dumb, silent, motionless in time, "A poem should be wordless / As the flight of birds." It should exist as a Miró or Paul Klee exists on the wall, unidentified, perceived rather than understood, not necessarily saying or meaning anything.

I passionately disagreed with such a definition, still do. I asked myself, why shouldn't a poem, which consists entirely of words, *both* mean and be? When T. S. Eliot was urged to explain his poetry he replied with an evasion, "It means whatever it means to you," but he did say *means*. MacLeish's poem contained a lot of meaning. How else could I disagree with it?

James Reston, my best source of summation and prophecy, warns the Class of 1982, "So everything is in peril, but so far nothing has collapsed." The *consistency* of the times is uncanny. All things agree with the state of the world, even the weather that becomes spectacularly worse, a wrath of storms with tornadoes in Oklahoma, blizzards in May. A professor of geophysical science at the University of Chicago advises people to wear football helmets in the home. While in Chicago this month, I saw on Wabash Avenue a sign over an entertainment hall, "Nude fashion show on stage, complete nudity." And I thought, it has come to this—a fashion show without clothes. A sign nearby said, "*Live* nude dancers," as if dead ones are what you've come to expect.

Flight

The coast is clear. "Fair weather along the coast
Till maybe Tuesday," says the weatherman
(Thunder over Kansas, squalls in Arkansas,
Whirlwinds in Wyoming, floods in Idaho)
In whom we trust for his unclouded vision
Of present clarities in Carolina—
A crystal gazer, warning me to make
My getaway before, say, Tuesday.
The coast is clear. *Now to escape the storm.*

These years of living by myself have taught me the luxury of fear, an extravagance I can't afford. The world and one's father may be to blame, but some fears can be unlearned, or the number reduced by counting over the things one doesn't actually quail at—lippitude, for instance. Pliny spoke of the fear of lippitude, a state of being bleary-eyed. He said Mucianus, a Roman consul, carried a living fly in a white linen bag as a way to ward off lippitude.

W. H. Auden, my grandmother Smith, and I share a fear of spiders, unlike E. B. White who calls them Charlotte and basks in their company. In New Zealand they told me of an eight-inch poisonous native spider that spins a web large enough to catch birds. Its cone-shaped web was formerly used by the Maoris as a cap to smother widows when their husbands died. I walked right into such a cap on exhibit in the Auckland Museum. In terror I turned and ran.

But of honeybees? No fear. When Pindar was young in Thebes, a swarm of honeybees settled on his mouth and left their honey behind (the same tale is told of Plato in his cradle, Saint Ambrose, Saint Isidore, and Chrysostom who was John of the Golden Mouth). Pindar had a honeytongue, whether he played his flute or spoke his poems—paeans and dithyrambs straight from the honeybees.

Boredom, though, is a thing to fear if one lives alone. It can lead to numbness and panic at the lethargy of life. Luckily I'm not easily bored except by Tiffany lamps and Meissen china, fussiness and figurines. A boring sight is Monet's haystacks—thirty pictures of a squat, shapeless haystack in the middle of a field (D. H. Lawrence in "Love among the Haystacks" found them a handy place for making love). A friendly farmer left Monet a haystack near his house at Giverny so that he could study it sunlit or rained on, then label it "Haystack (mid May) 1890." In the end it was not a waterlily pond or the Rouen Cathedral, just a haystack.

Tears are another luxury I can do without, or with fewer than Niobe all tears. In his autobiography, *The Other Half,* Kenneth Clark confessed he couldn't cure himself of a good cry. "I am very prone to tears," he wrote, "and cannot read my favourite poems, even to myself, without weeping." While giving a talk one night on some designs for Diaghilev's theatrical settings, he broke into loud irrepressible sobs and disrupted the meeting.

Katherine Mansfield wrote of sitting one day on a park bench in Leicester Square and crying into her black velvet muff. An old woman watched her for a while, then sighed and said, "Well, that's 'ow it is, my dear."

"As for me," said Thurber, "I don't even weep for Adonais."

There is, of course, courage, the thing itself. Once at the London Zoo I saw an English sparrow making itself at home inside a lion's cage. The lion, pent up and snarling, paced back and forth lashing his tail, while the busy sparrow picked about, deaf to the bellowing overhead, indifferent to being eaten or stepped on. I thought, "What courage! What a lionheart!"

Günter Grass, *From the Diary of a Snail:* "I do not give demonstrations of courage." Not in these days.

> Formerly
>
> In those days I had fewer head colds
> And no nostalgia. I knew
> Nothing of fear before the age of three,
> Because in those days people worried less
> Or didn't let on. And the world
> Was full of buttercups.
> Believe me in those days I liked it better.

One of John Gardner's modern fairy tales, "The Griffin and the Philosopher," tells how to be philosophic, no matter what. A solution to a perplexing problem is not to recognize it is a problem, therefore ignoring it. When the king asks the wise old philosopher how to rid the kingdom of a troublesome griffin, the philosopher assumes that not he nor anyone else knows how to get rid of a griffin.

"What griffin?" asks the philosopher.

In a recent review in the *Times Literary Supplement:* "Philosophical problems are often difficult because they are unclear. Part of the problem is, 'What is the problem?'"

Another lesson appears in Gardner's "Gudgkin the Thistle Girl," a Cinderella story of Little Gudge, who pricks her fingers to the bone gathering thistles for her wicked stepmother. With the help of a fairy godmother, Gudgkin manages to meet her quota of 2 × 88 sacks of thistles, wins the prince at the royal ball, and sees her stepmother thrown into a dungeon, which ought to wind up the plot. But Gudgkin has emotional problems. She has never before felt sorry for herself. Now that she has got everything, she says, "I pity all of us in this miserable world."

The prince tells her, "My advice to you is to make the best of it."

"Oh, very well," says Gudgkin. "It's no worse than the thistles."

The wife of Socrates is credited with making a philosopher of him. Xenophon in the *Memorabilia* deplores her peevish temper. Some think Socrates knew Xantippe's impertinence before he married her and took her for wife to try his patience and teach him philosophy. He didn't tame his shrew but stayed clear by walking the streets of Athens exhorting the populace to virtue ("To want nothing is divine").

Saint Jerome, who wrote that a wise man should not marry, tells how one day Xantippe, shouting reproaches from an upper story, emptied a chamber pot on Socrates' head. The drenched philosopher wiping his brow observed, "After thunder there generally falls rain."

In his life story *Speak, Memory,* Nabokov says the true purpose of autobiography is to follow through the thematic designs of one's life. The patterns exist, not consciously appearing till memory speaks and you root them out. They repeat themselves as if life were purposive and consistent, when only oneself is consistent, responding predictably to the vagaries of existence.

Autobiography is—has to be—tellable. Auden for one denounced it as "always superfluous and usually in bad taste," but he forgot that one man's life is everyman's. B. Franklin said autobiography is the nearest we can come to living a second time. Offhand I think of several patterns that persist in my life. One is the theme of my disappearing father, who abandoned my mother and me when I was two and emerged no hero in the tales she told—a scamp and a ladykiller. In a sense I was never his child. The few times we met he was almost a stranger, married to another woman, father of another child. Yet when I reached the point of asking who I was, it was Charley I resembled and belonged to, Charley Smith's girl.

Another design revealed itself at nineteen when I graduated from the University of Chicago and looked around for a future that failed to beckon. In some doubt I asked of the gods three gifts, so far unattainable: a man to love, a journey to take, work to do. (William Blake: "Honour and genius is all I ask, / And I ask the gods no more.") When they were graciously granted within a year and a day, I hastened to make the same three wishes again, and again, and again—love, travel, work. I hadn't imagined they would last a lifetime or nearly. By now the consenting gods must be bored with the monotony, always the same plea "One more time," and nothing in it for them. Maybe I haven't been humble enough in my beseeching. Or they are with reason jealous.

There was the design of reading, dependence on books. I became a confirmed reader aged four when I taught myself. After Charley left and my mother supported us by teaching music in the village school, she had no time to read to me. One winter's day on the Electric Light Pond where I was learning to skate, a neighbor boy, Harold Shafer, promised me a funny paper from his vast collection for every time I fell down, an offer that spurred me to hurl about and sprawl flat on the ice all afternoon. By his count of headers and backflops I fell down fifty times and he paid up. I started to read the adventures of Happy Hooligan, the Yellow Kid, Buster Brown and his dog Tige, Foxy Grandpa, Little Nemo, the Katzenjammer Kids. At five I signed up with the Worcester Public Library, and learned to skate. I still read the funny papers.

I became a writer at eleven when I entered high school and kept a secret diary with entries as cryptic as Pepys's. The reason for the squiggles (if, say, a boy kissed me in the hall) was to outwit my mother, who made a habit of looking for hidden rebellion if not proof of incipient immorality. In my desk drawer she had unearthed a small cache of pictures of movie stars cut from magazines. Each showed a couple embracing or gazing into the other's eyes. My mother was incensed. Before burning them in the stove, she said in despair, "You are exactly like your father."

Life changed its surfaces but the patterns remained. One way or another my life produced a single plot, even a symmetry. The design of *A Book and a Love Affair* reflected the main theme, the struggle to acquire a man and live happy ever after. Unlike my mother, whose upbringing had taught her rectitude and prejudiced her against men, whom she was inclined to call mashers and moral lepers, I've loved them all my life. In books they see the funny side—like Sydney Smith— and talk honestly about themselves—like Montaigne. Montaigne too believed we must find our nature and follow it. Sydney Smith believed the laughter must be kept.

I also collect proverbs.

On June 30 the Equal Rights Amendment died. For ten years the contest lasted, till thirty-five of the thirty-eight states needed to ratify it had voted to, of which North Carolina (with Florida and Nevada) wasn't even close. "Stop ERA!" we shouted. An agitated state legislator spoke of fighting in World War II, "and God knows I didn't want any woman marching along beside me!" "Our grand old flag is going down the drain," said another. "I'm trying to save women from their fool friends and from themselves," said our Senator Sam Ervin. For the first time since the so-called War of the Northern Invasion, North Carolina was a battlefield. Did we think God made a mistake creating *two* sexes? ERA would break up the family, harm old women and little children, legalize homosexual marriage, make women subject to the draft. "Women already have more rights than they can handle." Pass ERA? When elephants fly.

It's a simple twenty-four word declaration: "Equality of rights under the law shall not be denied or abridged by the United States or by any state on account of sex."

Rosalynn Carter and Betty Ford as reckless First Ladies campaigned for the end of discrimination. Nancy Reagan said nothing, gazing up at Ronny who was immovably opposed to the amendment. Whether the cause is just, on July 16 a women's band in Raleigh will perform feminist tunes, proclaiming "I am strong. I am invincible. I am woman!"

(Newspaper headline: "President Makes Vows to Women." Contrary to what they may have heard, Reagan told an audience of Republican women, "I am a ladies' man.")

Not many people, it's safe to say, care to look a weasel in the eye. Or sit in an Ecuadorian jungle on the banks of the Napo River idly studying a tarantula the size of one's hand as it seizes moths. Or stroke a giant tortoise's neck in the Galápagos Islands, with a sea lion settling to sleep on one's arm. It's a treat to watch Annie Dillard doing so, especially if you have read *Pilgrim at Tinker Creek* and know her capacity for living, as she says, "in tranquility and trembling" among the wonders and terrors of the world. Tinker Creek, in a valley of Virginia's Blue Ridge Mountains, is where she lives not only a pilgrim but, as Thoreau was, a preacher. She preaches Thoreau's doctrine, "Do what you love," and like him takes pains to clarify how it's done. A weasel lives the way he's meant to, and the principle is the same for all, though it would take both curiosity and clear thinking to live as Annie Dillard does. She makes it sound like a profitable enterprise.

The title of her book *Teaching a Stone to Talk* explains something of her method. A man she knows, living alone in his shack on the West Coast, keeps a palm-sized oval beach cobble on his shelf and performs a ritual several times a day to try to teach it to talk, which she thinks beats selling shoes. She doesn't know what he expects the stone to say— maybe a single word like "uncle." For her what it speaks is silence, nature's silence, which we're on this earth to witness. "That is why I take walks: to keep an eye on things. And that is why I went to the Galápagos Islands." She went to look closely at the palo santo trees, holy trees—silent, lifeless, covered with lichen. She went to Barter Island inside the Arctic Circle, where all she saw was colorless sky and a mess of frozen ice. And she goes back in memory to a farm where she lived at one time alone, where the silence was heaped in the pastures, on the fields, where there was only silence, and it "gathered and struck me. It bashed me broadside from the heavens above." She has a taste for cosmic silence. She likes to look through binoculars at mirages, confirming them for what they are, illusory. Since we're on the planet only once, she says, we might as well get a feel for the place.

The taking of these expeditions, which is Annie Dillard's lifework, has its perils. Once she was present at a total eclipse of the sun and lived to tell the tale. Early one February morning, she and her husband drove to a hilltop in the state of Washington near Yakima to watch the miracle. Many were about, bundled up in caps and parkas. "It looked as though we were scattered on hilltops at dawn to sacrifice virgins, make rain, set stone stelae in a ring." Then the light went out, and from the hills on all sides came screams. She prays that she, that you and I, may never see anything more awful in the sky. It was a near thing, as if people had died on the hilltops of Yakima and were alone in eternity. Afterward the two of them rushed down the hill and escaped to a breakfast of fried eggs.

One memory is of her encounter with Santa Claus, when on a Christmas Eve in childhood she heard a commotion at the front door and there in full fig he stood ringing a bell, whom she had no ambition to meet. She thought Santa Claus was God and ran for her life upstairs, refusing to come down. It was just a well-intentioned old lady who meant no harm. But Annie Dillard ran that night out of fear, and she is running still. "Why do we people in churches seem like cheerful, brainless tourists on a package tour of the Absolute?" she asks. We should be wearing crash helmets and life preservers. In the Catholic church she now attends is a singing group equipped with guitars and tambourines that calls itself "Wild Flowers." After a fiercely anti-Catholic upbringing, she attends mass to escape Protestant guitars, and this is what happens. No silence here. She listens and laughs all the way home. God being almighty can stifle his laughter.

So it goes at Tinker Creek and elsewhere on the globe. She is a wayfarer alert to the shrines and holy places after carefully selecting them for herself. She lights out for other landscapes or she stays at home thriving and surviving, no more scared than anybody. "I have not been lonely yet," she says, "but it could come at any time."

P. G. Wodehouse: "We shall soon be having Christmas at our throats." Duke is holding a series of workshop classes on "Unhappy Holidays, or Coping with Seasonal Stress," the idea being most of us find unendurable one more go at holly wreaths and jingle bells. The workshop studies ways to survive the holiday, offering support instead of tidings of joy. You pay a fee for the course but receive no academic credit.

While making a sound test before his radio address, Reagan thought his microphone wasn't connected. He began his speech, "My fellow Americans, I've talked to you on a number of occasions about the problems our nation faces." He paused. "And I am prepared to tell you it's a hell of a mess!"

During this bloody year there was war and rumor of war in the Middle East, San Salvador, Nicaragua, Iraq at war with Iran, Russia with Afghanistan. Prime Minister Thatcher joined the club by sending a fleet halfway round the world to the tiny Falkland Islands that were invaded by Argentina. A 74-day war resulted over a crown colony with a population of two thousand. The English sank the Argentine battleship *Belgrano* with several hundred men aboard, the Argentines sank the destroyer *Sheffield*. And the number they killed added up to more than the number they fought for. "We had to stick to a principle," said the Iron Lady. She didn't say what the principle was.

1 9 8 3

G. K. Chesterton's Father Brown: "If ever I murdered someone, it might well be an optimist." As they say, in one year and out another.

The Man of the Year on the cover of *Time* is not a man, it's a computer. Said to be more significant than a human being, it is identified with the home like television and microwave ovens—the computerization of America. "One of the things I have always disliked about computers," says Lewis Thomas, "is that they are personally humiliating, unable to function as badly as the human mind." Well, now. Computers have computer bugs that make monumental errors, screwing up the postal service, banking system, airlines, the Pentagon, and the Internal Revenue Service.

Headline in the *New York Times,* January 22: "Soup Lines for the Down and Out in Paris." For the first time since the Great Depression of fifty years ago, the Salvation Army in Paris is handing out free bowls of vegetable soup.

Elsewhere in the paper a tempting full-page spread on high-class, nourishing soups recommends the Oyster Bar at Grand Central Terminal, where a bowl of delicious oyster stew made with real cream costs only $6.75. Customers who can afford it order two bowls. I'm haunted by Thoreau, who spent 27¢ a week for food at Walden.

Four years ago Merv Griffin invited to his talk show a group of over-80s to report on "What are the pleasures of old age?" Four were actors glad to perform the star role of survivor—Pat O'Brien, Estelle Winwood,

William Demarest, Gracie Fields. One was a writer, Robert Nathan, whom Griffin greeted with "So you're 95!" Nathan happened to be 85 but took no offense. I missed Lillian Gish and George Burns, who may have sent their regrets.

Not one was senile, tuckered out, or peevish. Not one railed at old age or regretted the self's decay. Pat O'Brien declared "I've always been ageless." Estelle Winwood said, "Well, my dear, I don't do anything except play bridge every night and smoke three packs a day." William Demarest observed, "Women, they live forever, they've got nothing to worry about," and stared admiringly at Gracie Fields in a pantsuit. The writer, Robert Nathan, alone pondered the state of the world. Aside from the fact, he said, that our music is nothing but noise, painting hasn't grown beyond the Impressionists, there are no poets and no world leaders, life goes steadily on. "If there are any great men today, I haven't met them."

This month Estelle Winwood, a longstayer born when Chester A. Arthur was president and Victoria was queen, turned 100. She still wears lipstick, drinks sherry, plays bridge every night, and smokes three packs a day. When asked what she wanted for her birthday, she looked thoughtful and said, "I'd like something wonderful to happen."

I asked the CPA who makes out my income tax if there was any advantage in growing old. "None whatever," he said. "They sock it to you till you die."

Old-age retirement villages are called "glorified playpens."

Take heart. Grandma Moses was my age when she began to paint. "If I didn't start painting, I would have raised chickens," she said.

Donald Frame, a Columbia University professor who is the biographer of Montaigne, is here as a fellow at the National Humanities Center. He is the man who long ago taught me Montaigne's "scandalous serenity," and has become my friend as Montaigne is my friend, though Frame is four centuries younger. After fifty years of studying Montaigne, he shows the beneficent effect. At a recent talk he gave at the center on Montaigne's sense of absurdity, Frame's own sense of it was apparent in the way he fumbled his scattered papers, lost his notes, scratched his ears, let his glasses slide off his nose, captured and put them on crooked, smiled at his awkwardness, all the while listing the ways Montaigne found man a ludicrous figure and never ceased to recognize his absurdity in being a man.

We are absurd, Montaigne said, in our mortality, the brevity of our striving ("the goal of our career is death"). We are absurd in the inconsistency of our actions, contradictory in all things. Absurd in our incapacity to gain true knowledge, not knowing what knowledge is. Absurd in the difference between our aspirations and our accomplishments ("What of it? We are all wind").

This genial recognition, unlike a tragic view of life, led Montaigne to accept himself for the man he was—and the way men are. Unless he saw himself as the fool of the farce, the most vulnerable and frail of creatures, he would fall into vanity and self-reproach. "I seldom repent," he said, "and my conscience is content with itself."

Even a king on the highest throne, Frame ended, quoting Montaigne, must sit on his behind.

JOURNEY TO SICILY Goethe said, "Sicily is the clue to everything." He made this extraordinary remark on a tour of the island in 1787, two hundred years ago, and never really spelled out his meaning as to what the clue might be or what Goethe at thirty-seven would call everything. I can't believe he, or anyone else, would say it now.

On the other hand, Goethe's words gave me added excuse for going to Sicily this spring. He too was a tourist, but a truculent tourist who was offended in Palermo when his guide tried to explain the history of Sicily's glorious past. Goethe angrily rebuked him for ruining the sights with his "erudition" and walked haughtily away, turning his thoughts to the *Odyssey* and a drama about Nausicaa he meant to write.

I'm just as glad Goethe wasn't on our tour. Or Lawrence Durrell, either, who recently circled Sicily in a red bus with an assortment of tourists and wrote a book, *Sicilian Carousel,* in which he observed among other things that Americans are a "soft, pulpy and dozed people." We were Americans on my Sicilian journey, and I suppose acted the way Americans do, wanting orange juice for breakfast as opposed to the English who want marmalade. Durrell tolerated his fellow Englishmen but took exception to the aggrieved French who, he said, won first prize for bad manners and bad temper in moments of crisis. Like Goethe, he may have been on the lookout for a clue, though he seemed too busy setting down his impressions to notice if one exploded on the horizon, absorbed in his notebook the way a man studies his navel.

Mount Etna had been erupting for the last six weeks and the Mafia was fighting another heroin war when on May 21 Betty, Ted, and I joined a tour sponsored by Alitalia bound for Sicily. To distinguish ours from the stream of flights on TWA or Pan Am, this one was identified as "Heart and Soul," a name that promised a clue to the heart and soul of the matter, also reminding me I had brought mine along for safe keeping.

On a 747 superjet overnight from Kennedy, we landed Sunday morning at Rome's Leonardo da Vinci Airport so expertly the passengers applauded. In another hour we had crossed the Mediterranean to Palermo, where we piled into a motor coach and rode downtown to the Grand Hotel Delle Palme—an old hotel grand enough for Wagner, who completed *Parsifal* while a guest in 1882. Of the group of twenty middle-class, middle-aged tourists, a portly black-haired Sicilian-American Catholic priest, eating a candy bar, loomed large and comforting. When teased for his round belly, he confessed to the sin of gluttony that, by his benign smile, must count among the lesser of the deadly sins.

Because I'd been to Palermo before and soon ran into myself, I tended to compare it with past times. Sicilians now say O.K. With gasoline $3.50 a gallon, the traffic is paralyzed by tiny Fiats, and more parked cars than people occupy the sidewalks. We are warned of the prevalence of organized crime in a city noted for the Mafia (formed in Sicily in 1875 by a secret society of terrorists), where thieves reach out of a car window to snatch gold from your throat. Again the admonitions: Don't walk too near the curb. Don't walk at night. Don't *ever* walk alone.

Maybe life is worse than it used to be. Anyway, Oscar will tell us. My trust in tour guides is fortunately extreme, in their professionalism and stamina, but never before have I met the likes of Oscar, who will remain throughout at our side. Oscar is a wonder. Privately I call him Oscar Heart-and-Soul since it's clear his heart is in his work and his soul is steady. He is a small Italian with a small mustache and the kind of character needed for this business, being highly intelligent, patient, informed about everything from pizzas to Empedocles. As a boy in Rome he ran away to see the world from the Argentine to New York

City, where he taught himself English. Now after seven years of conducting tours, married with two children in Rome, he intends to retire at thirty-five, the absolute limit, he thinks, of a guide's endurance. I'm fascinated by Oscar's technique. He talks animatedly while tourists yawn or slumber, answers idiotic questions with a gratified air, laughs easily, most of all understands tourists in their peculiar guises. Lawrence Durrell's guide Roberto was bitter about them. "Travelling isn't honest," he said. "Everyone is trying to get away from something." Oscar is more tolerant, in love with life and Sicily, calmly resigned to loud complaints about them both.

On these days in Palermo, I sat up front in the bus beside Esther (a traveler from Hartford, Connecticut) under Oscar's microphone, which I dodged to avoid collision. Being Italian he brandished his hands with every word.

What *is* the clue? Part must lie in the remote past when the Mediterranean was the center of the Western world and Sicily, in its splendid location, was itself a center of civilization. It was also a battleground, where for centuries the Carthaginians fought for possession first from the Greeks then the Romans in the Punic Wars; where the Byzantines battled the Arabs, and in the eleventh century the Norman conquerors swooped down on this small island. With the Normans Palermo entered its golden age, one of the world's fabulous cities and capital of the kingdom of Sicily. The present city of poverty and flourishing crime dates from that magnificence, from the jewel-like Palatine Chapel to Monreale, richest of medieval cathedrals, built on a mountain overlooking the Conca d'Oro by William the Good. Its interior, covered with gold mosaics, so gleams with gold that, Vincent Cronin says, to cross the threshold is to throw a golden light over the rest of your life. Above the high altar, the six-foot hand of the Christ Pantocrator is raised in awesome benediction.

Even the towering Mount Pellegrino that dominates the city is of Norman fame and legend. A niece of William the Good named Rosalia disappeared one day in 1159, aged fifteen, into a grotto or cave on Mount Pellegrino and never emerged. All trace of her was lost for five centuries, till in 1624 a holy man dreamed she lay buried in a cave, and her bones were found near the summit and carried down to Palermo, where they promptly delivered the city from the plague. The grotto of Santa Rosalia, round which a church was built, is a sanctuary with votive offerings for her continued help, including a tire from a Fiat. There I caught up with Goethe, who visited the cave on April 6, 1787, and was captivated by the image of the girl lying in a glass case. A plaque in the sanctuary said, in effect, Goethe was here. So was Pope John Paul II.

On the highway to Selinunte beside the Mediterranean, the oleanders were blooming, with no sign of the golden celery once abundant in the fields for which the ancient city was named. Thucydides wrote of Selinunte, a thriving Greek colony of many temples, twice ravaged by the Carthaginians—a lost city mentioned by Strabo four centuries later as extinct. Now ruins were heaped on ruins in the silence, a few Doric columns and vestiges of seven temples, labeled by letters A through G for lack of better knowledge of them. They lay as if felled by havoc, earthquake or a thunderbolt from Zeus. Nearby was Segesta, a hated rival of Selinunte where, as well, nothing exists of a city but a strangely preserved temple to Demeter, empty, roofless, and Greek, alone on a hill like a small Parthenon. Twenty-five centuries ago slaves hauled up immense blocks of sandstone to build it. Then the wars with Carthage came to Segesta.

We spent the night on a hilltop on the southwest coast of Sicily, at Agrigento, another Greek city, one that Pindar loved and called "the most beautiful of mortal cities." A place of wealth and splendor, mortal indeed, it has more ruins than any other town in Sicily. Yet close to the site is a modern town with a fine hotel, the Hotel Jolly Dei Tempii. "What does Jolly mean?" we asked Oscar. "It means just that, jolly," he said, though it's the name of a string of hotels not all jovial like this among the gods. After dinner we walked out in darkness to the Valley of the Temples, a row of seven floodlit temples perched in lonely fashion on the site of the old city. It was a quiet spectacle among cypresses, less a meteoric display than a ghostly illumination of dead gods—with the Temple of Concord barely visible, the colossal Temple of Zeus gone the way of all wonders.

However, with Mount Etna erupting not far ahead, I looked most gladly on Agrigento as the birthplace of Empedocles, who tried to make himself immortal by leaping into the crater, achieving fame in Matthew Arnold's poem "Empedocles on Etna." Empedocles was a fifth-century B.C. philosopher and poet, a self-styled god ("I go among you as an immortal god") believed by his contemporaries to be divine. Followed by a retinue of servants, he wore a purple robe, golden girdle, long flowing hair, a laurel wreath, gold sandals. Empedocles suffered from hubris and self-love, at the same time holding to the philosophy that in the beginning Love alone was dominant and the sexes were happily one and the same, till Strife (Hate, Discord) came along and sundered them into male and female. To keep his death secret and insure he would remain a god ascended to Olympus, Empedocles threw himself into the flame of Etna and perished, while the volcano scornfully hurled back a gold sandal and proved him mortal. In *Paradise Lost* Milton committed him to limbo, "he who to be deemed a god . . . " Arnold's poem advised him in reproach, "Be neither saint nor sophist-led, but be a man."

Empedocles set an example. In *Sicilian Carousel* Durrell told of a member of his tour named Beddoes, wanted by the *carabinieri,* who after leaving most of his clothes on the brink of Etna took off and disappeared from the country. This is fairly common practice, they say, to which the polite Sicilians shut their eyes. In Japan the same trick is played at Mount Fuji.

By crossing Sicily from the west to the east coast, we skirted Etna, whose smoke rose like storm clouds and lava flowed like a slow river. Oscar, shuddering to see it, said nothing in heaven or earth could force him to climb up there, though this side trip was included in our tour. Virgil in the *Aeneid* described Etna as "singeing the very stars"; Sicilians think it is actually alive and angry, with a mind of its own. Etna *knows.* Yet at its base the countryside was green and fertile, houses climbed its slopes. The town of Catania, eighteen miles away, has twice in recorded history been submerged in redhot lava.

As we drove through the scarred streets of Catania, where fish stalls were lighted to make the fish scales shine, I held my breath to consider the way mortals meet catastrophe by electing the day after to start over on the same spot, building anew for the next disaster as if it were God's holy plan. Catania is a more perilous city to live in than Pompeii was. It has been destroyed by earthquakes, Carthaginians, Byzantines, Arabs, Normans, sacked by Frederick II when he was king of Sicily, attacked by pirates, severely bombed in World War II, and now is ruled by the Mafia. Why do people continue to live there, they and their descendants? Why do any of us live our lives on the edge of craters, in Catania only a little more vulnerable?

Matteo, our Sicilian driver, stopped the bus and got out to collect pieces of lava as souvenirs from the unsightly piles of four centuries ago that strew the roadside. My hunk resembled the piece of the moon I saw at Cape Canaveral, old and gray and inscrutable.

On reaching Taormina, which overlooks the Mediterranean within sight of Etna, we were urged to forget the Sicilian story for a day or two and relax at one of the loveliest seaside resorts on the planet. It is "lovely, lovely, dawn-lovely," D. H. Lawrence said, built in abrupt layers up a perpendicular mountainside, where at the top, perched on a cliff above the town, rose the Grand Hotel, Albergo Capo Taormina. There we were staying. When I reached my room on the fourth floor this afternoon, I burst into tears. What put me in a panic was the discovery that the hotel is built upside down. In order to get from the first floor to the fourth you have to go *down,* and the top floor is far below beside the sea, a bewildering architectural arrangement I don't understand and have no reason to trust. It makes me catatonic. I seem to be standing on my head.

As calmly as I could, I put on my bathing suit and went down to lie for hours under a yellow umbrella at the hotel's swimming pool. Where I lay was once part of the beach at Naxos, the earliest Greek colony in Sicily. Across the blue transparent water of the Ionian Sea was Greece. I glanced round at the blond German types who, Oscar said, come to Taormina and turn into tomatoes in the Sicilian sun. I thought of Winston Churchill who often visited Taormina, his favorite vacation spot, never once, it's safe to say, succumbing to claustrophobic fears. And of D. H. Lawrence, who occupied a villa for three years on a green slope above the town and on a day "of Sicilian July, with Etna smoking" saw at his water trough a poisonous yellow snake about which he wrote his poem "The Snake," admitting his paralyzing fear and unmanly cowardice in hurling a log at it. (Lawrence also abhorred Etna and, after the first enchantment, found the Sicilians soulless, maddening, exasperating, impossible.)

Tonight under the moon we danced on the hotel balcony, while my terrors in Taormina began slowly to subside.

A dream of Syracuse, a city I'd never seen, at last came true. We were driving south along the coast this morning while ashes from Mount Etna darkened the sky and scarlet bougainvillea grew like flambeaux along the roadside. Even the tomatoes had turned red in the fields, after being shown pornographic films, Oscar said, to make them blush and ripen early, his first attempt at stand-up humor. Inspired by the sight, he launched into an impassioned lecture on how to cook pasta the Italian way, including a recipe for his own tomato sauce—Oscar, *il cuoco*—with a warning never to combine garlic with the Parmesan cheese. Oscar may have been trying to divert our thoughts from Syracuse and too much expectancy of the once splendid Greek city, the rival of Athens and for a while surpassing her in fame and glory. Like Athens, Syracuse attracted many to her gates—Pindar, who lived several years in Syracuse; Aeschylus, who died in Sicily when an eagle dropped a turtle on his bald head; Plato, who came three times. Theocritus, probably born in Syracuse, composed idylls of the Sicilian shepherds; Thucydides and Herodotus wrote histories of her wars. In 212 B.C. Archimedes fought and perished in Syracuse when it was sacked by the Roman Marcellus, and he who had cried out triumphantly "Give me a place to stand and I will move the earth!" was given instead a place to die.

From the fifth century B.C. the people of Syracuse were ruled by tyrants, from the great Gelon to the great Dionysius who fought the Carthaginians in three wars, whose rule was cruel and absolute. Dionysius trusted neither his wife nor his barber, only his three daughters whom he named Justice, Self-Control, and Virtue. It was he who turned Syracuse into the richest of cities, with a high wall to enclose its wealth and keep it undefeated. Cicero—in his time a Roman official in Syracuse—told the story of Damocles, a flatterer in Dionysius' court given to extravagant praise of his ruler as the happiest man on earth, luckiest of mortals. Dionysius invited Damocles to ascend the throne at a banquet and see how it felt to be royal. And he, accepting, gazed on the homage paid him till he caught sight of a sword hanging over his head by a single hair. In abject terror he begged to get down, while Dionysius told him to be merry, this was the happiness men face who are in power. This was the contented state, said Horace, of him "o'er whose doomed neck hangs the sword unsheathed."

Alas. In Syracuse one had to reflect on its ancient history and enjoy the sea breeze from the harbor to find the city remarkable now. Papyrus, brought long ago by the Arabs, grows ten feet tall like flower stems in a stream, its thin reeds still used to make paper. The cathedral, built on the remains of a Greek temple of Athene, is baroque with Doric columns. That, plus a Greek theater and Roman amphitheater—not quite comparable to the amphitheater at Taormina that rises from the sea and dominates the town—is about it. A cave north of the city, a black hole known as Dionysius' Ear, has an entrance seventy feet high shaped like a human ear. The constant echo, echo, echo allowed Dionysius to lend his ear to whispers of treason among the slaves he had imprisoned in its depths.

As we left Sicily this morning, crossing on a ferry the windy Strait of Messina, the last sight was of Messina itself, one more city conquered and destroyed with appalling regularity. Goethe called it an accursed city, five times leveled by earthquake alone.

Someday a bridge will span the twenty-mile channel from Messina to the toe of Italy. Now there is only the ferry, where one is reminded of the dangerous winds, currents, rocks and whirlpools that used to terrify sailors who had to cross the strait between old Scylla waiting to devour them and the deadly whirlpool Charybdis. But on this clear day with no mirage or fata morgana visible to keep alive the fear, I had time to think of Goethe and wonder again why he said Sicily was the clue to everything. Had I found the clue, or any clue at all beyond the simple one, obvious to everybody, that men inevitably perish and civilizations predictably fail?

Recently David Broder, a Washington correspondent, on a visit to Sicily came to the conclusion that it was indeed a tragic country where roses bloom the year round and nightingales sing for six months straight, where the Mafia rules, the drug wars have taken over, the people are silenced by terror, where life is anything but good. Unfortunately Broder found in Sicily a disturbing prophecy of what America too may become, or is already becoming, with our own Mafia active since the 1920s, our poverty and drugs and violent crime, our erupting Mount Saint Helens, and of course our nuclear bomb.

TO ITALY It was June when we crossed to the toe of Italy's boot and the old city of Reggio di Calabria, like Messina the victim of wars and convulsion, many times rebuilt. Before us rose the rugged mountainous region of Calabria in the Apennines, with stupendous views, olive trees the largest on earth, and plentiful signs of acute poverty in a region known as the "killing field" where gangsters operate. After lunch in Cosenza, which Pliny praised not long ago (before Vesuvius erupted in

79 and killed him) for its apple trees and wine, we continued along the coast to Salerno where not long ago, September 1943, the Allied forces fought the Nazis in a battle that nearly pushed us into the sea. At day's end we reached Sorrento, a heavenly resort town standing on a cliff beside the Mediterranean. And the mountain ahead was Vesuvius.

I wanted to stay in bed Sunday morning at Sorrento's Hotel Parco Dei Principi and miss the day with Oscar in Naples and Pompeii. I'd been there before and dreaded to return, remembering the first time when at Naples B. and I went aboard the *Haruna Maru,* a small Japanese ship, for a trip around the world and from the deck stared up at Vesuvius at the start of the happiest journey of my life.

Yet one learns by going back, inevitably to a different Naples, another Pompeii under Vesuvius. For one thing, though Pompeii remains dramatically the same these two thousand years—its Temple of Jupiter still standing in the Forum, its houses open for the owners to return, its two agonized dying slaves at the baths—the exploits of Etna had softened the threat of a lesser volcano overhead. For another, the famous pornographic frescoes adorning the house of the brothers Vettii, shown only to adult males till recently when they were made available to women and, I suppose, little children, were a disappointment and a fraud. "Is this all?" the women asked, this glorification of the phallus. "How very boring."

Naples was exciting, crowded, alive with vitality and pizzerias (where the pizza itself originated) and the statue of Garibaldi heroic as ever in the square. I carried a copy of *The Diary of One of Garibaldi's Thousand* that Ted gave me as a guidebook, written by Giuseppe Abba, one of Garibaldi's red-shirted volunteers. In September 1860, after entering Palermo with his guerrilla army, Garibaldi crossed the Strait of Messina, conquered Calabria, and took Naples. In the name of Victor Emmanuel he united all Italy, with Sicily a part, under one king. An exultant Abba, to whom Garibaldi was Moses, Charlemagne, and Christ combined, wrote in his diary as they entered Naples, September 14, 1860, "It is a city magnificent even in its squalor. Never have I seen such an open display of filth."

Oscar told us, "For the rest of your life you will quake at the thought of the Amalfi Drive." Nor would Matteo forget maneuvering us down the steepest road in Italy, barely missing cars, buses, motorcyclists racing like hell's angels down the cliffside to Amalfi. "Aiuto!" muttered

Matteo, *Help!* Heart in mouth we made it to a fishing village on the Gulf of Salerno that till 1373, when the sea destroyed it, had been a fair city—Amalfi, where John Webster in his tragic *Duchess of Malfi,* without visiting the place, murdered the lady ("Cover her face; mine eyes dazzle; she died young"). Breath restored, we sat with sandwiches and beer directly opposite the Cathedral of Saint Andrea, gazing at its facade of black-and-white stone, one of Italy's most striking cathedrals. From this spot the First Crusade set out for Jerusalem.

Back in Sorrento Oscar took us to a nightclub, the Fauna, for the tarantella, a frantic dance native to southern Italy inspired by the tarantulas that inhabit nearby Taranto. From the fifteenth century it was thought to be a remedy for the spider bite that caused a manic desire to dance. By gyrating to music, one sweated out the poison and was cured, otherwise went mad. A member of our group, Mel from New Jersey, let himself be coaxed to the stage and hopped about with the cast in their folk costumes, looking more sheepish than manic. Between numbers, the local patrons rushed to the dance floor to flap their arms in the funky chicken, a popular number imported from America, which outdid the tarantella by dancers incurably possessed.

We went to Capri. A short bumpy ride in a small steamer took us from Sorrento over the Bay of Naples to the Blue Grotto. We might have picked the Green, Yellow, Pink, or White Grotto, since the island is full of grottoes, most at sea level. But the Grotta Azzurra is the one known to the Greeks, who avoided it as a place of monsters and witches, familiar to the Romans who probably cut the narrow hole in the rock.

The method was to transfer passengers from the steamer to rowboats hovering near, four to a boat. When our turn came, Betty, Ted, Esther, and I lay down in the bottom with feet outstretched. I lay directly under the two strong legs of the boatman, a swarthy fellow resembling a pirate. As we reached the tiny opening, I felt him pull with all his strength on the chains that shot us neatly inside the black hole without knocking us senseless or crashing the boat against the side. It seemed a limited career for a man, expert in a single maneuver that took powerful muscles, plenty of nerve, and no time to execute. For a while we circled the dark cave the size of a large field, and, hating caves (like Gladstone, who was seasick in the Blue Grotto), I kept watch of the exit and the shimmering Capri blue light that filtered through sunlit water. We came out the same way, with a lurch, two steady arms controlling the boat. Then the boatman handed us over, his courtly bow worthy of a gondolier.

The emperor Augustus, fond of Capri, turned it into a private estate for his royal pleasure. (On his deathbed he asked, "Have I played my part in the farce of life creditably enough?") His stepson, the emperor Tiberius, who was said to be sexually depraved and physically beautiful, built twelve villas over the island, shut himself up in exile, and refused to return to Rome. Tacitus speaks of Tiberius strangling little boys and girls after playing with them in the Blue Grotto. Later Capri became a stronghold of the Barbary pirate Barbarossa. Now it's a playground on a rock four miles long, a little mountain springing from the sea. By a funicular railway we rode up to Capri town—crowned with outdoor cafés and the flower gardens of Augustus—and to Anacapri, higher still, with palatial homes occupied at various times by Sophia Loren and Mussolini.

"In Rome I am full of new thoughts," Goethe said, and found himself reborn, renewed, fulfilled, and fortified. Why then didn't Goethe discover the clue to everything in the Eternal City? Before it fell Rome was the center of the civilized world, when Horace and Virgil walked in the Forum; when the Sacred Way was filled with shrines that now is full of cats; when the Colosseum rose bloody and eternal, built by 12,000 captive Jews; when miles of catacombs where the early Christians were secretly buried filled a space greater than Rome aboveground; when St. Peter's was built to honor a fisherman from Galilee whom the Romans crucified. Rome was still a place of clues—Michelangelo lying on his back to paint a portrait of God while paint dripped in his face; the bells of five hundred churches ringing in unison when a new pope was declared; Gibbon's history that began when "the idea of writing the decline and fall of the city first started in my mind."

"Come to Rome," Shelley said, whose ashes are buried in the Protestant Cemetery. Halfway there, a hundred miles north of Sorrento, we stopped at Monte Cassino. The name clanged in my mind—MONTE CASSINO—a black page of history written since last I passed by. During World War II, in the three months from February to May 1944, the Benedictine monastery was destroyed. High on a mountain above the town of Cassino, it had been founded in 529 by Saint Benedict, and here he established the Rule of monastic life that made Benedict a saint and his name immortal. Charlemagne had a copy of it. It taught in clear language not austerity but the good life (provided you were a monk) of simplicity, love, tolerance, humility—instructing the monks to live without grumbling and without possessions, to be of good zeal toward each other but not to sleep in the same bed, to receive all guests as if Christ himself.

Four times the gilded Abbey of Monte Cassino was destroyed: by the Lombards in 589, by the Arabs in 884, by earthquake in 1349, and by us, reduced to dust during the Allied bombardment. We had made the fatal error of thinking the Germans, who used it as a fortress to block the Allied advance to Rome, were quartered inside the abbey. But only monks and refugees were hiding there. After terrific fighting, when most of the abbey disappeared, the Allies captured the German position and ousted the German troops from the charred remains of the town.

Monte Cassino, beyond comprehending in its vast size, all gold leaf and ornate rococo, has been rebuilt. A mere thirty monks live there now. The remains of Saint Benedict and his sister Scholastica, his "twin soul," who occupy the same tomb, are intact. The village of Cassino far below is a scattering of whitewashed houses. And that is all, except for the signs pointing to the Polish Cemetery, the British Military Cemetery, the American Military Cemetery, and so on—30,000 graves.

In Rome at last it was Roman summer, hot, crowded with pilgrims there because Pope John Paul high-handedly proclaimed 1983 a holy year. The tourists were there, at least ours were, with tourist grievances complaining of the heat, crowds, pilgrims, accommodations, and other tourists. Till now harmony had prevailed, but no longer. The new Sheraton Roma offended by being outside the Roman wall and not smack in the middle of the Piazza di Spagna. Though a shuttle bus ran every hour for their convenience, the wailers and handwringers blamed Oscar, claiming he was indifferent to our welfare, uninformed as a guide, furthermore had been so throughout the tour, and what was he going to do about it? Oscar listened in silence, accustomed to edgy people with tired feet bent on finding fault (like Mark Twain, who said of himself, "One never knows what a consummate ass he may become until he goes abroad." Twain came to hate travel, hotels, and Old Masters).

I don't know which gave me greater pleasure—the Sistine Chapel or the audience with the pope. The audience was shared by a thousand others, but we had admission tickets inside the barrier, chairs to sit on, and a plentiful shower of godblessings. Each Wednesday if he is in town Pope John Paul, the 264th since Peter, spends an hour till 12:00 noon in St. Peter's Square (where two years ago during a weekly mass he was shot) spreading benisons, trying to save the world by words of faith. On the dot he appeared from the Vatican Palace in white and yellow robes, standing fearlessly like a charioteer in his tiny bullet-proof Popemobile that circled the square twice while he waved, beamed, blessed. I've never seen a face more cherubic, not surprising in a man who believes angels exist. Finally he mounted a canopied platform where, before a microphone, he spoke welcome in seven languages, his English clear, his Italian loud. The sun beat down and we sweltered. By noon he was deep into his sermon of exhortation, while people started to leave, not without broad smiles for he is known as the Publicity Pope who never stops talking. Since he will visit Poland next week, he had much on his mind to say of justice and peace. As we walked out, filled with beatitude and the sound of his voice still raised, I saw a sign painted on a wall: YENKEE FORA (Yankee go home).

The Sistine Chapel was too thronged to let one lie flat on the floor and stare at the ceiling. Thirty years after painting it, Michelangelo covered the entire altar wall with the magnificent Last Judgment. But it is upward one looks, craning the neck to study God and Adam, the creation of man and his fall.

Goethe was obsessed by the place. "Until you have seen the Sistine Chapel," he wrote in his Roman journal, "you can have no adequate conception of what man is capable of accomplishing." Even so he treated it casually in the year he spent in Italy, going often with two German artist friends to work on his own canvas. They tipped the custodian who let them enter by the door next the altar, and settled down to their easels wherever they pleased. They ate meals in all that sublimity and, said Goethe, "I remember that one day I was overcome by the heat and snatched a noon nap on the papal throne." Pure impertinence in the amateur painter Goethe was.

It was built as a private chapel for the popes. In the sixteenth century Palestrina sang *Kyrie eleison* in the choir and wrote 105 masses for the service. Montaigne heard mass in 1580 and in an audience with Pope Gregory XIII kissed His Holiness' right foot. The Pope, Montaigne said, had a long white beard and a bastard son "whom he loves with a frenzy." In 1770 Mozart at fourteen went to the chapel to hear the *Miserere* of Gregorio Allegri, returned to his hotel room and wrote it down from memory. Stendhal attended mass in 1817, listening with disgust to the celebrated castrati that he called "the excruciating cacophony of saw-voiced capons." Ruskin in 1840 found only "a little mummery with Pope and dirty cardinals."

In Rome I walked in a city that no longer gave me nightmares by its crushing layers of history, its walls built sixteen centuries ago by Aurelian, its ancient Appian Way that led from Rome to the Adriatic. One reason it mattered less was that the past looked diminished by tall modern buildings and expanded city. The Circus Maximus where thousands of Christians died was an empty lot. The ruins appeared inconsequent to the populace that ignored them. The fickle tourists had seen one ruined temple and one Diocletian bath too many.

Even the Protestant Cemetery that I remembered outside Rome among fields and countryside was hidden now behind a high gate in the midst of traffic, enclosed by buildings, small and tucked away. Shelley wrote of it to Thomas Love Peacock, December 1818, "The English burying-place is a green slope near the walls, under the pyramidal tomb of Cestius, and is, I think, the most beautiful and solemn cemetery I ever beheld." A local guide sadly informed us it contained an English poet whose grave, because he had drowned, was inscribed "Here lies a man whose name was writ in the water."

"Oh no," I cried. "Keats wasn't drowned!"

"Oh yes," he said, "drowned dead. That's why, you see, his name was writ in the water."

I didn't mind going down into the catacombs that before had scared me speechless. After the third century they were rarely used for burial. At the Catacombs of Domitilla—a Roman lady who became a Christian—one of forty catacombs in Rome, with sixteen miles of underground burials, a serene young man became our guide, a Brother of Mercy from Singapore who was given the dreary assignment for one year. He took us to a depth of forty feet in the cool tombs (where Saint Jerome spent his Sundays). Among the 100,000 niches, each empty of its nameless skeleton, we followed in single file through dark intersecting tunnels from which, if you strayed or made a wrong turning, you might not be found till your skeleton turned up in one of the niches. I was glad my courage proved greater than Goethe's, who like me was claustrophobic and strongly opposed to guided tours of caves and subterranean vaults. He managed to take a single step into the Catacombs of Saint Sebastian before he quailed and rushed to the surface to breathe again in sunlight and fresh air. Goethe laid it to his poetic sensitivity.

When I reached home late in June, my yard man, Mr. Utley, announced he had seen by the paper that I was dead.

"You couldn't have," I said. "Nobody else with my name lives in this town."

"Well," he said. "It was somebody named Helen."

In Milan Kundera's novel *The Unbearable Lightness of Being,* the character Tomas stands at a window staring across the courtyard, saying to himself "Einmal ist keinmal," that is, one time is no time, once is not enough.

He wasn't talking about the limitations and injustices of travel but of the quandary of being alive. It haunted Tomas as it haunts Kundera: "We are born one time only," and once is not enough; we may as well not have lived at all. Life is too fleeting to get the hang of it. Not having been a child before, or an oldtimer either, we need to be allowed another try, a second chance.

The answer, I guess, is reincarnation, which puts one in a worse quandary, being unstoppable.

Late in July I began a journey I've been meaning to take back to my hometown of Worcester, New York. I wanted to lay a couple of ghosts. It was time if ever to dispel the more persistent phantoms by looking with my eyes instead of my memory. Perhaps not everyone has to do that, but sooner or later I had to.

I flew to LaGuardia and took a limousine up to Rhinebeck, where my childhood friend Vernette lives. The driver of the limousine, without turning round to see if I was listening or awake, related the story of his unhappy marriages, on his mind because he was about to make a third trip to Niagara Falls for his third honeymoon. Said he'd rather be shot.

Even if she hadn't offered to accompany me to Worcester, Vernette herself was worth the journey. She is a lovable, roly-poly woman, so startlingly different from the tall, skinny, angular child I last saw at age eight that I embraced a stranger. Gradually her smile convinced me this was Vernette. We were in the first three grades together till to my sorrow I moved away from Worcester. Because she was unable to carry a tune she was terrified of my mother, the music teacher, who believed anyone can learn to sing if he isn't too stubborn to try. Like me Vernette had her childhood hauntings. On my arrival she drew a black picture of Lizzie with her pitch pipe as a holy terror in the classroom.

Vernette lives alone with three cats in a charming country house surrounded by twenty acres of lawn and woodlands, a red barn and a lily pond. She is divorced from a man who comes up from New York to see her. She sends him a ham at Christmas, he buys her gifts of ceramic cats. I like her composure, serenity, acceptance; she has found how to live with herself and is amazingly imperturbable.

This Sunday afternoon Vernette invited Frances Hadsell, also a child in our grade, for cocktails and reunion. Frances drove up from Pough-keepsie where she lives, bringing her husband who harped on memories of his own childhood, and some faded snapshots. She is no longer the tomboy I knew but a white-haired spectacled lady, proper, neatly dressed, who probably met me after these years with real misgivings. Over her gin and tonic she dropped the bombshell.

"Did you know your books have been banned from the Worcester library?"

The astonishing piece of news made me laugh in disbelief. When Vernette nodded it was so, I cordially agreed the town had done the right thing. They had read *Charley Smith's Girl* and found it scandalous, in particular the tale of my mother's divorce from Charley, the Methodist preacher. Miss Bessie Wright, who taught with my mother in the public school and is still alive in her old age in Worcester, had led the vigorous campaign of censorship, abetted by the ladies of the Fortnightly Society. Indignant threats were made to withhold funds for buying books if mine were found on the library shelves. I had revealed secrets known to everybody and had achieved a distinction I never dreamed of. H. L. Mencken used to be banned in Boston. I am banned in Worcester, N.Y.

Early Monday morning Vernette and I drove through the green hills of Upstate New York, along country roads of summer lined with hicko-ries, oaks, poplars, the landscape I like best in the land. It was a hundred miles to Worcester, beyond the Catskills to a small village with a population when I was a child, and a population now, of eight hundred—a village that had been the object of my love in a lifelong affair. Vernette too was ready to go back, not because it was the town where she was born and reared but because she marveled at my attachment, which appeared to her eccentric, an idealized version of the real place. So we went together to find out the way it was.

I wouldn't have missed it. On the surface Worcester was unchanged, as if nothing had happened to alter it for better or worse ("Nothing has," Vernette said). The houses were the same houses, their early twentieth-century architecture a fanciful combination of American Gothic, Greek Revival, Palladian, Georgian, Victorian, tastefully mingled with gables, cupolas, curlicues, bay windows, verandahs, and stoops. They looked freshly painted and prosperous, set back from the street behind clipped lawns and flower beds, wonderfully respectable, Protestant, Republican, self-respecting. As we drove slowly up and down tree-shaded Main Street, no longer a dirt road for buggies and Model T Fords, I could say the names of nearly every family who had lived there—the Goodenoughs, the Starkweathers—who for all I knew lived there still.

We passed the house of Miss Bessie Wright, the schoolteacher, and Vernette said, "Would you care to drop in for a social call?"

"Heavens, no," I said. "Would you?"

"I haven't written a scandalous book," Vernette said. "She wouldn't remember me."

We passed without pausing Sloat's Hotel, the Grange, the Methodist church and the parsonage where I used to live till Charley left us. We passed Vernette's former home, imposing and attractive, that she barely turned her head to glance at. But at a white frame house and barn on upper Main Street she stopped the car out in front and we settled down to stare. Or I stared while Vernette waited. The privy and the apple tree were gone. But here was my house, to which Lizzie and I moved after the divorce when I was two, for which she paid four dollars a month rent. How had it managed to stay untouched by time when I had not? It stood intact, the front door still framed by a border of small panes of colored glass, violet, yellow, deep blue, and so on. The yellow glass, the golden pane, at the height for a child to peer through, was the one I had believed mine, had made into a talisman, written about as golden—one small, dim, discolored piece of window glass.

It was uncanny, a town fixed and immutable, though the houses must have acquired bathrooms and television by now. Nothing shuttered or ramshackle was in sight, nothing to deplore—no motels at the edge of town, no pizza parlor within it, no billboards, no traffic, no industry. Because Main Street, Worcester, was recently declared an "historic district" for reflecting the genteel look of a century ago—its dozen stores of antiquarian interest for their facades—the village had got a tiny historic museum next to the drugstore, closed on Mondays. By peering through the plate glass window, we glimpsed a table with a pile of photographs and in the corner a Union flag, not much of a collection. This, I thought, was the spot where my offending book belonged, to be shown by special request to early settlers and local chroniclers.

It hadn't occurred to me to include the cemetery in our tour, since I seldom frequent cemeteries, but Vernette was a thorough sightseer. As we reached the crest of the hill, where as schoolchildren we marched on Memorial Day with baskets of lilacs, I saw what had happened. Here the change had taken place: the town I knew had moved its location and my childhood with it. The people I loved were gathered here—the Prestons, the Multers, Vernette's parents, Frances Hadsell's sister Delia, Chauncey with whom I fell in love when I was seven. This too was a well-kept town, green and flourishing, almost alive. Vernette pointed to the showiest tombstone in the grounds, a tall marble shaft like Cleopatra's Needle.

"Look, there's Gussie Multer," Vernette said. "She always put herself above everyone else."

I admired Gussie for that, the richest woman in town, some said the handsomest. Why shouldn't she keep it that way?

I don't have to go back again. I went searching for something—a lost childhood, a golden windowpane—and found with considerable relief I had in fact invented a version of the thing.

Thank you, Vernette. It's all right now.

Childhood

It hangs around—the taste of Necco wafers
And in my nose the smell of Mentholatum,
The horsehair sofa prickling my behind
As I sit peering through her stereoptican
At snow on Pike's Peak in Miss Bessie's parlor,
And ask politely "Please, may I go home now?"
It's there in Charley's deep voice singing,
When I am six, Champ Clark's campaign song. Like this:
    Every time I come to town
    The boys start kickin' my dawg aroun'.

It's in the mayflower baskets filled with trillium
And limp hepaticas to hang on doorknobs
And ring the bell, run for my life, die laughing,
Because the gift is secret. And it's free.

In the August heat that breaks records, I've found a book on mermaids—*Sea Enchantress, a Tale of the Mermaid and Her Kin,* by Gwen Benwell and Arthur Waugh. Mermaids neither sweat nor shed tears. Pliny believed they exist: "As for mermaids, it is no fabulous tale that goeth of them." Prufrock claimed "I have heard the mermaids singing, each to each," but they didn't sing to him.

In legend this sea girl with a fishtail was beautiful beyond saying, forever combing her seaweed hair, riding the waves on a dolphin's back. "The rude sea," says Oberon, "grew civil at her song." Lacking a soul or hope of salvation, she lured sailors to their doom and sometimes slept with a mortal man like the Eddystone lighthouse keeper—an affair that ended with her song echoing out through the night, "To hell with the Keeper of the Eddystone Light."

I gave up belief in mermaids after I saw a manatee in the Florida Everglades. On a boat trip among those ten thousand islands, through a wilderness of tropical marshes and tangled mangrove swamps, we nearly ran down a splendid female sunning herself in the mud soup of a shallow inland sea. This fat sea cow is credited with inspiring the myth of the mermaid, though her tail ends in a paddle, her color is wrinkled gray, she has a balloon snout and mustache. Shaped very like a whale, she weighs a ton and looks preposterous. A mariner of long ago, overcome by rum, must have caught sight of a manatee feeding on seagrass and taken her for a lovely maiden. Sociable, not bright though amorous, she squeaks and whistles but could never seduce a sailor.

The Nobel Prize for Literature was awarded this year to William Golding, author of *Lord of the Flies,* a consistent choice if you believe the world is mad. It says man is inherently evil, that even children if left free of restraint will turn to savagery and murder. A group of English schoolboys not yet adolescent, age six to twelve, alone on a tropical coral island, not only succeed in setting fire to the island but, in acts of wickedness and depravity, kill two of their number and are hunting out a third when rescue finally comes. At least a dozen are "littuns" who suck their thumbs and scream in terror. One of the littlest burns to death.

For years this best-seller has been required reading for high school and college students, who find it a believable adventure story. It has been called "Lord of the Campus." Golding was a schoolmaster for twenty years in an English grammar school, where he disliked the boys he taught and came to "understand and know them with awful precision." The children in his book have been evacuated after an atomic explosion in England (that suggests a world at war); their plane has been shot down, sweeping many into the sea. Among the survivors, Ralph at twelve is chosen leader, a confused boy who fails to keep order before he is rejected and nearly murdered. Piggy, fat and asthmatic, is decapitated by a rock the savages in fury hurl down on his head and spill his brains out. Simon, nine, called by Golding a "Christ figure," is martyred. The fourth boy, Jack, head of a group of choirboys, becomes the leader, a tyrant and dictator who spurs the rest in a bloodthirsty hunt for wild pigs to paint their faces, dance, snarl, kill and destroy, chanting "*Kill the pig. Cut her throat. Spill her blood.*" They turn from killing the pig to killing Piggy, from Piggy to Simon, from Simon to Ralph, their victims.

Golding calls the book a fable but contradicts himself by saying it is about "real boys on an island, showing what a mess they'd make." In fact they are human beings in a bestial state, in league with the devil. When they choose as a false god a pig's head on a stick, the head speaks in the gloating voice of the Lord of the Flies, Beelzebub—the god in hell to whom flies belong—saying "I'm the Beast. I'm part of you. I'm the reason things are as they are."

At the end a naval officer appears in a trim cruiser armed with a submachine gun. He says to Ralph, "Fun and games? . . . Having a war or something?" The contrived ending hardly matters; in such a world of hate and evil it's too late for anyone to be saved.

Those who admire Golding think the book deserved the Nobel Prize "for trying to tell the truth about human nature." Could have fooled me.

The Shrine of St. Jude Thaddeus of Dominican Fathers urges me by mail to send for a bottle of St. Jude Oil to protect me from the deceits and tricks of the devil. St. Jude, one of the twelve disciples, patron of desperate cases and lost causes, is of most avail in November, the

Month of Poor Souls, what the poet Ted Hughes calls "the month of the drowned dog." You touch the oil to a vulnerable part and pray for your life.

On television the Pentecostal evangelist Oral Roberts also urges me to send for a packet of "anointing oil," a drop of which you place on your body where it offends and Roberts is on your case. "Expect a miracle," he says from Tulsa, Oklahoma, the City of Faith, where he conducts a crusade to deliver us from demons.

If the devil still tricks and deceives, I suppose you can try antibiotics.

In November the country watched a television movie, "The Day After," depicting the end of the world by nuclear war. For weeks experts in child psychology debated the question who should be allowed to see it. They agreed that by age twelve a child is old enough to face the idea of the death of the planet and annihilation of the human race. Before then, at five or six, the child should sit next to his parents who hold his hand and answer any questions. Nicholas Mayer, the director, said the movie is a "gigantic public service announcement, like Smokey the Bear."

It takes place on a pleasant day in Lawrence, Kansas, and nearby Kansas City. Suddenly the people hear bulletins of a thermonuclear attack from Russia. In a matter of minutes the blast with accompanying mushroom cloud results in instant devastation, a ravaged earth.

The film says there is no way to survive the day after.

Encounters

It addles the mind to consider them all—
The blows and benevolences,
The collisions, pricks, stabs, arrows, bruises,
And more cordial encounters,
The doubts and despites, transitory as tumbleweed,
Vexations and griefs and indiscriminate rapture,
Plus an occasional insight into the quandary,
As if all could be well. Or once was well.
And now isn't.

JOURNEY TO SPAIN Maybe the place to go, after all, is Spain. It beats staying at home in December, quailing at the specter of another Christmas, another new year. Besides, winter in Spain is said to be mild and you miss nothing but the bullfights that begin in March. Nobody could drag me to a bullfight.

Betty, Ted, and I flew to Madrid on the night of December 4 by Iberia Airlines, in a half-empty plane where we could stretch out to sleep. At dawn the captain's voice wakened us, announcing we would land in Valencia because Madrid was fogged in. "Where is Valencia?" I asked Ted. It used to be the name of a popular song. He studied a map and sighed. "Valencia is on the east coast beside the Mediterranean," he said. "Must be three hundred miles beyond Madrid." We ate breakfast without panic, leaving it to the captain to set us down wherever he had to, and a few hours later landed safely at a fogless airport. It was Madrid. How can I ever get to Valencia?

In the airport we were met by a man from Marsans Tours and led to a waiting limousine. We looked around in surprise. Where was the rest of the tour? Were we, in fact, it? Since nobody turned up, we were taken through morning traffic to the Hotel Palace on the Plaza de las Cortes across from the Prado—a hotel in the style of 1912 with a dome of stained glass and a sweep of lounges so broad as to be intimidating. Before he left us, our greeter cordially explained if we wanted to go sightseeing we should show up each morning at the Marsans Tours office a few blocks away and take the motor coach provided for the day's outing.

By noon I had fallen in love with Spain, and this is a report of that love affair begun in Madrid in a gray December. I knew little about Madrid—an impoverished village unexpectedly chosen by Philip II (who sent the Armada against Elizabeth) as the seat of monarchy. Though Philip was obsessed with building the Escorial for his burial place, Madrid bristled thereafter with fortresses, grew with convents, flourished in baroque and rococo, coming into greatness with Cervantes (who died in Madrid in 1616), Lope de Vega, Calderón, Velázquez, El Greco, Murillo, Goya. And it flourishes still, with Picasso (who lived and died in France), Miró, Dali, Juan Gris, Lorca . . . Nowadays we were free to explore the majestic Royal Palace, unoccupied by kings since Alfonso XIII was deposed in 1931 and the Republic proclaimed. His grandson, Juan Carlos, tolerated by Franco and crowned king after Franco's death, lives modestly in a small palace outside the city.

In the Spanish Civil War, from 1936 to 1939, Madrid in loyalty to the

Republic was the battlefront against Franco's Nationalist forces. Aided by Hitler and Mussolini, Franco overthrew the Republic, assumed total power and ruled Spain as dictator for thirty-six years. During the war Hemingway as war correspondent stayed at the Hotel Palace where we were now, and in 1937 wrote his bitter novel against Franco and fascism. Camus said of that catastrophic war: men can be right and yet be beaten.

It's a tremendous European city of broad avenues, illuminated fountains, wide squares bedecked for Christmas. On the Gran Via we were at home among movie theaters showing American films, pizza parlors, bingo parlors, hamburger joints of McDonald's, Burger King, Wendy's. We walked with the crowds along the Puerta del Sol, Madrid's largest plaza, where it is folly to try to cross the street; and on the Plaza Mayor, where autos-da-fé once took place, now streaming with children clamoring at the stalls of bright Christmas tawdry for sale.

We went and next day went again, and then again, to the Prado, the stupendous art gallery where pride of place is given the Spanish painters. In the Velázquez room are fifty masterpieces of the one who surpassed the rest, a supreme realist. Kenneth Clark said of *Las Meniñas,* "Our first feeling is of being there" with the five-year-old Infanta Margarita of the golden hair, who pouts at having her portrait painted while the young Ladies in Waiting seek to persuade her, the two dwarfs try to amuse her, her parents reflected in a mirror watch her, and Velázquez himself waits before his huge canvas, paintbrush in hand. It is 1656. The pretty child died at twenty-two, but the picture lives.

The El Grecos are there, who turned his sitters into elongated bodies with melancholy faces, into spiritual El Grecos. And the Goyas, familiar and unfamiliar—the celebrated Duchess of Alba in the *Maja Clothed* and *Maja Naked,* her body as apparent in one pose as in the other. And Goya's masterpiece, *The Third of May in Madrid,* the execution of Madrid's defenders by a firing squad—not in Franco's war but the Peninsular War when Napoleon occupied Spain in 1808. Goya at sixty-two, too deaf to hear the shots, probably witnessed the atrocity himself. A man on his knees in a white shirt is about to die. While a lantern shines on his terrified face and outstretched arms, behind him shuffles the long line of the condemned whom nothing can save. To me this is more horrifying than Picasso's *Guernica,* now hanging in its own museum behind the Prado.

It's a strange thing about the *Guernica,* his enraged cry against

Generalissimo Franco, who on April 26, 1937, a market day, ordered the indiscriminate bombing that wiped out a small Basque village in northern Spain. I had seen the picture twice in New York before it was returned to Spain in 1981, and I had remembered it streaked red by the blood of dying soldiers in a general massacre. But the color is stark gray and black, with nine grotesque figures—a wounded horse, a wild snorting bull with a slain soldier at its feet, a dove, and four women: the torso of one who holds an oil lamp from her window into the night, a shrieking mother clutching a dead child, a woman fleeing in panic, another fallen inside the burning house—four defenseless women in a scene of murder. This time I heard their screams.

To see the fabled Escorial, we went by coach thirty miles from Madrid through country of scrub pine to a hillside above the village of Escorial, where after long search Philip chose to build his monument, half monastery, half palace. There, wanting solitude, he lived "on God's doorstep," and after ordering 30,000 masses said for his soul he died. The gloomy, walled-in structure with miles of corridors and courtyards includes living quarters for the monks; an ornate church in its center with a cross by Benvenuto Cellini; and the royal apartments, plain and austere save for the art treasures Philip avidly collected—Dürer, Titian, Tintoretto, El Greco (whom he disliked and dismissed), a surprising number by Hieronymus Bosch whose diableries he fancied. He wanted Michelangelo and Titian to come and decorate the Escorial, but both were in their eighties. Veronese declined.

The unpretentious throne room, a cold empty hall, contained only a backless throne chair, actually a campaign stool of his father's. Behind the chapel was Philip's private cell ("a cell for himself and a palace for God") with a window through which he witnessed the mass. In a crypt beneath the altar was the fulfillment of his dream—the Basilica or Pantheon of Kings where, from hither and yon, Philip gathered the corpses of his family and brought them for burial: his father Charles V, his mother Isabella, his third wife Elizabeth. By now eleven kings of Spain and most of their wives lie in marble coffins on shelves along the walls, with empty coffins ready for Juan Carlos and his wife Sofia if they care to join the rest. Besides a vault for other members of the family, here are some 7,000 fragments of corpses from all over Christendom—including 10 bodies of saints, 144 heads, 366 assorted limbs, fingers, and toes. To collect them became a compulsion. One relic, though, straight from heaven is missing, described by William Beckford in 1797 who said he was shown it on a silken mattress, "a feather from the wing of the Archangel Gabriel, full three feet long, and of a blushing hue more soft and delicate than that of the loveliest rose."

Philip had four wives. His second wife, Mary Tudor, Queen of England, whom he encouraged in her bloody persecutions, died childless and unloved, after which the Protestant Elizabeth, heir to the throne, scornfully rejected Philip's offer of marriage and made him an enemy for life. His fourth wife, his niece Anne of Austria, died in Madrid pregnant with her sixth child, leaving Philip withdrawn to the Escorial in the company of 150 Augustinian monks. He urged the burning at the stake of heretics as an act pleasing to God, and made no attempt to stop the terrors of the Spanish Inquisition that his progenitors Ferdinand and Isabella had set up the century before. He prayed at the Escorial while in August 1588 the Invincible Armada entered the English Channel with 125 ships sent by Philip to wrest England from Elizabeth (whom he plotted to assassinate) and restore it to the Catholic church. When he failed, as he said, in carrying out God's work, the blow to Spain was disastrous.

If Philip is regarded in Spanish history as fanatic and villain, how is Franco remembered? A few kilometers from the Escorial we stopped at the Valley of the Fallen, a memorial and crypt planned by Franco for the million men who fell in the Civil War. It is, in fact, a shrine to himself meant to rival the Escorial, and here he is buried before the high altar. Franco, who died in 1975, gave himself this gigantic monument overlooking the valley, blasted out of a mountain peak with a stone cross 450 feet tall. Masses are said several times a day, each hour on Sunday, in a showy, ostentatious cathedral whose walls are covered with copies of ancient tapestries; and the elaborate attendants wear white gloves. Above the altar is a dome with a mosaic of Christ. The audacity of it! Yet who can say what glorious monument Mussolini would have erected for his tomb had he survived World War II, or how Hitler would have immortalized himself for all eternity? Franco alone, the littlest dictator, prospered as fascist and emerged from the slaughter hero and saint.

It was the right day to go to Toledo, the old capital of Castile, blanketed in dense eerie fog. Forty miles south of Madrid on a granite hill surrounded by a gorge of the Tagus River, what visibility there was revealed a medieval city, Gothic and somber, a kind of walled fortress perched on a rocky shelf, with winding narrow streets and cobblestone alleys. It looked as if El Greco had painted it, as he had done many times during the forty years he lived there, loved a woman and had a son, died there in 1614. Toledo belongs to El Greco and they say has changed little since his time. In the immense Gothic cathedral with, incredibly, 750 stained glass windows, the most exalted possession was El Greco's *El Espolio* in the sacristy, Christ in a vivid scarlet robe about to be torn from him while a workman readies the cross at his bare feet so soon to be pierced by nails. Behind the high altar and on the wall opposite, the two gaps for the famed *Transparente* gave the illusion of light from heaven, streaming saints and angels. A lane outside the cathedral was the Street of Life and Death.

Presumably life and death go on in Toledo, whose houses looked deserted without windows on the street. The sun must shine, the skies aren't always dark, silhouetted by mysterious towers, spires, pinnacles as El Greco saw them. But for us passersby—a beaming Japanese couple trundling their baby in a carriage, a French honeymoon couple, a man from Paraguay, a lady from Toledo, Ohio, whose bewildered glance showed this place didn't remind her of home—it stayed in the enveloping fog almost unseeable.

At Madrid a plane like ours of the Iberia Airlines was hit head-on while arriving in heavy fog at the airport; ninety people dead.

Segovia is a town fifty miles north of Madrid in Old Castile. Under clear skies we climbed to distant mountains where, at a peak of the Guadarrama range, we crossed to the Spain the Romans occupied before they were ousted by the Visigoths who were ousted by the Moors. About these mountains of hottest fighting in the Civil War, Hemingway wrote *For Whom the Bell Tolls*—of a guerrilla camp of Loyalists hid behind fascist lines to blow up a bridge, and of an American, Robert Jordan, who died in the attempt to stop Franco. Segovia goes back to the first century A.D., its proud spectacle a Roman aqueduct built two thousand years ago in the time of the emperor Trajan. They call it the glory of Segovia and the work of the devil, its massive arches stretching from hill to hill over the town captive beneath.

Nearby Ávila lives in the past of Old Castile, enclosed by battlemented walls built in the twelfth century. It appeared lost in the Middle Ages if, Betty said, you ignored the car-wash signs. Ávila is dedicated to

Saint Teresa, born here in 1515, called the most important woman in the sixteenth century. She's important to me because of the candid autobiography, *The Life of Teresa of Jesus,* she wrote to account for her busy mystical life. My fondness for saints baffles me since, being secular, I have no desire to become one. Perhaps the reason is such extraordinary things—marvels, miracles, illuminations—happened to them, like hanging on a sunbeam or talking with fishes.

Teresa of Ávila entered a Carmelite convent at eighteen. One day at nearly forty she fell in tears into a trance and saw Christ rising from the sepulchre to show her his wounds. Soon after she saw the Trinity. As her visions increased, the scandalized nuns feared she was possessed of the devil, who in his appearances took to impersonating God. For a while Teresa feared so herself when he threw her down a flight of stairs and she had a peculiarly bright vision of hell. Being most of the time a sensible person, a witty one who laughed often, she replied to a brother who thought of meditating on hell with one word, "Don't!" She had raptures, during which she became lifeless while her soul flew toward heaven. In 1651 Bernini made his famous sculpture of Saint Teresa's ecstasy (as she described it) when an angel pierced her heart with a golden spear "so that it penetrated to my entrails" and left her afire, consumed by the pain and passion of love. "A rapture is absolutely irresistible," she wrote.

In the church at Ávila, at a gold baroque altar a bejeweled Teresa offers her blessing. She was tall with white skin and rosy cheeks, black curly hair, intense black eyes. The impassioned poet Richard Crashaw wrote a hymn to Saint Teresa, "O thou undaunted daughter of desires," who had the eagle in her and the dove. When she died her body smelled of violets. I saw her little finger, kept as a sacred relic.

Her appeal is heightened too because Saint John of the Cross was her associate. In my poetry course I talked about Saint John, his dark night of the soul and climb up the penitential stair that inspired T. S. Eliot upward in *Ash Wednesday.* I hadn't thought of Saint John as flesh and blood, but Ávila kept his presence and two of his bones—a small frail Castilian given to ecstasies, who, said Teresa with amusement, would if one spoke to him at once fall into a trance. For seeking with Teresa to simplify the Carmelites to a barefoot order, both were threatened by the Inquisition. In 1577 John was kidnapped, taken to Toledo, lashed and tortured by the friars till he nearly died and worms bred in his tunic from the blood of the scourgings. Each night the brothers formed a circle and flogged him. In his prison cell he wrote the *Spiritual Canticle* that says, "Where there is no love, it is for you to bring love." During the last years of his life he wrote *The Dark Night of the Soul:* "On a dark night, kindled in love with yearnings I went forth."

To think the name Torquemada exists in Ávila, that such fierce love and hate flamed in the same town. Torquemada was a Dominican friar who in the Inquisition was made the Grand Inquisitor by Ferdinand and Isabella. According to Prescott, the historian, he burned to death 10,220 persons to defend God and rid Spain of the hated Moors, Jews, heretics. Full of years and merit as torturer, he returned to Ávila where, sixteen years before the birth of Saint Teresa, he died.

Next morning we were picked up at the Hotel Palace and climbed into a larger motor coach for a circular tour of Spain. We were leaving winter behind in Madrid, heading south to Andalusia and the Mediterranean. And of the people in the bus, gathered in the slow season from other tours, most were Afrikaners—eager young couples never so far from home—others from Brazil and Chile. A fractious fellow of Venezuela wearing a leather wine bag slung round his hips, a clown of ribald song, gave no trouble. Our tour guide had a way of handling nuisances and eccentrics.

It was a pleasure to settle down comfortably with Mariano. I knew I was well off, as I've been before—with Niki in Greece on the Four-Day Classical Tour, Herbert in the Andes, Oscar in Sicily. This time Mariano was in the catbird seat, a Castilian educated at the University of Madrid, who while practicing law was struck one day with an urge to travel. After passing examinations he became a guide to "everywhere," he said, "all over the world." How much knowledge does *that* take? Now with a family in Madrid, Mariano was happy in a life to which he appeared addicted. He was a short stout man, amiable of manner, whose deep voice shifted effortlessly from Spanish to English, dwelling fondly on words like "artistical" and "touristical." Unlike Oscar, Mariano wasted no gesture or emotion except on the subject of the siesta, which he recommended when he had exhausted himself and turned on soft music to lull us. He had the courtesy of a Spaniard. He made travel like this seem a reasonable lifelong pursuit.

I'm glad Mariano was there to talk about La Mancha. Beyond Toledo in central Spain we came to a vast barren plain through which the highway passes from Madrid to Andalusia. Though the multitude of windmills dotting the horizon have nearly disappeared, tilted at no more, for reminder an occasional billboard pictured a lean Don Quixote astride his horse Rosinante. The knight of the doleful countenance—the Man of La Mancha—wandered over this treeless land in search of giants to joust with and defeat. The novel begins, "In a certain village in La Mancha" where Cervantes placed it, of whom his celebrated contemporary, Lope de Vega, said there was no writer as bad as Cervantes or anyone so foolish as to read his book and praise *Don Quixote*.

While we rode along it began to rain, allowing me to chant to myself "The rain in Spain stays mainly in the plain of La Mancha."

Our destination was Córdoba, on the Guadalquivir River, to which the Arabs came in the eighth century and stayed immovably for nearly eight hundred years. It was one of the most magnificent and populous cities of the ancient world, Moorish in character, till in 1236 it fell to Ferdinand III of Castile and became part of Christian Spain. Though it declined greatly in power, the Moors remained till at last they were expelled.

The glory of Córdoba, which is the great mosque or Mesquita, was begun in the eighth century. In a city that once contained six hundred mosques, the Mesquita stood alone, incomparable in its beauty like the Taj Mahal, an enchanted place of 1,200 columns in an endless series of parallel aisles linked by interweaving arches to look like a multicolored forest of onyx, jasper, marble. It had nineteen bronze gateways, four thousand bronze and copper lamps, and in its center was an immense gold and crystal shrine that held the Koran. On their knees the Moorish worshipers circled the shrine seven times, till the stone floor grew hollow and worn by centuries of prayer.

The Christians couldn't allow a pagan mosque like this to remain the magical creation it was. In the sixteenth century they walled it in and ripped out the center, demolishing more than three hundred columns to build a Gothic church in the middle of the temple and turn the Mesquita into a Catholic cathedral—with baroque high altar, chancel, choir, chapels dedicated to the Virgin, saints fitted into niches. The incongruity of it is saddening, a dreadful mistake, the harsh imposing of one religion on another—the Cross for the Crescent. Emperor Charles V told the church fathers, "You have destroyed what was unique in the world."

The days spent in Seville were sun-gold. There is a city easy to love, with palm-lined streets and orange trees, whose inhabitants are rumored to be happy and carefree, at the same time preoccupied with death in their fondness for bullfights and worship of grim bleeding crucifixes. The Moorish maxim "Life is much shorter than death" fits the mood of Seville that lives with a carnival air ready for the next fiesta. It's the city of Don Juan, the legendary rake and seducer, of Molière's *Don Juan* and Byron's *Don Juan* and Mozart's *Don Giovanni* (who had 700 mistresses in Italy, 800 in Germany, 91 in France, 1,003 in Spain); the city of Rossini's *Barber of Seville* and Bizet's *Carmen*. Carmen they say was a real girl stabbed to death at the entrance to the bullring, and the cigar factory where she worked is one of the sights. For a while I wondered why Shakespeare hadn't put his Moor Othello in Seville instead of Venice, till Ted reminded me how unpopular Spain was in England after the Armada.

Our hotel, the Alfonso XIII, formerly a palace, is the one Hemingway objected to for its "comfortless grandeur," but he didn't like Seville anyway or its bullfights. If the King of Spain dropped in I could offer him hospitality from the impressive array of bottles in my room. A cunning device is a set of push buttons lined up over the bed, each button with a little picture above it to indicate the service available. The trick is to punch the right button in the middle of the night. Each of us, Betty, Ted, and I, managed independently to push the wrong one about 4:00 A.M. while trying to turn on the light. Instantly a smiling bellboy knocked at the door with a bottle of wine and two crystal glasses on a tray. At Betty and Ted's door he appeared *twice* in one night and bowed out hastily when they shook their heads in alarm. It must happen all night long.

The shops of Seville were festive, stocked with bright objects nobody needs—castanets, tambourines, painted fans, embroidered shawls, flamenco dolls, holy images. Otherwise there was an Arabic Tower of Gold, a Tower of Silver, and a splendid cathedral built over the ancient Moorish mosque. It had sweet saintly Murillos, Seville's own painter, and a mural of Saint Isidore of Seville, the encyclopedic saint who in the seventh century kept bees and wrote *Origins,* setting down all knowledge. Like Pliny he included such items as that the stars have a soul. At the corner of the cathedral—the largest in the world after St. Peter's and the Mesquita—was the lofty Giralda, a minaret with a revolving statue of Faith turning uncertainly not to Mecca but to the four winds like a weathercock. Inside the cathedral Christopher Columbus lay in an elevated coffin borne on the shoulders of four stone figures. May he rest in peace after his stormy voyages following his death in 1506, when his body was shipped overseas to Santo Domingo, transferred for safety to Havana, and just before the Spanish-American War returned to Spain and placed in the cathedral. Spain honors the Italian Cristóbal Colón more gratefully than we do.

Above all I loved the flamenco dancing Seville has made her own. It was created in Andalusia by the gypsies, fiery improvisational dancing that, no less passionate, has become traditional, strict in its routines. In the small nightclub the dancers seemed caught in a spell, oblivious of all but the movement of the dance. On the iron spiral staircase they gathered to wait their turn, marking the beat, catching the staccato rhythm before sweeping down to the stage. Between each man and woman, whirling in perfect accord, the desire grew and the being desired, convincing proof that one sex is meant for the other. Yet the flamenco song that accompanied the dancing was most often tragic in tone, like the wailing Portuguese fado song, like all love song every-where.

I could see why Mariano enjoyed this Spanish tour. Last night he studied the dancers with open joy, and today, after the drive south from Seville to Jerez de la Frontera, he was more than pleased with the local sherry. In a town surrounded by miles of orderly vineyards, we stopped at the wine cellars or *bodegas* of Sandeman (who makes sherry in Jerez and port in Portugal). Sherry was invented in Jerez, named by the English *sherris* to approximate the sound—in Spain called *vino de Jerez*—a white wine stored aboveground in huge casks to mature for five years before being fortified by dark sweet wines or brandy to give it a distinctive flavor.

Just before noon, we sat down at a long table in the storehouse with wine glasses and bottles before us to sample the sherry produced there, from very pale dry to amontillado to sweet dessert sherry to cognac. The first two appealed to me, especially the amontillado that I used to read about as a child in Poe's "The Cask of Amontillado," and scared by the sinister tale vowed never to touch. Now the amontillado made me feel, as it was itself, mellow and well aged.

To reach the Costa del Sol, the Spanish Riviera, we drove from Jerez to the shining city of Cádiz, on a rock peninsula surrounded by the Atlantic, called by Byron the prettiest town in Europe. It looked too modern to have been founded by the Carthaginians, and the paella we had for lunch was surely unknown in Carthage. Then, where the Atlantic and Mediterranean meet at the Strait of Gibraltar, the Rock came in view rising straight and sheer from the sea. In Spain they call it the "Spanish Rock," though the British have held it nearly three centuries since Spain lost it in a sea battle off Málaga. "Some fine morning," said Mariano, "we'll get back our Rock. Wait and see."

The Costa del Sol is for playboys, a narrow coastal strip on the Mediterranean stretching from Algeciras for 150 miles of sunny beaches, luxury villas, imposing hotels. A few years ago these were fishing villages in the poorest region of Spain, now resorts frequented by the jet set, film stars, maharajas, and King Fahd of Saudi Arabia, who has a palace and mosque here in a royal return of the Moors. After speeding along the Sun Coast, aware of passing Ferraris and anchored yachts, we came to the town of Benalmádena and the Hotel Triton, a resort hotel grandiose in size. Before dinner the owner of the Triton, a friendly but aggrieved Swiss gentleman, stopped to chat with the three of us in the deserted lounge and point out its emptiness. Privately we agreed it was like being lost in the Escorial, away from our group and Mariano, who were staying at sensible hotels. But dinner tonight was a consoling filet of sole and cold asparagus, nougat ice cream and Chablis.

I liked being idle if not rich for a couple of days on this glamorous strip, thriving with shops, pubs, orange trees, and "Hamburguesas." Too soon we climbed into the motor coach and went on ten miles to Málaga, where Picasso was born, a Mediterranean port city framed by the highest mountains in Spain; and on a hundred miles to Granada, high among the Sierra Nevadas where the peaks are like cathedrals.

Granada is a city of pomegranate trees. It was the last possession of the Moors in Spain, theirs till January 1492 when the last Moorish king, Boabdil, surrendered his kingdom to Ferdinand and Isabella. By then the rest of Spain was Catholic and the hated Moors of Granada were ordered to become Christians, given four months to accept baptism, be expelled, or die. The Inquisition, founded twelve years before, was ready to deal with them. As a race they perished, who had conquered Spain and dominated it so long and so well.

The steep climb to the Alhambra was through a luxuriant park, where the Duke of Wellington planted elm trees, to the entrance Gate of Pomegranates where nightingales sing. The Alhambra isn't a single palace but several palaces, enclosed by a fortified wall overlooking the city. A dazzling jewel of many-colored tiles, gold mosaics, marble pillars, lacy filigree arcades in honeycomb style, emerald pools and fountains, it was built in the thirteenth century in the lavish style of Moorish sultans. Of the many courtyards the most exquisite was the Court of Lions, where twelve crudely carved marble lions supported a fountain with alabaster basins. Of the many halls the most elegant was the Hall of Justice, where Ferdinand and Isabella took formal possession of the Alhambra and Columbus stood spectator at the ceremony. Later that year he sailed for America.

The last resident king, three hundred years later, was Philip V. After he abandoned the cold damp palace, it became a desolate place, neglected and empty, till a lawless population quietly moved in—smugglers, vandals, thieves, beggars, stray dogs. Napoleon's troops, quartered there in 1808, defaced and nearly destroyed it. Yet when Washington Irving went to live in the Alhambra for four months in 1829, he found a rare curiosity that he came to love, wandering freely through marble halls, looking from his window on tangled weeds in the gardens of the summer palace, the Generalife. Irving occupied the once sumptuous apartments of Philip's queen, Elizabeth, while for neighbors along the corridors he had "a ragged brood who inhabit the Alhambra," a disreputable company of tramps and beggars. Bats and owls flew in and out.

Having written *The Conquest of Granada,* Irving began a series of sketches, *The Alhambra,* again revealing his sympathy for King Boabdil, a merciful man, and for the heroic Moors in their struggle against Christian conquerors. The custodian of the palace, Doña Antonia Molina, her nephew Manuel and niece Dolores looked after Irving, made his bed and served his meals. He ate breakfast in the Court of Lions and dinner in the Hall of Ambassadors, bathed in the pool of the Court of Myrtles. They told him legends of the place, and he eagerly set them down. His self-appointed guide, Mateo Jiménez, a tall youth in a tattered cloak, claimed to be of a clan that had inhabited the Alhambra since the conquest. His family lived in a hovel above the gate.

Irving gathered no tales, though, from the nearby gypsies of Granada, three thousand of whom lived and still live in caves once the hiding places of the Moors. The gypsy settlement, the Sacromonte, is on the mountain opposite, where the flamenco is danced for tourists and the caves are gaudy with hangings. "The gypsies," wrote Laurie Lee, "are one of the aristocracies of Spain."

Nor did Irving mention the tombs of Ferdinand and Isabella, in a royal chapel behind the Metropolitan Cathedral of Granada. Side by side they lie innocent in marble, whom time has transformed into falsity—the two relentless leaders of the Inquisition. Down in the crypt beneath the chapel their bones are kept, each in a pitifully small leaden box—five boxes in all including their daughter mad Joanna who inherited the crown, her husband Philip the Fair (whose embalmed body Joanna carried about with her everywhere), and one child.

Like Irving, the poet Lorca believed the fall of this noble Moorish city to Ferdinand and Isabella was a disaster. Lorca called Granada "a paradise set apart from the world," a city of gypsies about which he wrote songs that made him beloved in Spain:

> O city of gypsies,
> Who that has seen can forget?
> City of musk and sorrow,
> City of cinnamon towers.

Lorca was born in a nearby village and died tragically in Granada at thirty-seven when, at the outbreak of the Civil War, he was shot by Franco's men, his body thrown into a common grave—Lorca, who wrote so longingly of "nightingale yesterdays."

When at last we drove back to Madrid and the same Hotel Palace after a trip of a thousand miles, it seemed several months later. In Madrid time had stood still and the city, assuming the date was appropriate, was even yet celebrating Christmas. Our last night there the streets were ablaze with light—floodlights, lighted fountains, silver stars and reindeer outlined in the sky. Madrid was thronged with merrymakers in fancy dress singing carols, some kissing in public (till lately illegal in Spain), some dancing in front of the Galerías Preciadas, a department store downtown, under a skyful of fireworks. This, we said as we joined the commotion, was our gift to ourselves, observing peace and love in Madrid this December.

"What could you possibly see of Spain in two or three weeks?" people were inclined to ask on our return to the States. A few years ago I spent two weeks driving with friends across America, stopping at the national parks, visiting Abraham Lincoln in Springfield, Illinois, Mark Twain in Hannibal, Missouri, and somebody's cousin in Twin Falls, Idaho. Those who heard with amazement how long we had taken for the trip exclaimed, "Two whole *weeks?* You could have made it in five hours by flying."

1 9 8 4

Here comes the year that wears George Orwell's label. Imagine his naming an ominous novel *1984*, indifferent to the fact that eventually the year would arrive and we would have to live through it. Already the debate begins as to how accurate Orwell was in his predictions. Some say he was wrong. A full-page advertisement of the United Technologens in the *New York Times* announced, "Thanks to the electric microchip and the technology that brought it into being, 1984 has not become *1984*." It takes an electric microchip to save us from the bomb and the arms race with Russia.

Saul Bellow says we as a people are greatly concerned with perishability.

Orwell was a dying man of forty-seven when in 1948 he reversed the numerals for his nightmare picture of a catapulting world ruled by hate and terror, in which man had destroyed the meaning of life. In explanation he wrote, "I do not believe that the kind of society I describe *will* arrive, but I believe that something resembling it *could* arrive."

These are rough times for Eros, the Greek god of love, who is the winged boy atop the fountain at Piccadilly Circus. Now ninety years old, he has been retired to mend his scars and restore his youth, leaving London loveless.

At the Piccadilly Hotel there's an Eros bar, where nothing really erotic is encouraged. I used to stare at the beautiful naked boy, wondering what he was doing in the middle of Piccadilly as a memorial to the

8th Earl of Shaftesbury, or why they choose to call Eros the Angel of Christian Charity.

It seems to me anyone who writes books about travel has an obligation to enjoy himself. Take Paul Theroux. He says a travel writer *travels for the reader,* who, I think, deserves to be glad he went. Faced with nothing but vexations, the reader is sure to grow restive and like the author sick for home. What he wants is a companion with neither a jaundiced eye nor a nose for trouble.

Theroux's *The Kingdom by the Sea* is a dispiriting journey of three months around the coast of Great Britain, where he refused to be taken for a sightseer or go near the sights, managing even to miss the sound of churchbells. As he boarded a train on May Day for Margate, his starting point, "No," he thought. "No sightseeing: no cathedrals, no castles, no churches, no museums." But what about me, the reader? I *like* sights.

Instead Theroux stayed at cheap seaside hotels and boardinghouses, ate wretched food, talked with landladies, walked in drizzle, and reported his suffering: "It was a mystery to me why no one had ever come to Britain and written about its discomforts."

At Sandwich he said, "I saw a man with a frightened face walking a tottering dog." Sandwich is a quaint old town, one of the Cinque Ports that, before the sea receded, supplied 40,000 herrings each year to the monks at Canterbury. Thomas Becket landed there in 1170 on his way to Canterbury to be murdered. Theroux might at least have escorted me the twelve miles from Sandwich and let me stand in Thomas Becket's footsteps. "I don't want to go to Canterbury," he told someone who suggested it.

Along the deserted beaches he always expected to find a murder victim or a suicide. He came upon very old people under blankets staring out to sea as if they were waiting for Godot. They made him feel eighty years old. "I hate Brighton," he said. "It's a mess."

A man needn't *shun* pleasure. At Minehead on the Bristol coast where he walked lonely and alone, he could have carried in his pocket Hazlitt's "My First Acquaintance with Poets" and listened to Coleridge, who never stopped talking on a jaunt through Minehead down the Bristol Channel. Theroux went in the opposite direction, making notes in his diary while from Cornwall to Wales to northern Ireland to Scotland the towns whispered to him, "Move on!" "Go home!" Holyhead appeared to be dying of gangrene. "I came to hate Aberdeen more than any other place I saw," he wrote. "I chose to stop at Dundee because it had a reputation for dullness."

He makes me ashamed, dragging him away from home like that.

I had a bad time with John Steinbeck in *Travels with Charley* when he crossed America in a pickup truck accompanied by a French poodle with bladder trouble. One thing I hate is getting lost, but lost Steinbeck was determined to be. As he said, "I was born lost and take no pleasure in being found." It became an endurance test for him and Charley, whose complaints he recorded. The only state they liked was Montana. Steinbeck dutifully talked with Americans he came across: waitresses in diners, a parking lot attendant, a hitchhiker, people living in trailer courts. "Why had I thought I could learn anything about the land?" he wondered. He deplored the littering, the traffic-jammed highways while pounding out the miles, misled by maps, assailed by doubts and such desolation that twice he sent for his wife to meet him, in Chicago and Amarillo, Texas. It was a relief to get the damn trip over.

E. B. White, given the same assignment by *Holiday,* turned back at Galeton, Pa., saying "I might as well be home in bed."

The best travel writer I know is Peter Fleming, who before his death in 1971 pushed on cheerfully to the impenetrable jungles of Brazil, to Outer Mongolia and Chinese Turkistan, accommodating himself with equal pleasure and equanimity to the hardships, the natives, and the scenery. In his travel books, *Brazilian Adventure* and *News from Tartary,* he said he allowed himself to entertain high hopes while traveling, "not because I expect them for a moment to be realized, but because I enjoy entertaining high hopes."

Wisps of March

I wandered lonely as a cloud,
One small white cirrus in the sky
Unqualified to scud or threaten,
No cloud less turbulent, no nimbus I,
No massy cumulus to cry
Havoc from heaven, which is why
Jesus wants me for a sunbeam.

Notes on writing (during a bout of pneumonia):

Bertolt Brecht, *Diary:* "Of all the arts, that of writing is the vulgarest and most ordinary. It is too public, too unambiguous and open to checking. The writer's own views lie plainly visible as does his wish to force them on the reader." Example of ordinary writing, vulgar and open to checking: Brecht, *Diary,* entry for March 2, 1921, "Spent the night sleeping."

The critic Anatole Broyard believes figures of speech should be removed from the language, on the ground they inevitably debase it. From Frederic Prokosch's *Voices, a Memoir:*
"She darted across the room like a desperate canary."
"One of the petals fell on his nose and clung to it wistfully."
"Gertrude Stein looked very voluptuous as she licked her spoon, which she did with half-closed eyes and a slow, stately rhythm. Her tongue suggested the bow of an expert fiddler who is playing a languid and delicious adagio."

Elie Wiesel: "Why do I write? Perhaps in order not to go mad."
Borges: "Why do I write? To ease the passing of time."
A writer may assume he is elected to write, chosen by God. Kathleen Raine declares she is a poet by heaven's will, her gift "merely God-given." In her autobiography *Farewell Happy Fields,* at her birth her father placed a rose in her hands and her poet's fingers clasped it. At three the chickweed "filled my beholding as full as a rose window." Her friend Willa Muir told her to stop writing honeydew.

Ann Truit in her journal *Daybook:* "The pain of poets seems to me unmitigated" (more honeydew). "Why hold that poets are so sensitive?" asked Louis MacNeice. "A thickskinned grasping lot who filch and eavesdrop."

"Writing is an estimable profession," observed John Cheever. "But the grandeur of life escapes us."

Time brightened April by announcing the end of the sex revolution. Over and done, they said. The obsession with recreational or revolving-door sex, tiring after too many whirls, has lost its appeal. Back we go exhausted, with renewed faith in true love, courtship, fidelity, and marriage.

In a perfect piece of timing, a study of *The Lecherous Professor* appears as the revolution winds down. Everyone agrees the academic world is by nature conservative, characteristically unaware of recent events like the breakdown of morality. Belatedly sex attacks the professor. An AP release said of four hundred interviews and case histories gathered by two women at the University of Cincinnati about their male colleagues, "This may well be the most chilling indictment of higher education ever published." It exposes the blackmail method of promising an A to a student for sexual favors, an F if she refuses. There used to be a rule that professors keep their office door open while conferring with a student. If doors are shut and lechery prevails, I suggest an ad hoc committee be appointed to study the problem. Why did only male professors get interviewed?

"Sex and cheerleading are two different things," said a cheerleader on the news show "Good Morning, America."

With no travel plans—only a vague desire to go to Zanzibar or the Promised Land—I spent the summer on Guess Road. (James Reeves: "Approve the traveler who never went.") I live on Guess Road, perhaps the only Guess Road in existence. "Is this a joke?" friends write, with an arrow pointing to my address. The other day Ray Bradbury, who lives in California, wrote, "*Guess* Road? Sounds like the story of my life." He knows a man in L.A. whose address is Elusive Lane.

It runs through the countryside and relaxes into farmland that soon will turn into outskirts with a four-lane highway as traffic grows and man disposes. Soon the jig will be up for a community of rabbits, squirrels, raccoons, owls, quail, moles, hummingbirds, meadowlarks, mourning doves, and singing titmice. The bobwhites are already gone. Nobody's seen a possum lately. The cardinal sings "Ciao" instead of "Cheer cheer."

This winter my nextdoor neighbor, three acres away, heard an ominous sound in the night and went to investigate. A huge feathered object came hurtling down from the pine tree he was standing under. A wild turkey, close to extinct on Guess Road, landed on his head and with a screech disappeared. A gray fox sometimes inhabits my wood. Three white-tailed deer wander across the lawn and into the trees, nothing more decorative than they.

The country colors remind me of Dylan Thomas's "Fern Hill" that was applegreen, sungold, lambwhite—like my green willow, gold jasmine, white dogwood, not to deny the scarlet azaleas and Rose of Sharon Baptist Church. Guess Road. I guess I've taken it back and forth to town, oh, ten thousand times. Town is worth the trip, famed for the Dukes and Bull Durham tobacco (smoked by Gladstone, Tennyson, Disraeli); for Mr. Bennett's farmhouse where the Civil War ended seventeen days after Appomattox; for Dr. Rhine's extrasensory perception and Dr. Kempner's extraordinary rice diet.

Inventory

This is the place. This is the house I love.
The river runs below, the countryside
Is not yet lost in traffic lanes, three deer
Ran through my dooryard only yesterday.
And I've magnolia trees and mockingbirds
And partiality enough to claim
This is the place. This is the world I love,
Where nothing matters now but that I keep
My wits intact, my thought uncomplicated
By too much memory or expectation.
Who would believe in such a hiding place
It takes survival tactics to remain?

Mike Royko, a Chicago newspaper columnist, asked an expert on body building, "Does it develop the entire body?"

"Everything but the brain."

He should try aerobic dancing. Not only does it build the body, it takes using your head to be light and airy (an airhead), to grasp the language of aerobics, a vocabulary of bounces, stretches, lunges, flick kicks, cha-cha, can-can, charleston, and water pulls. After five years I perform these on command, which is better than I ever did at learning decorum.

If Walt Whitman were alive, he would sing the body aerobic.

Aerobic Dancer

First we zig and then we zag,
We nip and tuck and call the tune

And face the music, counting heartbeats,
As if, alas, all heartache were
Cardiovascular.

With fall coming on, Sears Roebuck wants to sell me a new outlook on life. It is a Mature Outlook, available by mail order, just follow directions. My outlook is so mature it's going to seed. "That's a nasty outlook to face," said Ogden Nash, "but it's what you get for belonging to the human race."

Bloomsbury's Lady Ottoline Morrell once consulted a psychiatrist in Lausanne whose specialty was eliminating unwholesome outlooks. He emptied her head of its prospects and vistas and advised her to give up thinking.

Having written five travel books devoted to the cities of the world—*Cities, Places, Travels, Destinations,* and now *Journeys*—Jan Morris has fulfilled an ambition and returned to Wales. My guess is she ran out of titles. She sounds weary of the U.S.A., toward which her feelings are less than fraternal, having found here neither Auden's Just City nor Saint Augustine's City of God. She had no fun in Fun City, Las Vegas, bored with its tomfool architecture and the casinos of the Strip. Her conclusion was, "Ah, but there is to the very presence of Las Vegas, I came to feel by the end of my stay, a suggestion of true evil." It reminded her of towns in Sicily where half the population consists of murderers, kidnappers, extortionists, and the other half pretends not to notice.

On a five-day visit to Houston or Boomtown, "a bit of a dump," big, brash, and improbable, nothing pleased her—the skyscrapers or the oil people in big hats—so much as a supermarket with six kinds of English marmalade. The significance, she said, of this Texas city to the Houstonians, who are under the impression it is paradise, is that the first word uttered by a man on the moon was "Houston." Neil Armstrong said it to NASA, making it Houston's moon.

Miami turned out worse. After five days she found it by normal standards not a city but a vast jelly, "an amoebic coagulation of separate settlements," reminiscent of the 1930s of mock-Italian villas and Dorothy Lamour at Eden Roc.

Santa Fe, she reflected, was the "artiest, sculpturest, weaviest and potteryest town on earth," with galleries of trivial pictures, gimcrack shops, Indian trading posts, a motley population infested with poseurs and pretense, a town full of sham and adobe.

Jan Morris looked at four cities presumably typical of America and worth investigating. She found them corrupt, phony, disappointing (on an earlier trip she couldn't bear Indianapolis and thought Washington, D.C., an alienating city "almost expressly designed" to be destroyed by a nuclear missile). Of the above four, I've been to Santa Fe and love the place. However, a traveler is free to come and go, no law or ordinance against it, though little he knows how much it would please him if he stayed a week.

I call them, in Shakespeare's words, "the quick comedians." Or in Wordsworth's, "What you will / Republican or pious." In the Reagan-Mondale debates before the election in November, Mondale fell so far behind in the polls that, someone said, he couldn't win unless Reagan was revealed as a transvestite. At Kansas City, Reagan's best line was "I will not exploit my opponent's youth and inexperience." At Louisville, his worst line was, in explaining why he doesn't go to church, "I think the Lord understands."

"You know what I stand for," he said, as if we actually did. "I am still the champ."

When the storms died down Reagan carried every state except Mondale's own Minnesota. People who cried "Send him back to Hollywood" must have voted for him. The claim is that Geraldine Ferraro's appearance on the Mondale ticket did nobody any good. She provided novelty as a woman who said "I will be a leader," and George Bush, elected vice-president, provided further novelty by bragging after their debate he had "kicked a little ass."

Charity Begins at Christmas

There are people, said Günter Grass,
Who would bend the banana straight
For the benefit of mankind. (There are those
Who would hook a rainbow trout
To keep the poor fish from drowning.)
They are the guileless ones, the pushovers,
Like whom I have a life mission,
Though not either of the above.

Now we're done with 1984, I see that Orwell came close to predicting the way things are and the world is. Had my bout of pneumonia finished me off, I would naturally have blamed Orwell. He was right about current atrocities: terrorism, mass killings, war, human misery, evil and hate. He was wrong, fortunately, about peace and love. We have a faint hope of gaining on them both by 2084.

As John Leonard, the book critic, observed, "It takes a long time and a lot of practice to become a human being." For one thing, the number of imponderables grows, like how do you know when you are one?

So I'll end the year in the vicinity of lions.

1 9 8 5

AFRICAN SAFARI   Nobody told me what it was like to go on safari in Africa. Travelers seldom come back and make the journey visible, though Teddy Roosevelt and Hemingway showed well enough how it used to be. Roosevelt went out from Nairobi on foot in 1910, accompanied by five hundred black porters (to him savages) dressed in blue, walking in single file with an American flag flying. Roosevelt shot 296 animals (including 9 lions, 5 elephants, 13 rhinos, 7 hippos), after which he wrote an exultant book, *African Game Travels,* its two hundred illustrations devoted to horizontal victims, with captions: "Lion shot by Mr. Roosevelt," "Mr. Roosevelt beside dead hippo." He kept a diary of shots and misses (like that big-game hunter Louis XVI, who in his career ran down 1,274 stags): "The bullet went a little high, breaking the gazelle's back above the shoulders." "Hartebeest shot through face, zebra between neck and shoulder." Standing with gun over the body of a giraffe, he admired "the beautiful coloring of my prize." He found safari life exhilarating—the sport of killing "great fun," the white man of acknowledged superiority—and slept soundly each night in a pitched tent.

Hemingway was a big shot too, like Roosevelt a happy predator. In *Green Hills of Africa,* 1935, "I did not mind killing anything, any animal, if I killed it cleanly," he wrote. "It was funny to see a hyena shot at close range." "I hit him [the lion] with the Springfield and he went down and spun over and I shot him again." Hemingway's finest story of Africa, "The Snows of Kilimanjaro," had nothing to do with safaris or killing. It told of a snow-capped mountain, "wide as all the world, great, high, and unbelievably white in the sun."

A total ban on hunting wild animals was declared by Kenya in 1977.

As a tourist on safari, I had a few qualms beforehand and several doubts. Why go so far to see an elephant, when I avoid zoos these days and circuses? I imagined the scene in a Land Rover on a smooth paved road through Kenya, borrowing someone's binoculars to catch a glimpse of zebras no more than a smudge on the horizon, a progression of indistinct giraffes, or faroff unrecognizable animals like oryxes, kudus, gerenuks, dik-diks, and bongos. I didn't even have a camera. I had a bottle of malaria pills, pills for dysentery, a bodyful of inoculations for cholera, yellow fever, and tetanus. "Why don't you just take a nice trip to Europe?" Dr. Wysor asked, "where you don't need all these shots?"

Nobody told me it would be the excursion of my life, close to mystical, close, as Symond said, to being in on creation.

We arrived at Nairobi's Kenyatta Airport on December 31, thirty people mostly from Connecticut. Together they had left the snows of Hartford with the conductor of the safari, Symond Yavener, a professor at Central Connecticut State University, and his wife Martha. I was the stranger, there because last year in Sicily I met Esther from Connecticut and we became friends. She had telephoned to invite me along. "You'll love Symond," she said. "We all do." Since his background was Russian, I pictured a burly, bearded academic in a fur cap. Instead he was a slender, clean-shaven, warmly smiling man in his fifties, born in Hartford, who takes his friends on holiday tours in Egypt, Russia, now Kenya, concerned for everyone in his care. It seemed likely I would love him too as predicted.

Nairobi, the safari capital of the world, a mile up and cool in the highlands, looked surprisingly European, a city of flowers and tree-lined streets that not long ago was a squalid frontier village and before that a waterhole used by Masai herdsmen. It started life in 1900 when the British built a railroad north to Uganda. We drew up at the newest hotel in town, the Inter-Continental, white and glittering in chrome and glass, with corridors of smart boutiques, gardens of crimson bougainvillea, a swimming pool. Opposite rose the towering cylindrical Kenyatta Center, the cone-shaped Congress Hall, and a statue of the black leader Jomo Kenyatta. Though an inviting city, warm and flowery, after two nights under way with a stopover in Paris Esther and I wanted only to find our hotel room and sleep. Besides, tonight was New Year's Eve. The party in the Yaveners' suite lasted till midnight, when in my opinion our future together brightened steadily. Kissing will do that for you.

It was a safari of two thousand miles. We set out from Nairobi next morning in a caravan of six minibuses, each with an adjustable roof for standing to gaze over the top. The group had transformed itself into white hunters in bush jackets, khaki pants, sun hats, weighted down with cameras and binoculars, dressed to kill. Esther and I had the extraordinary luck to share a bus with four wholly congenial people: Alice Ann and Vincent, a nuclear engineer; Elie and Jack, he in insurance in Hartford. Our driver was Geoffrey (spelled as Chaucer did), a Kikuyu of twenty years' experience with safaris, a large, capable, amiable man in whom God himself would put his trust.

The new member of the company was Joe—Andrew Joe Chira— also a Kikuyu, in charge of the expedition, a so-called courier or director of operations. He had spoken to us briefly yesterday in the hotel, a reassuring leader obviously well-educated and able, who carefully explained the rules of the road: never step outside your van except at designated sites, never take a picture of a Masai warrior without his permission, never make unnecessary racket to alarm the animals. We were in good hands with Joe. He was prepared to bring us back in one piece.

We took the main road south, between Nairobi in the highlands and Mombasa on the coast, traveling by ourselves to avoid close formation with the other buses because of the dust. In no time the landscape changed into immensity, the endless flat grassy plains of Africa where the blue bowl of sky went on forever. The first animal we saw was a solitary eland (a kind of antelope with spiral horns), then three or four galloping giraffes, a troop of gray baboons that traipsed along chattering beside us. Somewhere the road changed into a deeply eroded dirt track full of potholes like craters, and Geoffrey used all his strength and skill to control the lurching, bouncing bus that acted like a startled gazelle. Before noon we reached the entrance to the largest game park in East Africa, Tsavo East (divided from Tsavo West by the Nairobi-Mombasa highway), where the soil was deep red and the thornbush grew and everywhere on the sunlit plain were wide-topped acacias or umbrella trees whose foliage giraffes eat. Hundreds of red, tapering ant hills rose like spires, the work of termites and taller than a man. The road grew worse, swampy and rutted, kept by government policy out of repair to discourage tourists from careering about in a world not theirs, where man was the intruder. Now in the midst of wild animals— not safely distant as I had supposed—we watched delicate gazelles frolicking without a care, grazing hartebeests, the lovely impala that leaped, Geoffrey said, at least thirty feet. We could expect lions, and there they were—a lioness with her two cubs under an acacia tree gazing sleepily at us, others scattered about the field, resting, yawning, royally indifferent to our presence. Time after time Geoffrey stopped the bus for the strange confrontation, we the caged prisoners, they the ones who were free.

We reached the Voi Safari Lodge in time for lunch, a sumptuous hotel situated in the middle of a wild game park! A resident baboon sat clowning on the roof, and the signs said "Keep quiet. Do not disturb the animals." From the terrace Symond stared out at the tremendous expanse beyond us, the spaciousness of these green plains of Africa, and he said, "It sends a shiver down my spine. It's limitless."

After lunch we climbed into the buses and went back for another game drive, this time running into wild elephants and baobab trees, both with huge trunks—the mammoth African elephants with wide ears waving, their skin dyed by the red soil of Tsavo. They say forty thousand live in the park. An ostrich sailed by like a plumy old girl being pursued, and the only sound was of cameras clicking to catch every last beast. Except for us, the landscape was sky with a ridge of acacias across the horizon. Then suddenly in the far distance we saw it, Mount Kilimanjaro, a diffused snowy mass of heavenly height, the Delectable Mountain—more cloud really, more ghost than mountain, its peaks not yet visible. But there it was, rising in Tanzania on the border of Kenya, and tomorrow it would be nearer, it would be right overhead.

At the Voi Safari Lodge where we spent the night, I had a talk with Joe, who was wearing a T-shirt adorned with big red apples above the words "Henderson, N.C."

"Do you know what N.C. means?" I said. "It means my home. It's where I live."

Joe laughed. "Sure, North Carolina." He knew about the States. His other T-shirt said "Yes to Michigan."

Joe, a good-looking, modern African of about forty, with small mustache and skin like ebony, has been a courier for thirteen years—a life he chose, after two years at the University of Nairobi, because he likes animals and people, except, that is, the British. Till Kenya gained her independence in 1963, they were the masters and Joe's people were the servants, often the slaves. His tribe, the Kikuyu, far outnumbering the rest, is the largest of the forty-six tribes in Kenya and the most advanced, most politically conscious—a carefree, adaptable, friendly people used to foreigners. I asked Joe which nationality he preferred in his acquaintance with tourists. "Japanese," he said to tease me. "They are grateful."

"Not Americans?"

"Yes, Americans, always the Americans, easy to please and full of loud complaint like children."

Joe has children, a daughter Helen, two young sons Mark and Kendall. "English names," he said and laughed. They're not brought up Anglican, though, but Roman Catholic.

This morning when we left Tsavo East Lodge, Joe was with us, in the front seat beside Geoffrey. To play no favorites he rode in a different van each day. It was a joy to have him tracking the wild game, especially so for Geoffrey, who could steer the plunging bus without having to scan the terrain for more beasts. Joe saw everything before we did. Impalas floating on air crossed and recrossed our path; a huge red elephant stood imperturbable in the road till the other five buses caught up and gathered round. (I thought of Fellini's remark, "Sometimes pulling a little tail, we find an elephant at the other end.") Joe, beckoning us out of the bus, led me over to touch the enormous red ears and rough hide. The elephant lifted its wrinkled trunk and flapped an ear but didn't bellow or charge. As we knew, rangers in Land Rovers patrolled the reserves day and night to see the rules were obeyed, to protect animals and people from each other, to impose heavy fines for leaving the bus.

By mid-morning we entered Tsavo West, the other half of the park that sprawls over eight thousand square miles. It was made famous some years ago by two man-eating lions that created terror by carrying off a victim night after night. In one month they ate twenty-nine men. Finally shot by a Colonel J. H. Patterson, who wrote *The Man-Eaters of Tsavo*, they were mounted and sent to the Field Museum in Chicago, where I remember as a college student quaking to see them.

Now in jungle bush wilderness the going was strenuous, the pitching bus more unruly than yesterday, worse than the natural shocks flesh is heir to. I marveled how people with weak backs bore the jolting over ruts and descent into bedrock. Yet the six in our van chatted and laughed as if riding on a mattress, while Joe and Geoffrey talked not in Swahili, the language that replaced English in 1974, but Kikuyu.

At Mzima Springs, again we left the bus to stand beside a crystal stream and gaze at the ferocious olive-green crocodiles who would eat your heart out, and the half-dozen fat hippos who showed their wide snorting nostrils above the water, while we kept silent to avoid exciting them. Hippos have nasty tempers. A clumsy gray wildebeest on the hill above peered down at us, and a sign said "Beware of dangerous animals." The name Mzima comes from the wild date palm. In this green oasis I counted sixty-seven nests of yellow weaver birds hanging like gold baskets from a single tree. A capuchin monkey was perched in a nearby acacia eating a package of cheese crackers. While we were gone, it had climbed into the coach and snitched what it could find. At the northern end of Tsavo West we crossed the Shetani lava flow, a barren treeless expanse covered with black lava rock from an extinct volcano that is said to have buried a whole village. Against this inky blackness we lined up Joe and Geoffrey for their picture, after Joe explained why the Masai refuse permission: they fear their soul may be captured by the camera. Joe gladly gave us his soul if we wanted it.

The close encounter of the day was a visit to the Masai, when we stopped inside the park at a *manyatta*, a Masai village. Tall warriors or herdsmen (who fill both roles), wearing red cloaks and carrying long spears, their skin painted with red ochre, greased hair in braids, strode out to greet us crying "Jambo!" (hello in Swahili). They led us through the opening to the small fenced-in village that consisted of a cluster of windowless huts made of mud and cow dung, encircling a noisome dung heap where the animals were kept at night. Such swarms of flies filled the air and batted our eyes we had trouble focusing on the populace—the smiling women with shaved heads, laden with bracelets, dangling earrings, beaded wire collars and coils of necklaces over bare breasts; or the bedecked naked children and babies whose bodies, faces, eyelids were a mass of flies. Geoffrey wrapped an arm around me to protect me from the importuning women who tried to touch my mouth pleading for my lipstick, while Joe stayed in the bus, his expression stoical, and Jack bought a spear he later used in a hopeless attempt to clean the stinking dung from his shoes. The Masai, a nomadic people rich in herds of cattle that graze among the wild animals, drink daily the milk and blood of cows. They clean their gourds with cow urine, and the smell of dung is fragrant to them.

Shortly we entered another game reserve, the Amboseli National Park, an immense open savannah beside the foothills of Mount Kilimanjaro that rises snow-blanketed through shining cloud to more than 19,000 feet, Africa's highest mountain. The Masai call it the White Mountain where the sun god lives, out of reach as if on Olympus. A barely moving herd of buffalo crossed the plain like a slow express train, a hundred zebras ran in single file among black-headed herons and warthogs, and we came upon a kill, three greedy lionesses eating the dismembered body of a zebra, one of the three with distended belly satisfied and licking her paws. They didn't look up when we stopped beside them, close enough to touch if the window were open. To them we didn't exist.

For the next two nights we stayed at the Amboseli Serena Lodge, where each pair of roommates occupied a separate entry along the flowery garden walk, with black-faced vervet monkeys playing about, sitting on the doorstep. During the day we were off in the bus till twilight, when the sky turned from shimmering gold to apricot, and we left the plains reluctantly, allowed to remain only in the daylight hours. The night belonged to the predators, the hungry lions, leopards, cheetahs out stalking and killing their prey that, playful as ewe lambs, had danced so heedlessly before dark.

By now I had moved up to sit beside Geoffrey, with his cordial permission, in the belief it would be less bumpy there, easier to write in my notebook. I was wrong. My notes were like the tracks of the secretary bird, undecipherable. I learned that Geoffrey was fond of Juicy Fruit gum and making jokes. When I reminded him he never asked me questions, though I asked him so many, he thought about it a while and said, "What's your tribe?"

"Northern," I said. "We fought the Southern tribe to save the Union." Geoffrey probably knew that from watching television.

Once he pointed to a herd of elephants. "Look, there's a male elephant with five legs."

I stared in astonishment. "Is he searching for a female?"

Geoffrey pondered before giving the answer worthy of a philosopher: "I think he's just feeling wonderful about being alive. He's a male elephant and he's proud of it."

Occasionally the joke was on Geoffrey. When he told us a strange bird was the bustard, calling it bastard because his vowels slip a little, Elie cried out, "Never mind about them. We have plenty of bastards at home."

From Amboseli Park we drove north again toward Nairobi and the central highlands, with Mount Kilimanjaro shining like a beacon over our shoulder, its base such a deep blue it seemed to float. Two lions rested at the roadside. Soon we were traveling in lush green hill country, past Thika and the flame trees, on our way to a tea plantation at the foot of the Ngong Hills belonging to the Mitchells, an elderly British couple who have spent their lives in Kenya. At the spacious home with clipped lawns and English gardens, Mrs. Mitchell served a buffet lunch and entertained us with talk as one of the last of the true colonials.

Beyond her acres she pointed to what had been the coffee plantation of Isak Dinesen, whom she knew as a distant neighbor. For seventeen years Baroness Blixen lived in Africa and for ten of them managed a six-thousand-acre farm in these highlands, till in 1931 she gave up her bankrupt farm and went back to Denmark. She had lived elegantly in a stone manor house with Persian rugs, silver and crystal, where she entertained the Prince of Wales, and her lover was a white hunter of big game, the son of the Earl of Winchilsea. In *Out of Africa* Isak Dinesen wrote possessively of the Kikuyu and Masai whom she lived among and loved. Though conscious of her rank, she found them more civilized than the British snobs whose racial prejudice and exploitation of the natives appalled her. She wrote of shooting lions, of the stillness of Africa, of being perfectly happy with a feeling of belonging there "as God had meant me to be." Hers was a Kenya that has disappeared, a British colony in white man's country where legal ownership was possible only to the privileged ruling class, and their servants and field hands were the dispossessed Kikuyu.

Sometime in the afternoon we crossed the equator, not far from Mount Kenya that actually rises on it. A board on stilts bearing a picture of Africa said, "This sign is on the equator, altitude 6,389 feet." A few scattered huts belonged to natives who cheered as we tumbled out of the van to take pictures of ourselves between the Tropic of Cancer and the Tropic of Capricorn, where night equals day.

Though I had heard before of the Mount Kenya Safari Club, it came as a shock to find a luxurious resort and country club at the equator. To reach it we drove through bamboo forests to a long entrance canopied by trees, emerging at a lavish estate on the slopes of Mount Kenya, with peacocks on the lawn, golf course, tennis courts, heated swimming pool, all meant for the Beautiful People who are its members. Every room had a fireplace, and on each of the nights we spent a man came to light the fire in case we felt a chill. From our windows was a closeup view of Mount Kenya, a pyramid imposed on the sky. Gifts from the management, such as a small carved wooden Laughing God ("A very special small Thought for our Esteemed Guest") appeared magically on our pillows. The club was founded as a game ranch in 1959 with the movie star William Holden its principal shareholder. He and actress Stefanie Powers lived here for some eleven years before his death. Now part owner, she spends much of her time in the green haven, and because of her generosity (in providing an orphanage for young wild animals abandoned by their mothers) has been made an honorary member of the Kikuyu tribe, which means she can marry a Kikuyu if she wants to. It is Kikuyu country; Mount Kenya is their mountain, the dwelling place of their god in the heart of the highlands.

This was the day a miracle happened, a *dies mirabilis*, Saturday, January 5. This morning nearly everyone chose to give up the game run at the Samburu Game Reserve well to the north of us, shuddering to recall the jounces and jolts of yesterday. The Mount Kenya Safari Club beckoned, offering irresistible pleasures and a day's relaxation in a playground of wealth and considerable style. Besides, by this time several were down with dysentery.

"Why do you suppose you and I haven't got it?" Esther said.

"Intestinal fortitude?"

"No joking matter. You may be next, you know." Esther decided to stay behind with the rest.

In the end only four went, with a driver named Gordon. Joe couldn't go, Geoffrey was too exhausted from hauling us over the rough roads. Bill and Elsie came along (Bill is making a documentary film of Kenya) and untiring Mr. D'Arcy. I sat in the front seat with Gordon, a driver on safaris since 1961, accommodating and patient without the easy friendliness of Geoffrey or the laughter.

A game reserve in Africa scarcely differs from a game park, except that here we left the road entirely and lit out across the desert-white plains among elands, gerenuks, oryxes that resemble a unicorn (all of them antelopes). We chased the comical warthogs who ran distractedly at twenty-five miles an hour with tail in air, leaving them to follow a herd of reticulated giraffes, near enough to see their eyelashes. At one time eighteen giraffes surrounded us, the handsome kind found in northern Kenya with glossy tan coat and regular web pattern of white stripes. Flowing through the reserve was the swampy Uaso Nyiro River, where the lion, cheetah, buffalo gathered to drink and a pair of tiny dik-diks the size of a cat fluttered by, the smallest of the antelopes.

We were completely by ourselves now, remote, isolated in a solitude of thousands of wild animals—they and we alone in the whole immensity of Africa. All at once the overwhelming realization hit me. In an absurdly small minibus we were alone on an endless plain with no horizon, in a thunderous silence that was like the beginning of the world. And the numberless animals close around us, created on the sixth day, were as they were then, and had always been, part of that cosmic silence. Among them a sense of peace, the kind that passes understanding, settled over me, and I made the great discovery: this was what a safari was about. This was why I had come. Nobody told me beforehand, nobody warned me what to expect, but it was there, oh, it was surely there. I prayed it wouldn't leave me or let me forget. I shut my eyes and listened to take the stillness in, to carry it away for future need—the measureless calm, the timeless serenity. I had never been so happy or so much at peace.

Just then we dived into another ditch and, climbing out, Gordon nearly ran down a male lion, with his shaggy head and black mane, asleep in the checkered shade of a thorn tree. Startled awake, he leaped up to face us with a vacant stare, snarled to show his ferocious teeth, turned slowly around and lay back down to sleep. He wasn't afraid of us or anything on this earth. He too was at peace.

When we returned to the Club at dusk, I felt like a changed person, complexities of life resolved, the world forgot, temporarily born again. We had driven many miles that day toward Ethiopia and Somaliland, as far north as the Buffalo Springs Reserve and Samburu Reserve, on to the small frontier town of Isiolo (where Joy Adams had lived with her husband George, a game warden, and raised the lioness cub Elsa of *Born Free*). Near Isiolo under an acacia we ate our picnic lunch packed by the Club and drank the African Tusker beer. Ten zebras passed in procession as we ate. It was a feast of chicken, ham, cheeses, passion fruit, so abundant I shared mine with a Samburu family of five who had walked that way from town. The Samburu call themselves "the world's top people" (the best, the most northern), like the Masai tall and proud and much adorned. In English the wife thanked me and begged me to write her a letter from America. Face alight, she printed her name in my notebook, Mercy Nyanu of Isiolo, Kenya.

On our return Joe asked how the day had been, teasing me for my insatiable love of game drives.

"It was about the same thing as yesterday, wasn't it?" he said.

"Oh no!" I said, "not at all, Joe, not the same at all."

"What was different?"

"The silence."

He looked at me and his eyes widened. "The silence," he said. Maybe he understood, I like to think he did. I couldn't say what was inexpressible for the peace I'd found, there in a still country.

On Sunday morning Symond urged Joe to talk to us about Kenya, anything that came to mind. At ten o'clock we gathered in the conference room of the Club to listen.

"O.K., ladies and gentlemen," Joe began, looking ruefully at his few scribbled notes. He said he wouldn't talk about present-day politics but would tell us the Kenyatta story, since he had been old enough to witness part of it, the worst and the best. After seventy or more years of British colonial rule, independence had come in 1963 through the leadership of Jomo Kenyatta, a Kikuyu, who fought long and bitterly against white racism and discrimination. The English had taken over the central highlands of the Kikuyu, robbed them of their homes, forced them to work on the plantations of the white masters. Joe's own people, he said, were debarred by law from holding land. They knew the humiliation of slaves, made to wear dog collars, whipped, kept behind barbed wire, given maize as payment for their work, refused permission to leave the compound.

In 1952 the storm broke with the first organized revolt against English occupation and rule, an uprising of the Mau Maus, the freedom fighters, of whom Kenyatta was accused of being leader. They hid in the Aberdare Mountains and forest of Mount Kenya, waging guerrilla war against settlers on the highland farms. Thousands of blacks died in the fighting compared to the few whites who were murdered. The British imprisoned Kenyatta for the next nine years in an outpost on the

Ethiopian border, treating him like a criminal. At last in 1960 the white highlands were opened up to black ownership and divided into small lots for the Kikuyu, who had led the fight for *Uhuru,* freedom. Three years later Kenya became a republic with Kenyatta as president. But he was no tribalist; his tribe would be shown no favoritism among the strongly divided racial groups, each with its own language and tribal customs. His cry was the Swahili "Harambee," let us pull together. Some day, Joe said, Kenya must become a union of the tribes, but progress is slow especially among the lawless Masai, fiercely resistant, unwilling to change their ways. Kenyatta, who disliked American capitalism as well as Russian and Chinese communism, considered all Kenyans brothers of one family. All must be free, he said—the animals too. And in 1977 he stopped the killing. Loved by his people, he served them and died in 1978. Today Daniel arap Moi is president, not a Kikuyu but a member of a minority tribe, the Kalenjin, and tribal rivalries remain, the dream unfulfilled.

Joe was sorry, not surprised, that our few questions dwelt more on marriage customs than African independence. He didn't say that Kenyatta, already with two African wives and a number of children, took as a third wife Edna Clark, a white Englishwoman whom he married in London and who bore him a son Peter. For a fourth, most cherished wife he took Ngina, a pretty Kikuyu girl of Nairobi, who gave him four daughters and for whom Mama Ngina Street is named. Though divorce is now possible in Kenya, it seldom occurs because both the wife and the marriage dowry must be returned to her parents. Someone called out, "Is the bride a virgin?" but Joe merely shrugged. He described the ordeal of the circumcision ceremony at a boy's coming of age, the testing of courage before the whole tribe and the need to make no outcry. According to custom, girls also were circumcised before they could marry, and still are by the Masai. The new president has made this primitive rite unlawful.

After Joe's lucid talk we wandered out to the lawn to watch a group of African Chuka drummers and dancers, gaudily arrayed and painted. As a result several of us were late to lunch and, since the dining room was full, were ushered into the ornate "members only" room, where we sat opposite Stefanie Powers, slim and beautiful as in her films. To some this was a crowning moment of the safari, with rumors of Charlton Heston (who acted in *Nairobi Affair*) somewhere on the premises. *Out of Africa,* with Meryl Streep as Isak Dinesen and Robert Redford as her English lover Denys Finch Hatton, was being filmed nearby, and Kikuyu were hired to play their menial part in the Hollywood tale of fifty years ago.

On Sunday afternoon we left the glamour world, a curious one to find on anybody's safari, and drove through the mighty rain forests of the Aberdare Mountains to the Mountain Lodge, a treetop hotel surrounded by dense foliage. The original "Treetops," made famous by Elizabeth's visits as princess and queen, was destroyed by fire by the Mau Maus, later rebuilt. The Mountain Lodge rested on concrete stilts, a rustic wood treehouse perched forty feet above a water hole where animals gather, a route taken by elephants. At night the broad area beneath us was floodlit to encourage the animals to appear, and silence was enforced. On a balcony on the top floor, we sat riveted for hours waiting and watching, though Esther's and my room, #3, had a balcony of its own with the same view. This was game hunting at its most restful, listening to the animals breathe. From the treetop lookout we saw hyenas, waterbuck, buffalo, a sleek cheetah, yellow-billed storks, and the incredible sight, a *white* rhinoceros. I fully intended to stay up all night while the drama unfolded, but the air grew cold and, having bought a warm blanket for a hundred shillings (repaid on return in the morning), I slept instead. Hot water bottles, a British touch, were provided if anybody wanted to be British.

I tell you, it was hard to leave this spectacular place. Yet more spectacles lay ahead. Through miles of forest, across the Laikipia Plains and over the Aberdare Mountains, we dropped down to the great Rift Valley. This is the largest rift on earth, a dry valley formed between two volcanic faults running the length of Kenya—a stupendous gash, some of it as wide as forty miles between walls. On our way to Lake Naivasha, we stopped along the road to visit a small craft shop run by Kikuyu, full of native masks and carvings, where Joe told me to buy a neat mahogany sign on which the word *Karibu* was carved. Welcome, it said. I asked, "Haven't they got one that says Love?" and Joe laughed and shouted to the owner, "We want one that says Love." The owner regretfully shook his head, none in stock. Hereafter my house in North Carolina will say welcome in Swahili.

For a change the road became relatively smooth. Tall Masai herders in red cloaks guarded their flocks in the fields, able if need be to kill a lion with their spear. Along the road they waved and laughed, teeth flashing, while their women carrying heavy loads of firewood shuffled along bent double and Geoffrey said, "Today we see the people." We passed villages of squalid one-story huts with a middle hut calling itself "Hotel and Butchery." Road signs warned in English, "Wild animals on the road," and "A word to the wise."

Lake Naivasha is the jewel of Kenya's Rift Valley chain of freshwater lakes, with water birds and blue waterlilies, ospreys, herons, ibis, pelicans, pink flamingoes, white egrets. At the Safariland Lodge, each couple had a separate house on a broad estate beside the lake. Ours was House #40, large enough to live in for the rest of your life, surrounded by flowers. Across the lawn the dining area resembled a luxury hotel. (W. H. Auden once said he had grown too crotchety to like a luxury hotel, but that sad decline hasn't happened to me.) Instead of a boat ride on the lake, we spent the January afternoon in the outdoor pool with Elie and Jack. Symond came over to deplore the distinction of being put in House #1 and invite us to a party tonight. After dinner we walked there under yellow-barked acacias known as fever trees, though I had thought Kipling invented fever trees beside the great, gray, green, greasy Limpopo River. Symond and Martha gave lovely parties to the Connecticut travelers.

Until recently it was the season of torrential rains, but not a drop fell on us. Next morning we drove off in six minibuses from Lake Naivasha southwest along the wall of the Rift, over the Rift Valley floor through Masai country to the Masai Mara Game Reserve. Again the roads turned terrible, eroded with pits and morasses, washboard roads. The Masai Reserve, owned by the Masai tribe and leased to the government, is part of the great Serengeti Plain of Tanzania, the northern extension. There in the rolling grasslands is the most famous game reserve in Africa. We were back with the animals—herds of dazzling untameable zebras, no two striped alike, long columns of wildebeest or gnu with heads like an ox, Thomson's gazelles, Masai giraffes with blotched coats, 47 (by count) Egyptian geese, and the largest collection of lions in the world (remember the old riddle, how do you catch lions in the desert? You strain off the sand, and the remainder will be lions). Again we stopped for a kill, this time a freshly dead, massive black buffalo being torn apart by lions gorging themselves first on its brains, while in a semicircle discreetly aside the scavengers waited to move in.

The spotted hyena took precedence, next the jackal, after him marabou storks, and nine vultures sitting in a row.

I thought of the books I had read about lions, in particular those by George B. Schaller (*Serengeti, a Kingdom of Predators*), a zoologist who spent three years in the Serengeti keeping company with lions, studying them till at times he was sick of them, "thoroughly saturated." He marveled at their courage and cowardice, their appetites, watched them kill each other, watched a lioness eat her cub. Once he followed a lion for twenty-one consecutive days and nights. With amazing endurance he drove his Land Rover by the light of the moon or by flashlight in pitch dark, without headlights that would alarm the animals. And in his solitary researches the one important difference he noted between man and beast was that, while man is the greatest, most dangerous predator on earth, better at killing even than the lion, the lion is far more accomplished in the mating game. Male lions do little in life but eat, sleep, and procreate. Only courting keeps them active and attentive during the day. A lion whom Schaller observed steadily for 55 hours mated 157 times through the day and night, with one lioness 145 times and, briefly distracted, 12 times with an available standby. "I was interested in lions as individuals," Schaller wrote. In lionesses too, it seemed. His persistence in keeping count, and awake, was to me heroic.

At the border of Tanzania, closed since 1977, where we couldn't enter without a visa, Geoffrey steered the bus toward the hippo-filled Mara River, stopping often, cheerfully joining in the excitement as if he had never seen a hippo before. A handsome topi—an antelope with purple coat—stood poised on a rock and Esther cried, "Topi on the rocks," like ordering an African cocktail.

The Mara Serena Lodge within the Masai reserve, our home for the next two nights, was singular, as the others had been, this one built in the style of a Masai manyatta, though not of cow dung. Each of the grouped cottages was made of brown mud and shaped like a Masai hut but roomier inside. It resembled a beehive with small hyraxes scampering about. The Lodge itself sat high on a saddle overlooking on one side the immense plain and distant mountains, on the other the Mara River where the animals congregated. It had a tarmac airstrip that accounted for the occasional plane flying over us (sometimes a balloon). Most of the staff of the Lodge were Masai, dressed in smart uniforms, young and attractive and courteous, some of them college students eager for a chance to go to America for further study. Kenya has no money for grants. "Stay and teach us!" they said when they learned I was a teacher, quite seriously urging me to stay on at the Lodge for the next year or two. I said I'd love to.

The Masai Mara Reserve is so crowded with animals we went hither and yon all day without destination. We were observers being observed, closely by the keen-eyed giraffes, warily by antelopes, indifferently by elephants. Geoffrey said, "We go nowhere, in all directions," and we did, bouncing up and down like yo-yos across the sandy plains, driving in zigzags, playing games invented by Geoffrey who, crying "Jambo!", would tear off after a herd of swift bounding impalas, never of course hitting one. (Geoffrey has never hit a beast nor lost a passenger.) If a driver spotted something exciting, by a prearranged signal he would alert the others, and soon all six vans gathered in a circle like a pioneer wagon train in Wyoming. Together we surrounded a pride of lions whose dozen lionesses had nine tiny cubs among them, each cub fighting to drink from the nearest mother, rubbing her face lovingly before moving on to the next.

Just then a large lion swaggered over to our van and, mouth open, thrust his head forward to stare at me through the window.

"What's on his mind?" I said. As our eyes met, I stared back hypnotized, eyeball to eyeball with a lion, till Geoffrey yanked me away.

"Not so close," he said sharply. "Turn your face, don't look at him. He might take a notion to spring."

With the top of our van open, he could easily leap down and destroy us.

When a van drove too near ours and got mired and stuck, Geoffrey jumped out and, using his considerable weight, rocked the other van for several minutes to free it, while the driver watched anxiously. At the moment the field was full of lions.

"That was brave, Geoffrey, and that was dangerous," I said when he crawled back in beside me.

"Very dangerous," he said, "and against the law."

Later we learned a police patrol equipped with loaded rifles stayed close to us all day to guard our safety among the lions.

"A giraffe," wrote Isak Dinesen, "is so much a lady that one refrains from thinking of her legs." We saw a baby giraffe approach its majestic mother cautiously, trying to suck, giving up when she pushed it away with a swift kick. Giraffes aren't maternal. They give birth standing up and will let a six-foot baby drop on its head, then walk haughtily away as it hits the ground with a thud.

"There's a lone antelope," Geoffrey cried, a mild piece of news since there are said to be 74 species of antelope in Africa, abundant and gregarious, appetizing to the predators. What he meant was a *roan* antelope, with backward curved horns, rare and seldom seen. A cheetah crouched nearby in the bush, the fastest mammal alive, faster than a racehorse, capable of sprints up to 70 mph. A deadly hunter, it looked with its black spots almost exactly like the leopard we never saw, the shyest of beasts, most solitary and nocturnal. A family of twenty female elephants with two babies among them waited soundlessly while one of the mothers chased a hyena across the field. Nothing, not even a lion, dares attack a grown elephant, largest land animal on earth. It must feel proprietary, since the elephant made its appearance first in Africa. Trained for battle, African elephants crossed the Alps with Hannibal.

At the Lodge after dinner we gathered in the lounge to watch a group of eight garishly painted Masai dancers, who came whooping in dressed in loin cloths, carrying spears. Each took a turn leaping high in the air, trying to soar higher than the rest, making piercing cries. During this noisy performance a young Masai woman, a receptionist at the desk, left her post and startled us by joining briskly in the dance. She wore a neat business suit and glasses, her hair in a bun, sensible oxfords on her feet, but she kept up with the wildly yelling, nearly naked males. Just then the dancing was interrupted when someone cried "Hippo!" and we jumped up and ran out of the lodge down to the river to see him standing huge and peaceful in plain sight in the moonlight.

Afterward when I stopped at the desk to praise the young woman for her dancing, she said she often took part because she loved to and they were her people.

"Is it a kind of war dance?" I asked.

"No, not in the least," she said smiling. "We are leaping for joy. The dance means happiness. We leap and yell because we are happy."

Throughout the night a couple of hyenas yelped under our window as if they were happy. I have nothing against hyenas. They made an agreeable soft howl, not shrieking or laughing in the bloodcurdling way hyenas are said to do.

On the last day of the safari, we left Mara Serena Lodge unwillingly, at least I was unwilling, and quickly climbed into our buses. After directing the departure, Joe got in our van beside a subdued Geoffrey. Elie and Jack had flown back to Nairobi because Elie had taken ill. All the chatter and laughter were gone out of us. No longer did the wildebeests or dancing gazelles catch our eye. We were weary travelers done with pleasures too extraordinary to leave behind.

In three hours we had climbed the steep slope of the Kikuyu Escarpment and were back on the superhighway, at the outskirts of Nairobi. "Welcome to Green in the Sun," the signs said. I hated this return to the city, to any city, among the crowds and rushing traffic. At the Inter-Continental Hotel, Joe and I had only a moment to say goodbye—no more happy hellos, only *kwaheri,* goodbye.

"Send me the story you will write about the safari, about my people," he said. And I promised to.

"Asante sana," I said, thank you very much, dear Joe, dear friend.

He pressed my hand and disappeared down the long corridor to return to his own life, about which in the end I knew so little.

And the journey was over and we had a city to explore of theaters, cafés, churches, nightclubs, museums, none of which the black man had been permitted to enter till independence came to Kenya. For lunch Esther and I went to the famous Thorn Tree in the courtyard of the New Stanley Hotel, where in the middle of the café was a huge thorn tree planted in June 1961, replacing an earlier one, its trunk a post office covered with messages pinned there to arrange a meeting with friends or to tell someone he loved her.

That night Alice Ann, Vincent, the Yaveners, Esther and I had dinner on the roof of our hotel, dining in a style more European than African, though Martha the gourmet ordered eland and there was gazelle on the menu. The lights of the city looked no different from those of Paris or Rome. The orchestra played "I Left My Heart in San Francisco," as if that were the place to leave it. In our hotel a policeman on every floor patrolled all night, in a red shirt that said "Pinkerton," carrying a club to protect us. We were told not to walk alone, especially not in the slums of Nairobi, in grubby narrow streets where formerly all blacks were forced to live.

Next day Esther and I sought out the great National Museum, without the curiosity to visit the Nairobi National Park just outside of town; we had seen enough wild animals. At the museum was the skull of the oldest human being yet discovered, a Neolithic man of two and one-half million years ago, found by Dr. Louis Leakey in the Olduvai Gorge in the Serengeti of Tanzania (where a sign says, "This is the world as it was in the beginning"). It made me think again of creation, for in East Africa is said to have been the origin of man. His species began here where the world began. I marveled most at his survival, frail hunter and killer among the greatest concentration of wild animals on this earth.

Two charming Kikuyu girls, clerks in the craft shop of the museum, told us eagerly, "It is very good to be a Kikuyu. We love each other." Many appeared to talk that way, as if valuing themselves after years of servitude. This was their country, their people.

We had lunch on the balcony of the old Norfolk Hotel, a landmark from British colonial days, before walking back through the busy streets of Nairobi, past the university (established under Kenyatta, tuition free) and the resplendent Jamia Mosque and the synagogue, past the teeming open market, the Kentucky Fried Chicken and Wimpy Hamburgers, the "Curl Up and Dye Beauty Shop," the flowers and the jacaranda trees.

At midnight our flight on Air France left for Paris, where on arrival it was snowing hard, threatening delays and canceled flights. We were miserably cold in wintry Paris so soon after Nairobi, bundled to our ears and shivering. After some delay we boarded the crowded 747 to New York, and I sat between Symond and Elsie, Clarence's wife, whom I had judged severe but found to be funny and delightful. Cursing the paperbacks she constantly reads that to her dismay turn out sexy, she said she had bought *The Happy Hooker* thinking it was a book about crocheting. Symond and I talked through the night, of Montaigne whom he loves, of Russian poets, of the safari that had overwhelmed him as it had me, a journey he will take over again same time next year. Then at Kennedy I lost them, my Connecticut friends, when they went their way and I went mine to catch a late plane home.

I was returning to the everyday world, the safari had been only a dream. This illusion of peace would take a few days, no more, to dissipate. I knew it couldn't last in my customary life and I knew I wouldn't find it again, not that kind of silence, that quiet in an unquiet world, that peace. Lay it to love and yesterday. In Shiva Naipaul's story of his African journey, *North of South,* he says, "The tourist has this advantage: he *knows* it is a dream," from which he has always to return to wherever he comes from.

Trying to write about African safaris, I've grown as absentminded as Adam Smith, whose state was called impenetrable. I sympathize with one who didn't have both oars in the water (a type dismissed by Dr. Johnson, "We did not take to each other"). Adam Smith was the most distracted fellow in history, who in company would fall into a trance, laugh and talk to himself till roused, when he instantly began a public harangue and couldn't be stopped. According to Boswell, "the most absent man that I ever saw" made it a rule in company never to talk on a subject he understood. How much we have in common.

This learned professor of moral philosophy, author of *The Wealth of Nations,* had a "vermicular" or wormlike gait and never married. At breakfast he was known to take a piece of bread and butter, put it in the teapot, pour hot water over it, and complain the tea tasted odd. When he was four, he was stolen by gypsies and after a few hours found unharmed, howling in a nearby wood where the gypsy woman had dropped him. She must have thought he wasn't worth keeping. A biographer of Adam Smith, John Rae, observed, "He would have made a poor gypsy."

Catching up on the news, I see that 1984 had been rejected as a lousy year, headed for certain catastrophe. In his State of the Union message, President Reagan was rhapsodic about our emergence as a flawless people. We are, he said, vibrant, robust, alive, invincible in spirit, more secure than ever, standing tall and poised for greatness. We are a coming nation of yuppies, not to be confused with the long-haired yippies of the 1960s. Yuppies are young conservatives who support Reagan. Reagan has delivered us.

As I scan the *New York Times* with report on every page of murder and demolition, I find myself twenty years ago sitting beside a man on the London Underground absorbed in reading the London *Times.* At each item of news he gasps and whispers to himself, "Oh my God, oh my God!"

The movie "A Passage to India" puzzled me as it would have puzzled E. M. Forster, whose novel has puzzled everybody since 1924 when it appeared. The book and the film tell quite different stories, though each shows the infinite harm the British have done as conquerors and overlords. When he went to India in 1912, Forster was shocked by the spectacle of racial prejudice, the insuperable barriers to friendship and sympathy between the races. His character Dr. Aziz is a Muslim insulted by the treatment of his people, resentful of the discourtesy, the snubs, the exploitation. They in turn despise him as an inferior, and the book ends (unlike the movie) with Aziz further embittered, permanently estranged. Under British rule he knows there can be no trust without equality; they must be driven out: "My heart is for my own people henceforward. I wish no Englishman or Englishwoman to be my friend."

To Forster even more significant than the race problem was the human problem. In these opposed and separate worlds it too is insoluble; they can't understand each other. When the attractive Aziz innocently invites the two English ladies, Adela and Mrs. Moore, to visit the Marabar Caves in the hills beyond Chandrapore, he brings disaster to them all. Adela Quester has come to India with the elderly Mrs. Moore, whose son Ronny is the city magistrate, an arrogant prig whom Adela is expected to marry. In the cave each woman separately hears the terrifying echo, a meaningless "Ou-boum" that fills her with a nameless fear. Mrs. Moore, nearly fainting, discovers in the echo a denial that undermines her hold on life. It contradicts her Christian faith that God is Love. The echo says, "There is no love, nothing has value, life has no meaning." From this moment she is sunk in apathy and despair, her spirit broken. Her son sends her back to England alone, and on the journey she dies.

Adela too has a mysteriously destructive experience in the caves. Already disturbed by thoughts of sexual love, she feels someone behind her and seems to have an erotic encounter that sends her, frenzied and hysterical, flying in terror down the hill. She accuses Aziz of following her into the cave and molesting her. He is arrested; a trial results in which the English are roused to anti-Indian fury. When her mind clears and she realizes Aziz must be innocent, Adela withdraws the charge too late. She leaves for England rejected by Ronny, spurned by English and Indian alike. The mocking echo has been prophetic. Love has everywhere failed.

This part of the story, the meaning of the Marabar Caves and their echo, the film doesn't attempt to clarify. Forster said the book was about "the difficulty of living in the universe." He refused to say what happened to Adela in the cave. The fact is that *nothing* happened in the cave. Yet there the two worlds are torn further apart.

Paul Scott's splendid novel *The Raj Quartet* also shows British rule in India ending in disastrous failure. It takes place during and after World War II, when Anglo-Indian conflicts grew steadily worse. Dr. Aziz's prophecy comes true in Scott's novel, the barriers of race are too strong, the English are driven out.

Scott was well aware of his debt to Forster. There are many similarities (*raj* means rule), though Scott probes more deeply the violence and brutality Forster hadn't witnessed and was incapable of describing. The young Englishwoman Daphne Manners, in Mayapore as a nurse, falls in love with Hari Kumar, an Indian educated in England. When the two make love in the Bibighar Gardens, five or six Indians suddenly appear and after beating Hari unconscious attack Daphne and rape her. At the inquiry that follows, Daphne refuses to implicate her lover. The brutal district superintendent of police, Ronald Merrick, who had wanted to marry Daphne, can't charge Hari with the crime but manages to hunt him out, torture him, destroy his life. Merrick tells Hari, "I'm a ruler and you are the ruled." He tells him, "There's no love, no justice, only power and fear."

Daphne, who believes the child she is carrying is Hari's, dies in childbirth, and the rape with all its implications darkens the rest of the massive novel. Eventually Merrick is murdered, strangled and hacked to death. One of his murderers scrawls the word "Bibighar" on the mirror.

For the second time since January I've been in on Creation. It happened in Africa where the species man had his beginnings, and it happened again at the University of Toronto, where my son David and I went to see a miracle tale of the fifteenth century which started with Creation and ended with the Last Judgment. Moving as it was as spectacle, I kept thinking how deeply this account must have shaken anyone living at the end of the Middle Ages who took it for gospel truth.

The Towneley or Wakefield Cycle of mystery plays was performed in Yorkshire about 1475. It presented during the festival of Corpus Christi a sequence of biblical episodes acted in the marketplace by various trade guilds or "mysteries." The actors performed either on pageant wagons wheeled in procession past the audience, or they may have had fixed stations arranged in a circle for one play to follow another.

For two days, from morning to dusk, we sat on the grass at Victoria College while the drama unrolled at the several stations encircling the quad. Each of the twenty-seven plays was acted by a different group from American and Canadian colleges, who provided their own costumes and staging. They spoke a modern English version of the story of good and evil, the struggle between God and Satan for man's soul.

The first scene was a majestic Heaven, erected at the elevated entrance to the main building of the college, with Hellmouth below to the left and the Garden of Eden, consisting of a small tree with a red apple in its crotch, on a mound at the right. God in gold robes and crown, surrounded by angels, proclaims from his throne, "I am the first, the last also, one God in majesty." As he lifts his hand, painted panels depict the six days of Creation, and children dressed as animals appear on earth, to whom God descends to speak fondly. Meanwhile Lucifer or Satan, seating himself on God's throne, boasts in his pride of being equal to God, and the scene shifts to Hellmouth, belching smoke and horrible demons, where Lucifer is deposited, a fallen angel lost eternally to evil. To take his place, "Now make me man," God says, and gives Eve to Adam for his bliss and to keep him from sin: "Touch not the tree. Look at it but let it be."

The second play, "The Fall of Man," reveals Adam and Eve in flesh-colored body stockings under the tree with Lucifer in snake's clothing, there to tempt Eve to his own disobedience and fall. She bites the apple and hands it to Adam, while God observes their attempt to hide their nakedness. Adam wrestles with his figleaf, which he all but loses as an angel drives them from paradise.

Cain appears, striding through the crowd on the lawn, fighting his plough in anger at the work he must do, cursing God who has given him only sorrow and woe. Cain, a defiant, blustering villain, cries out, "By all men set I not a fart." Despising Abel, the meek, obedient one, he knocks him about before killing him on the mound where the Tree of Eden stood. "Are we not brothers, you and I?" asks Abel.

Below that mound Noah builds his ark. Noah's God, resembling the pope, declares, "Man that I made I will destroy." In a fresh attempt at Creation, he orders Noah to get busy with the ark, which the old man feebly undertakes while struggling to put his nagging, kicking wife aboard. Noah can't control his wife any better than Adam could, but unlike Adam he is obedient to God. A pert little angel with a watering can to start the Flood sprinkles Noah's wife to make her obey. God's hand is in all things, and Satan's also. God's creatures, male and female, must start over.

Again the scene is played on the mound of Eden—the hill of death that will lead to the Crucifixion—when Abraham's obedience is tested as he prepares to kill his son. In a striking tableau the slim young boy in a wig of bright red hair submits to his father's will, crying "Alas, what have I done?" With a touch of dark humor, Abraham hesitates to plunge the knife, turns Isaac over on his face and asks in bewilderment, "What shall I to his mother say?"

Minstrels sounding trumpets direct our gaze to a stage across the quad where Pharaoh, first of the tyrants and sons of Cain, sits like a god on his throne. To escape his power, Moses leads God's chosen people from their captivity in Egypt, the Red Sea (four long strips of red cloth painted with fishes) parts to let them pass, and Pharaoh is drowned beneath the red banners. God's commandments on large tablets are brought down by Moses from another mount, which is Sinai, each commandment one of obedience: "Do this and you shall live." While David, lover of God, plays his harp, another tyrant, Caesar Augustus, hears a prophecy of a child to be born whom he resolves to destroy.

At the Annunciation we are back at God's throne, where in a scene recalling the Creation God makes clear the connection between Adam and Christ. In a new creation, a new birth, the son of God will atone for Adam, the Cross will atone for the Tree, Mary will atone for Eve. The angel Gabriel is sent to Nazareth to reveal to Mary her divine role, while Joseph, a foolish old man like Noah, is sadly perplexed by his wife. Knowing his impotence as a husband, he doubts Mary's purity till Gabriel persuades him the maiden is chaste who will bear God's only begotten son.

The celebrated "Second Shepherd's Play" belongs next but was given last night in a special performance in the original Yorkshire dialect. The plot is a rowdy farce of drinking and quarreling among the shepherds Coll, Gib, Daw, and Mak the sheep stealer—who has trouble with his wife like Adam, Noah, Joseph. To hide the sheep he has stolen, Mak pretends his wife has given birth and with her help wraps the sheep in swaddling clothes and places it in a cradle. The shepherds, discovering Mak's low trick, toss him in a blanket and lie down to sleep, when suddenly above this comic nativity scene stands an angel singing "Gloria in Excelsis" to tell them that in Bethlehem a child has been born.

So the first day of the cycle ends with the "Gifts of the Magi," Mary and Joseph's "Flight into Egypt," and the attempt of the third tyrant, Herod, to kill all male children in his search for the boy Jesus. All day the hot sun has beat down on us. We have been transfixed by the simple tale with its amazing unity, its parallels and interweavings, the steady pace toward evil and God's struggle for man with a mighty foe.

Who would miss tomorrow's story and the outcome?

Day two began with a drizzle that grew to a downpour, a cold, dark, somber day for the Crucifixion. The scene was unforgettable—the crowds of jostling umbrellas, the tension on faces as we followed a nearly naked Christ dragging the cross on his way to Calvary, as if we too were part of the mockery and the scourging.

Already Christ has performed a miracle of resurrection at the tomb of Lazarus, four days dead. We have witnessed the conspiracy of the Jews, sat with the disciples at the Last Supper when Christ says "Each of you will betray me." At "The Buffeting" and "The Scourging" Christ has been cursed, made to endure the brutality of the soldiers, taken to the last of the tyrants, Pontius Pilate, where he is mocked with a crown of thorns.

On Calvary—the mount where the Tree of Eden stood, where Christ has undergone agony in the Garden of Gethsemane—he is nailed to the cross and slowly we watch him die. We hear Mary's lament at the foot of the cross—Christ's Cross and Adam's Tree.

Thus the dark story ends. In the final pageant, God who created man pronounces a judgment upon him. Christ descends to show his wounds. The blessed souls come to stand at God's right hand, holding fast to their new, slippery halos, while the wicked who denied him are driven shrieking to the jaws of Hellmouth to start their punishment, administered with glee by Titivillus and the weird dancing fiends. Satan sinks into Hell's pit.

Standing in the rain, we join the angels in singing "Te Deum Laudamus," free at dusk to go our own way, wet and cold, bemused perhaps by the persistence of evil in the world, perhaps in a temporary state of grace and rejoicing.

A traveler who made the Grand Tour in the eighteenth century wasn't a tourist, globe-trotter, or sightseer. The words *tourism* and *sightseeing* appeared with Baedeker in the nineteenth century and described travel on Thomas Cook's Tours made by ordinary people called tourists, often deplored as vulgar and obnoxious. The one thing V. S. Pritchett, world traveler, dislikes about travel is other tourists, whom he views with distaste—the faceless hordes who take a package tour and do the attractions. But then, Lady Mary Montagu, an earlier traveler, like Pritchett wanted to keep the world to herself. In a letter of 1739 from Venice, she wrote in outrage at the English infesting the town "who torment me as much as the frogs and lice did the palace of Pharaoh."

When the Age of Tourism began, the Grand Tour died. It was confined to the upper classes, frequently undertaken by the son of a British aristocrat fresh from Oxford or Cambridge wearing a tricorne and under his arm a silver-topped cane, sent abroad with a tutor to complete his higher education. He spent a year or two in the capitals of western Europe, absorbing, it was hoped, languages and a cultivated air in France, Germany, Switzerland, most of all Italy. With his companion he moved languidly from place to place, on horseback, in his own carriage, or if need be sharing a coach or diligence. Expecting to be welcomed by people of his own class or better, he preferred to visit Venetian palazzos and flirt with contessas. Otherwise boredom set in.

Horace Walpole, who in 1739–41 made the fashionable Grand Tour of Paris, the Alps ("such uncouth rocks"), Florence, Rome with his friend Thomas Gray, soon wearied not only of Gray whom he snubbed but of such plebeian sights as churches and monuments. Walpole was twenty-three, the youngest son of England's prime minister and a fearful snob, elegant in his tastes. To his friend Richard West he wrote from Italy: "I have left off screaming Lord! this! and Lord! that! The farther I travel the less I wonder at anything . . . and men are so much the same everywhere, that one scarce perceives any change of situation."

In 1809 at twenty-one Lord Byron made a grand tour that he called *Childe Harold's Pilgrimage.* Though the autobiographical poem follows closely his own journey, the Childe is a melancholy, romantic youth escaping from his sinful past ("For he through sin's long labyrinth had run"). Byron himself settled for a conventional Grand Tour, accompanied by his Cambridge friend John Cam Hobhouse and his valet Fletcher, taking along seven trunks and three beds. For two years they wandered aimlessly about, sailing first to Lisbon where Byron swam across the Tagus River, traveling on horseback to Seville and Cádiz, where he devoted eleven stanzas to a bullfight that sickened him. Twice he fell in love and wrote a poem to "The Girl of Cadiz" and in Athens to the "Maid of Athens" (who was twelve). He stopped in Missolonghi where fifteen years later he would die. He traveled through Albania, in Turkey swam the Hellespont, wrangled every day in Greece with Hobhouse, declared he hated objects of interest, learned to swear in Turkish, and in general had an amusing time, though "Nought that he saw his sadness could abate." He wrote Augusta, "I don't know that I have acquired any thing by my travels but a smattering of two languages and a habit of chewing Tobacco." He told his friend Trelawny, "If I am a poet, the air of Greece has made me one."

The Grand Tour was definitely for the rich and disdainful. On the whole I'm glad to be a twentieth-century tourist. The risks are much the same, the complaints equally loud of discomforts, vexations, delays, price of lodgings, bad food, bad weather, unsavory natives. On the Grand Tour one might run into a highwayman or Barbary pirate instead of the Mafia; the streets were dangerous, the thieves bold and numerous as now. One had to carry more excess luggage then, such as trunks, knife and fork, sheets, blankets, towels, a bathtub, a bed, certainly a loaded pistol.

Travel is faster now, available to anyone with a passport. But since world terrorism has taken over, survival is more squarely on the mind. An Air India 747 superjet with 329 aboard explodes in the sky, everyone killed as if a whole town had vanished. A TWA superjet is hijacked by Shiite terrorists. Bombs explode, usually in airports, in Lebanon, Rome, Madrid, Athens, yesterday in Frankfurt. A newspaper editorial begins: "Before long, a terrorist will get an atomic bomb." Then a man can blow up a city by himself if his demands aren't met. And that is the way the world is.

The Grand Tour was never like this.

With nowhere to go this summer, I read travel books—Peter Matthiessen in search of the white leopard and the great white shark, Sir Edmund Hillary high in the Himalayas, Han Suyin's journey to Tibet, Marco Polo's travels to China, Coleridge's to Xanadu, James Hilton's to Shangri-La.

And Pausanias. What a traveler. Eighteen centuries ago in the time of

Hadrian and Marcus Aurelius, Pausanias spent ten or twenty years wandering over Greece, coming in the nick of time to witness the sights of the ancient world before they disappeared or crumbled into ruins. He saw the gold statue of Apollo at Delphi, the gold statue of Zeus at Olympia, Athene in the Parthenon. He visited the theater at Epidaurus, the battlefield of Marathon, the lion gate at Mycenae, noted the remains of Pindar's house at Thebes, stood before the grave of Leonidas at Sparta who died defending the pass at Thermopylae. He saw other wonders: bits of clay from which Prometheus created man; Leda's egg from which Helen of Troy was born.

As for the sights "not well known to everyone," those too Pausanias took amazed notice of—the Altar of Pity in the marketplace in Athens, erected by "the only Greeks who pay honour to this very important god in human life and human reverses." He stopped to watch men killing some animals beside a grave, pouring the warm blood down a hole into the tomb for the dead man to drink. He waited in vain beside the river Alpheus to hear the trout sing like thrushes. He discovered the wild strawberries on Mount Helicon, the honey of Mount Hymettus, the white blackbirds, the tortoises of Arcadia. He learned as a traveler in Greece the greatest lesson of all: to believe in heaven and not in hell. Pausanias had no trouble accepting Mount Olympus as the abode of the gods (which he didn't climb to verify) but, frankly skeptical, of Hades he had considerable doubt. "It is not easy," he wrote, "to believe that the gods have an underground abode in which the souls of the dead assemble."

In Arcadia he heard a story (also told by Pliny) about a poor old man of Psophis called Aglaus who never in his life strayed beyond his small farm. When Gyges of Lydia, the richest king in the world, sent to ask the Delphic oracle if any man was happier than himself, the oracle replied, "Aglaus of Psophis is happier."

"I did not really believe the story I heard at Psophis about Aglaus," wrote Pausanias, "that he was happy throughout his entire life. It is absolutely impossible to find a man permanently untouched by tragedy."

Euripides: "No one is ever always fortunate."

Marco Polo noted a quaint custom popular in China. Strabo, another great traveler who lived in the time of Christ, found it among the Basques (where it still existed in this century)—the practice when a child was born of putting the father instead of the mother to bed. As if giving birth, he would groan at the ordeal while the hovering women attended him and in a nearby ditch or wood his wife bore the child. The word *couvade* (from *couver,* to hatch) means the male in the childbed.

Marie de France of the twelfth century wrote a fine tale about a man who thought he was in labor, about to bear a child. In her fable "The Peasant and the Beetle," a peasant lay sleeping flat on his face, exposing his backside to the sun, spreading himself so wide that a passing beetle crawled inside. The peasant woke and feeling a strange pain ran to the doctor, who in mockery told him he was soon to give birth. The peasant alerted his friends, and they gathered and sat in a circle awaiting the awesome event. After a while the beetle came out the same way it went in.

Peter Matthiessen's journey to the Himalayas is titled *The Snow Leopard*. In September 1973 he went for a walk of two hundred miles up snow peaks and over glaciers to the Crystal Mountain on the Tibetan Plateau, invited to the expedition by George Schaller whom he knew in Africa, and whom I admire for his ability to live with lions. Each man is a persuasive revealer of the right way to pursue wild animals. But they strongly disagree. Matthiessen never saw the white leopard, content to imagine its presence. Schaller, who had already seen a white leopard, was there to study Himalayan blue sheep, which he found in abundance when not eaten by white leopards. Matthiessen, a Zen Buddhist, a contemplative, had a mystical feeling he also caught a glimpse of the yeti or abominable snowman, a dark shape that quickly sprang behind a rock. He didn't let on to Schaller, a less credulous observer and no meditator or believer in visions, however long were his thoughts in the stillness of the African plains.

Peter Matthiessen recited to himself the Buddhist mantra, *om mani padme hum,* and wrote: "I climb to my old lookout, happy and sad in the dim instinct that these mountains are my home. I know this mountain because I am this mountain. I can feel it breathing at this moment."

You see how intoxicating travel is.

> I should be content
> to look at a mountain
> for what it is
> and not as a comment
> on my life.
> —David Ignatow

People stop me on the street to ask in astonishment, "But what will you *do* in Tibet?"

"Look for Shangri-La," I say. "And goldclad temples and abominable snowmen."

"I look on paradise askance," said Peter Matthiessen, though I don't see why after his mystical quests. If he means earthly paradise, it's always somewhere to be found, however trampled by men and missionaries. A twelfth-century map in Corpus Christi College locates the Garden of Eden in the Babylonian plain (that is now Iraq) at the mouth of the Tigris-Euphrates—a region whose history is the oldest in the world, dominated by many gods and races (the Sumerians, Hittites, Babylonians, Assyrians, Persians, Parthians) who came and went like a scattering of winds. Alexander the Great was very near Eden in 331 B.C. but didn't run into it, nor did Sir John Mandeville who sought in vain, honest to confess "I was not there. And that grieveth me."

I admit to grave inconsistency in having written a book *The Journey Is Everything* claiming it's the journey itself not the arrival anywhere that matters, only to go kiting off in search of paradise in a remote place like Tibet which is called Shangri-La.

Robert Louis Stevenson stoutly declared, "I travel not to go anywhere but to go; I travel for travel's sake." He proved it in his *Travels with a Donkey,* a leisurely amble on an ass named Modestine.

JOURNEY TO CHINA   I was happy to go to China. Even the distance from here to there seemed easy, a piece of cake. After twenty-two hours, six meals, and two movies, we reached Hong Kong on a warm Sunday in October, a dozen of us who had traveled with the roving Cranfords before.

The journey took us to the People's Republic of China and, if you cared to risk it, on to Tibet. We were directed by CITS, China International Travel Service, the official and inscrutable Communist government agency. They revealed our itinerary with reluctance as if it were a state secret and assigned hotels arbitrarily, sometimes recklessly, after we were inside China, which was opened to tourists as recently as 1978. A courier or "interpreter" named Si Qin joined us, a national guide appointed by the government to keep an eye on us and send in a daily report of what we were up to. I liked having him there to interpret what he could. Since tourism is so new in China, the results are highly unpredictable.

Besides Si Qin, there were the local guides. David Wang met us at the airport in Hong Kong and took us to the Golden Mile Holiday Inn downtown on the Kowloon peninsula. He was the first guide I've met who was barely able to endure tourists, with especially low tolerance for American tourists. Whatever his reasons, it was clear David couldn't stand the sight of us. In the bus he recited a few facts that duty imposed on him, namely that on July 1, 1997, England will lose Hong Kong, a British colony since 1842. Meanwhile in growing alarm, unwilling to become part of Communist China, Hong Kong wastes no time in making capitalist dollars off the tourist trade. "Were there eight days in the week," David said, "the shops would stay open eight days and nights. So hurry up, ladies, run out and spend your money. Buy, buy, buy!" He laughed at his wit and our stupidity.

My room at the Holiday Inn was pleasant except for the view from the window of slums opposite, where garbage thrown from squalid rooms had piled up in drifts on the window ledges, dribbled and splashed to the alley below. Hong Kong calls itself a "window on the world," and this was one window.

In the brilliant sunlight, Betty, Ted, and I walked down to the harbor, familiar to me from the time B. and I arrived in Hong Kong by boat on a trip around the world. Then as now the harbor swarmed with Chinese junks and sampans ceaselessly moving. Sunday was couples, slender young lovers dressed in matching jackets and pants, who sat embracing unabashed on park benches, proving the adage untrue that Orientals kiss only their mothers.

Hong Kong may not be China (supper at our hotel was bratwurst and sauerkraut), but it looks Chinese—99 percent are Chinese—with climbing-ladder streets, tremendous throngs flowing along, laundry flying overhead on bamboo poles—Chinese, not British at all.

On Monday morning the women fled straight to the Chinese Custom Tailors two blocks away (one of 2,500 tailor shops in Hong Kong) to be measured for a suit of ultrasuede, ready to wear in twenty-four hours. David waited glum and wary to accompany us on a tour of the city, whose traffic, says the Guinness Book of Records, is the heaviest in the world. He called it a place of "well-doing people," about whom he elected to tell "true" stories whose authenticity I doubted since I had heard most of them before. One concerned a rich Chinese lady, closely resembling Bess of Hardwick, that old harridan of Elizabeth the First's reign, who believed she would never die so long as she kept building castles. Another was about a Chinese poet who wrote the words that appeared on his tombstone, "As you are now, so once were we," when anyone knows these words have appeared in Western churchyards for centuries.

He took us to Hong Kong Island and we rode the vertical mile to Victoria Peak, where the wealthy live surrounded by celestial views. To the Chinese the site of his house is crucial to dispel evil spirits, though the poor make do with mirrors to deflect the evil onto someone else. Down the mountain we came, to the beach at Repulse Bay, where Chinese babies played in the sand among huge stone sculptures of Buddha on a lotus flower, of the God of Wealth, of the Goddess of Mercy. And on to the Aberdeen Fishing Harbor, home of thousands of fishermen who spend their lives on their junks and bury their dead in the fishing grounds. They are born, they die, and life is circumscribed by a boat. After shaking David, we hailed a ride round Hong Kong harbor in a flat-bottomed sampan steered by an old barefoot shouting woman, brown as the water she lives on and as dirty, who rammed one boat after another heaping curses on it, while children on nearby junks held out butterfly nets to catch any coins they could wheedle.

Dinner at the Hong Kong Hotel was a ceremonial feast of roast lamb and red wine among banqueting Chinese using knives and forks. As we came home at midnight, the road to the Peak was a strand of pearls like Gibraltar's peak and as improbably beautiful. No wonder the British put off giving up either one.

It was like taking a slow boat to China to fly to Shanghai by Chinese Airways, though waiting for planes is a custom not limited to the Far East. Lois Cranford gave me a magazine article brought from home, "How to Survive Your Trip," that she found, like soap, useful for travel. It said to stay alert and watchful, which we did after we found that, unsuspecting, we were being sent not to Shanghai but to a village near it of Ching-gian, to a small country inn that received us at nightfall with stunned dismay. The sight of twelve unexpected guests so agitated the owners they could think of nothing to do but throw us out. While the Cranfords pleaded our case by gestures and Si Qin politely nodded his agreement, we sat on our luggage till they figured a way to feed and bed us. In the end the chickens furnished the eggs and the family, I guess, slept in the barn.

The master plan, gradually revealed by the mysterious CITS, was to show us post-Mao China without delay, in a village containing a model factory, model hospital, model school, model commune. At the factory we watched the making of large wooden painted ducks, purpose unknown. At the hospital we watched an acupuncture on an old woman with arthritis who hardly winced when the doctor inserted in her shoulder three long needles topped by corks and set the corks aflame to heat the needles. At the kindergarten we watched the model children watching us till Betty T. took a picture of a child with her Polaroid and handed him his likeness, at which a near riot occurred. Each child raised such a howl that Betty was urged not to do it again.

We spent the afternoon at a model farm, a carryover from the calamitous decade of Chairman Mao's Cultural Revolution when the farmers lost their land to the state and were forced to live collectively or starve. Though Deng Xiaoping has abolished the system, many still live in communes, sharing land leased by the government, growing crops, building their own houses. The model house displayed by its proud owner had no water, no heat, no electricity, no plumbing, almost no furniture. Outdoors his wife bent over a tub doing the family wash. Across the court in the communal kitchen a pot of soup bubbled on the iron stove. Nearby the communal privy stank worse than did a stray goat and a water buffalo. Yet the farmer's lot is obviously better since Mao's death in 1976, and the People's Republic is eager to say so.

Shanghai seemed greatly changed from the way I remembered it. The Communist Party of China had been formed in Shanghai since my time, the People's Republic had been established, and what was the wickedest of cities, the most depraved, had become relatively clean and healthy, the poverty less, the cholera (in epidemic stage then) and malaria gone. The Bund was now a boulevard along the waterfront; the clock on the Customs House chimed out "The East Is Red." A Friendship Store had been added, everything for sale from Chinese rugs to precious jewels, with a sign on the door "Foreigners Only"— offensive I thought in a republic of the people that shuts the people out.

From my room in the Cherry Holiday Villa, the first thing I saw this morning was a hundred Chinese lined up in a field as if to be shot. An instructor led them in a vigorous workout of body and spirit by the Tai Ji Quan method, known as Gathering Celestial Energy, and they swayed, leaped, prostrated themselves in a stately Oriental way.

Tonight we went—who would miss it?—to the Acrobatic Theater, where the Shanghai acrobats, the most skilled on earth, dazed the audience with their routines. When two shapely girls made their "celestial flight" across the top of the stage, a wave of awe swept over the crowd. A panda performed a tumbling act to loud cheers. A man balancing three eggs on his head brought down the house.

Already Communist China seemed extraordinary to me, a strange world mixing the old and new. I saw almost no cars on the crowded streets, no filling stations, no baby carriages, no women in skirts and none with bound feet. I saw a man carrying a sofa on his bicycle. I saw a disturbing sign of Communist control, billboards showing a couple with a baby in their arms, eloquent in its message that, since 1981, the Marriage Law forbids couples to have more than one child. Severe penalties, sterilization, loss of one's job and place in the community result from defying the law. In China where children are cherished, the billboards say, "Why such happy, well-behaved children? Because you have only one child."

We took the train to Suzhou, sixty miles from Shanghai. Our carriage had tables for four with white lace tablecloths, at which we drank jasmine tea on our way to a town settled three thousand years ago, famous for its legendary gardens. Buddha said the world is a lotus pond, and lotus ponds appeared everywhere among its landscape gardens decorated with pavilions, temples, rock sculptures, given such names as the Garden of the Master of Fish Nets (begun in 1140), the Tarrying Garden, the Pavilion of Fragrant Snow and Azure Clouds. Only one, Si Qin said, was sadly "degraded" by being called the Humble Administrator's or Plain Man's Politics Garden. It had no flowers but had a Pavilion of Expecting Frost.

Suzhou, a network of canals, is the Chinese Venice. It straddles the Grand Canal of cargo barges and tugboats, the longest manmade waterway in existence. A proverb says, "In heaven is paradise. On earth, Suzhou." So Marco Polo thought, who in the thirteenth century found it a noble city rich in silks, courtesans, and rhubarb, with "quite six thousand bridges of stone," a boast that nobody believed, then or now.

In Shanghai the Cherry Holiday Villa sent us off for the flight north with a box lunch of pastries and boiled eggs. Chinese planes seldom serve meals but offer gifts instead—key chains, handkerchiefs, bill-folds, boxes of walnut cake. On the plane I read in the *China Daily News* a letter to the editor which said, "I was naturally delighted to see in your paper a quick response to the need to overcome bureaucracy, redress wrongs, and whatnot. But I was shattered on reflection to ask why these shortcomings in government policy aren't seen *before* they come to light." Strong language of rebuke in a communist country.

Landing in Beijing, with not a moment to lose we were rushed straight to the Temple of Heaven, while on the way our young, pink-cheeked guide whose mother won't let her ride a bicycle lectured breathlessly on the history of China through the dynasties to the end of Imperialism. Heidi was so indoctrinated with zeal for the new China and its "perfect" system of government (one that would eliminate all temples of heaven) that she found no irony in this required visit to Tiantan Park, whose sacred temple included a Hall of Prayer for Good Harvests, a Vault of Heaven, an Altar of Heaven. Here once a year the emperor would come to intercede with heaven as only a son of heaven could do, till in 1911 the monarchy toppled, the Chinese Republic under Dr. Sun Yat-sen was declared, and the prayers of the last em-peror, the six-year-old puppet Pu Yi, abruptly ceased.

In the bus Martha called out, "Where's the Friendship Store?" but Heidi followed a strictly organized plan. The moment had come to take us to our hotel. For reasons known only to the CITS, we were to stay at the Diaoyutai State Guest House, a former palace with imperial gar-dens and a lake, that in 1959 was transformed into an elegant com-pound of fifteen villas for foreign dignitaries, luminaries, ambassadors, kings and queens and visiting heads of state. Queen Elizabeth had been a guest; President Nixon stayed here during his visit that established relations with the People's Republic, as did Carter and Reagan. Kissin-ger was in House #5. Last week Vice-President Bush occupied our quarters, House #3, in rooms without keys where the appointments are palatial and the gold fixtures in the bathroom show what the Chinese can do to improve the plumbing when they try.

Heidi's tight schedule gave us no time to dress for dinner or sip a cocktail in our well-stocked rooms before being dashed off through closely guarded gates to a restaurant, then to a Chinese opera that was performed as a dance drama, a field of art being explored by Comrade

Sun Ying. Though the choreography was strenuously acrobatic, the story was traditional, laid in the third century, a tale of tragic love between a dancing girl and a drummer in the court of Cao Cao, where for loving each other the boy's eyes were gouged out and the girl was led off by the executioner. A narrator in the balcony outlined the plot, while on a panel a summary of events appeared in Chinese. It was very odd, an opera in which nobody sang, yet a great leap forward from Mao's Cultural Revolution when only eight "exemplary" political plays were shown on the Chinese stage, under the direction of Mao's dragonish wife, the hated Jiang Qing.

"It's a great wall," said Nixon when invited to examine it. Today we drove fifty miles from Beijing north to Badaling where the first section of the Great Wall to be restored was completed in the 1950s. Once about three thousand miles long, meant as a barrier to invaders, some parts are collapsing, some in ruins. At Badaling the Wall is magnificently whole and draws multitudes of Chinese, who bring the children in a ritual visit to stand and stare.

From the highway we turned off to a rough road in the midst of mountains and climbed to the rocky regions where the Wall starts. From the carpark we followed a path lined with fusty shops, like the Great Antiques Store that sold T-shirts, to the broad pavilion at the foot of the Wall. There we began a climb so vertical I had to hold fast to the rail to keep from tumbling backward. In incredible mountain scenery that grew more spectacular the farther we went, past layers of green mountains in seemingly impregnable country, the temptation was strong to keep on going, never to descend, never to return.

All too soon, though it was hours later, Heidi gathered us into the bus. And suddenly we were down from the mountains on the way to the Ming Tombs twenty-five miles outside Beijing. Through an arched gate we entered the Sacred Way, a mile-long road lined with stone lions, camels, dragons, unicorns, elephants, plus twelve warriors in battle dress to guard the dead. Beyond was the secret burial place of Ming emperors from the fourteenth to the seventeenth century. Not all the tombs were excavated, some mere chunks of shattered marble. I walked alone down 150 steps to a cold underground storage chamber for an emperor's occupancy, the tomb of Ding Ling who was buried in 1640 with many wives and many chests of precious stones. Poor Ding Ling.

Beijing is a splendid city of eight million people, three million bicycles. It became China's capital when Kublai Khan with his Mongols ruled in what Marco Polo called Cathay and Coleridge called Xanadu. Marco Polo, greatest of medieval travelers, crossed all Asia to reach China, stayed twenty-four years in the service of Kublai Khan, and came home to Venice to report the fabulous tale of an emperor with many wives and countless concubines, five hundred elephants, twelve thousand barons—only to be labeled a liar by the Venetians. Kublai Khan had taken kindly to Marco Polo and requested there be sent from the pope at Rome one hundred persons of the Christian faith "able clearly to prove that the law of Christ was the best and all other religions false and naught." Up to now he hadn't been able to choose among four possible gods—Christ, Mohammed, Moses, or Buddha—respecting them equally because he didn't know which ruled in heaven, the true god. Pope Gregory, missing the golden chance, sent two friars who soon gave up the hard journey and returned home. In the end Kublai Khan was converted to Buddhism, partly because the Buddhist magicians in his court amused him more than the Christians he encountered.

I like the story of two Confucian scholars who sat on a bridge at Peking's Summer Palace looking down at the fish. One said, "See the happy fish." The other said, "How do you know they are happy?" The first replied, "How do you know I don't know they are happy?"

I was happy this morning at the Summer Palace not to have known the Dragon Empress Dowager Ci Xi, who in 1888 restored it for her chosen residence. In a vast Park for the Cultivation of Old Age nine miles from Beijing was the palace among pagodas and temples, a hundred buildings with gilt roofs and poetic names—the Palace of Joy and Longevity where she lived, the Hall of Happiness and Longevity, the gardens of Virtuous Harmony and Listening to the Orioles Pavilion. A marble boat of Purity and Ease, used by the empress for tea parties, sat immovable on the edge of Lake Kunming at the foot of Longevity Hill.

She was a wicked woman, ruthless, tyrannical, murderous, who likened herself to the Goddess of Mercy and ruled China for nearly fifty years till her death in 1908. Daughter of a Manchu mandarin, she was picked at fifteen to become Concubine Yi in the harem of the emperor Hsien-feng, made herself conspicuous to catch his attention, and bore him a son. At the emperor's death from debauchery at thirty, she saw to it her weakling child was named his successor and herself Empress Dowager. She gained a power that was absolute, opposing all reform, bringing ruin to her country.

Ci Xi likened herself to Queen Victoria, her contemporary, whose portrait stood by her bed and whom she rejoiced to have outlived. In Marina Warner's biography, *The Dragon Empress,* she is quoted as saying, "Do you know I have often thought that I am the cleverest woman who ever lived and that others cannot compare with me. Although I have heard much about Queen Victoria . . . I don't think her life is half as interesting and eventful as mine." Victoria wasn't a voluptuary who had 120 courses at her meals and consorted with eunuchs.

It was Sunday and Beijing had taken the day off to wander through her bedchamber, her Pavilion of the Fragrance of Buddha; go boating on her lake and climb Longevity Hill to the Pavilion of Precious Clouds. Like the Summer Palace of Catherine the Great outside Leningrad and the Summer Palace of Empress Maria Theresa in Vienna, this was the same picture of the People finally allowed inside. Three years after Ci Xi died came the revolution and the founding of the Chinese Republic. The infant Pu Yi whom she chose to be emperor died in 1967 as a humble gardener in Beijing.

If only it were true that Communism, when the opportunity came, did return a country to its people. The Forbidden City is theirs, a complex of six main palaces with flaring yellow roofs and vermilion walls, in which for four centuries twenty-four Sons of Heaven lived in idleness, luxury, complete seclusion, absolute authority. Since October 1, 1949, when Mao as founder of the Party in China proclaimed the People's Republic, the people have been free to enter through the Gate of Heavenly Peace. It leads to the Hall of Supreme Harmony, the Hall of Perfect Harmony, the Hall of the Preservation of Harmony—all the harmonies that couldn't be kept and perhaps never existed. Now the Imperial City stands idle opposite Tiananmen Square and the gray government buildings, the Great Hall of the People, and the Memorial Hall of Mao Tse-tung who liberated them.

But did he? Chairman Mao, like Lenin, was a Communist revolutionary who, since his death in 1976, has been exposed as a cruel dictator and repressor of human rights. The Cultural Revolution of 1966 was a catastrophic mistake of Mao's, the death of a culture, a ten-year reign of persecution and terror when thousands died, the economy was wrecked, the frontiers of China shut, religious freedom denied, temples, churches, libraries, universities closed or destroyed by the Red Guards, works of art smashed, writers exiled, books banned. In his attempt to teach order and obedience, Mao, abetted by his fourth wife (one of the terrible Gang of Four) forced people into submission and Mao uniforms, commanding them to be boundlessly loyal, as his little Red Book said, to "study Chairman Mao's writings, follow his teachings and act according to his instruction." Every Chinese had a copy; his picture, like Lenin's, was their icon, Mao was their living god.

In the Memorial Hall, built in 1977 for his tomb, where we marched under abrupt signs, "Take Off Your Hat," "Keep Quiet," here was not merely Mao's monument impressively huge but his body on exhibition under glass. Like Lenin he had been embalmed and mummified, though as we filed past the crystal coffin he looked, beneath a covering red flag, more waxen a corpse than Lenin in Red Square. Both ears were intact (one recently was lost), his head and face were peculiarly shiny. He looked unreal, restored and rosy, not imperishable but nine years dead.

Outside in the great square, hundreds of pilgrims moved in silent lines toward Mao's tomb. In the opposite direction hundreds more entered the Forbidden City. For nearly an hour we watched them while Ted talked of heroes revered as divine by the people, like Mao, Lenin, Gandhi, winding up with Marcus Aurelius.

I heard no mention of the present head of the Party, Deng Xiaoping, though the relaxed air reflected a change. He is eighty-one, soon inevitably to be replaced, when Mao's kind of oppression may again be imposed. Deng says he is leading a second revolution, but he is a dedicated Communist in a one-party government. Who knows whether this is only a respite from the tyranny and terror Mao imposed?

A chartered military plane of the Chinese Air Force flew us to Xian, a city practically unknown outside China till the terracotta soldiers were discovered in 1974, one of the most astonishing archeological finds of all time. When the first emperor of China and builder of the Great Wall, Qin Shi Huang, died, a whole army was buried with him, thousands of life-size clay figures to protect him in the next life. They were found by accident by some peasants digging a well and are in the process of being excavated.

Xian was, say the guidebooks, once the largest city on earth, capital of eleven dynasties. It's a city of two million people, all of whom ride bicycles. When we arrived tonight in dense fog, we drove from the airport without lights in hazardous traffic where nobody had his lights on, since Chinese bicycles have no lights but do have the right of way and rule the road. When our driver tried to signal the hordes ahead that he wanted to pass, they paid no heed.

Next morning it was the same, the city blanketed with fog, the bicycles eight abreast sailing through the streets, bells ringing. On the massive stone walls were large signs, "Sighseeing on the City Wall of Xian," and "Go Forward." (I like that idea: go forward and see Xian with a sigh.)

On our way to the tomb of Qin Shi Huang, we stopped at the picturesque Huaqing Hot Springs at the foot of Lishan Mountain, where for centuries Chinese rulers came for relaxation. In the pavilion, among pomegranate and persimmon trees, the people waited in long lines to pay one yen for a steam bath. Over the desk of the hotel where we had lunch, a sign said, "MASSAGE, to release the blood. Whole body, 30 yen. Half body, 20 yen." It didn't specify which half, but I suppose you take your choice.

White birches lined the road that led to the diggings. Among the hills dotted with ancient tombs, our guide pointed to a conspicuous burial mound, the emperor's tomb beside the Wei River, but to my surprise we passed it by. Not yet excavated, it is believed to hold rich treasures and the bones of courtiers, eunuchs, concubines who were buried alive to join him in death. The soldiers who guarded him were buried a mile away to form an enclosure surrounding the tomb.

Under an enormous protective roof like a great shed covering three acres is the site itself, sixteen feet deep, only one section of the tremendous army of clay. This is Pit #1, with six thousand soldiers of the infantry division standing ready to attack in columns of six soldiers across, separated by trenches. Though some are headless, each warrior is clad in gray battle dress, each a real person, his face different from the rest. They look grimly determined and startlingly alive.

Beyond them lie the second and third pits, said to contain several thousand more officers and men, horses and chariots, still sealed till they can be unearthed and restored. On walkways we wandered silent among an invincible army buried and forgotten twenty-two centuries ago.

It was 8:00 P.M. by the time our plane reached the ancient city of Chengdu, capital of Sichuan province more than a thousand miles southwest of Beijing. Chengdu looked quite modern with its People's Road, People's Park, and Cultural Park, its supply of first-class hotels, each of which our local guide, Mr. Shi, proudly brought to our attention. The one I particularly noted was the new Jinjiang Hotel, where we had heard we were to stay. Yet Mr. Shi, a little fellow five feet tall with a round beaming face, showed it off and passed it by. In his zeal to give us the history of Chengdur (most of his words ended ringingly in the letter r) he had apparently forgot where he was going.

We turned off the main Renmin Road into narrow slumlike lanes and drew up at the Wang Jiang Hotel where, even in the dark, it was plain there was some mistake. This was a Chinese hotel, not permitted to foreigners, and, we soon discovered, a real fleabag. In the flaking brown lobby we were coldly assigned rooms with keys that didn't lock, plumbing that didn't work, beds hard as granite, ragged curtains at the window, dirt everywhere, and in the dimly lit corridors a couple of dead mice. Our luggage hadn't arrived and wouldn't be delivered till next day. The late supper served by angry waitresses was in tune with the surroundings. It was awful.

At the down-at-heels Wang Jiang, not found in any guidebook, we stayed for the next three nights. Once the error was made by the inaccessible CITS, to try to rectify it would be like trying to overthrow the government. Though he never stopped smiling, Mr. Shi managed to look downcast and apologetic. "Tomorrer," he said, "it may be betterr."

After the first shock I was resigned to being there, obviously alone in my view that, having had opulent quarters with gold fittings in the State Guest House in Beijing, it was only just we should be shown, amid squalor, how the Chinese themselves fare. This kind of accident wasn't supposed to happen, and our guide, Si Qin, was dismayed. When I asked if he would report the conditions in this hotel, he said, "Yes, I must, oh yes." I trusted his courtesy and tact. Like us, Si Qin was a stranger, far from his home in Inner Mongolia, sent down to represent, his card said, the "Chinese People's Association for Friendship with Foreign Countries." He was used to being resented by the local guides, scorned for his Mongol accent, feared as a spy for the government. He had learned to endure worse treatment during the Cultural Revolution.

For the next days Mr. Shi provided a nonstop tour of Chengdu and its countryside, voluble in praise of the new China "that solves all problems." In a suit two sizes too big, bursting with smiles, he assured us that every family managed to eat. The statue of Chairman Mao soared three stories high at the exhibition center, and a large billboard said, "You'd better have one child only."

Mr. Shi took us to the Grand Buddhist Monastery named Precious Light, colossal in size, where in the temple five hundred statues of Buddha, each one different, lined the walls. Mr. Shi said to start counting from the first Buddha till we reached the number of years of our age, and that one would be our own guide and benefactor. Mine, if I counted right, was a flattering youth with black hair and curling mustache whom I was pleased to claim.

On one occasion he arranged a tea ceremony to meet a painter celebrated for his bamboo paintings. After a flowery introduction by Mr. Shi and an address of welcome by the artist in Chinese, we gathered round his drawing board while he painted a likeness of bamboo with panda. This art, very close to calligraphy, is done in black ink, every brush stroke bold and final. In a half hour he had finished a panel of a giant panda clinging to a leafy branch of bamboo, every blade distinct. I've read somewhere of a Chinese artist who painted bamboo for ten years and won the right never to look at a bamboo shoot again.

"Now," said Mr. Shi, rubbing his hands in glee, "we go to see the pandars." The giant panda, found only in China and her national treasure, is a native of Sichuan and lives among bamboo groves, nearly impossible to capture. The Chengdu Zoo has the biggest collection in the world. "It's pandemonium," H. C. said. There we saw six giant pandas and a group of rare, smaller brown ones that looked like raccoons, uncaged and playing about. Thirteen-year-old Mei-mei with a record of seven cubs was delivered last week of another baby, at birth the size of a rat. Her subdued mate lolled by himself as far from her as possible. Pandas sit and gape at nothing but bamboo, eating forty pounds a day.

At six this morning we left for the Chengdu airport, carrying a box lunch of a green apple and a very hardboiled egg. We were a solemn company, not sorry to leave this terrible hotel but truly sorry to part from each other. Most of the group were taking a plane east to Canton and Hong Kong before returning home. Three of us, with the Cranfords, were on our way west to Tibet. I hated to lose my traveling companions, hated to lose Si Qin, my good friend. But nothing except bad weather over the Himalayas could keep me from taking this journey, which even as we boarded the plane seemed unattainable. Those we were parting from, unaccountably reluctant to go in search of Shangri-La, expressed aloud their doubt that we were in our right minds to set out over these mountains in near November.

TO TIBET I am a pushover for paradise, ever hopeful of a temporary Eden on this planet as a verifiable place to visit. Africa came close with its stillness and peace among the wild animals, except for the undeniable drawback of trying to live with lions and stay alive oneself. In my mind there was always Shangri-La and the ultima Thule (D. H. Lawrence: "I wish I were going to Tibet . . . to the ultima, ultima, ultima Thule"). When James Hilton wrote his novel *Lost Horizon* in 1933, he was free to describe Tibet as a hidden Buddhist paradise where life approached perfection and was nearly everlasting, since at that time nobody had been to Tibet. Up to 1980 it was inaccessible to tourists and nearly everyone else—a kingdom back of beyond at the roof of the world, sealed off and isolated by the Himalayas, the highest mountains in the highest country on earth. Lhasa its capital was the Forbidden City, secret, closed and sacred, where Lamaism as a form of Tibetan Buddhism was the ruling power and half the population were Lamaist monks. Tibetans called their country "Land of the Religion."

But in 1951 the Chinese moved in. Under Mao Tse-tung, Tibet was forced to become a "national autonomous region" of the People's Republic. For centuries the Chinese had refused to recognize Tibet as more than an outpost of China; under Mao they forcibly occupied the country, taking over the government. During the Cultural Revolution most of the Tibetan monasteries and temples were closed or destroyed, only a few spared and turned into museums. In 1959 after a brief uprising put down by the Chinese (in which it is said 87,000 Tibetans died), the Dalai Lama, God-King and living Buddha, from the age of four the temporal and spiritual ruler, fled to exile in India followed by a hundred thousand of the faithful. Now after more than thirty years of Communist rule, the Chinese have allowed Buddhist ritual in the surviving monasteries, and the Tibetans live as best they can in submission to two conflicting worlds, the old and the new, the godly and the ungodly.

On the three-hour flight from Chengdu to Tibet, over a wilderness of ice and snow, the Himalayas looked different in sheer magnitude from any mountains I had ever seen. They weren't like the Alps, say, or the Andes where one flew over snow clouds—they were more forbidding, more fierce and sharp-peaked, higher, colder, mightier, frightening in their immensity and grandeur. I looked away from the window to the comfortable plane only partly filled with Tibetans and Chinese, at the pretty Chinese hostesses wearing aprons to serve the jasmine tea, at my four friends half asleep beside me. And I considered our plight, sky-high over the Himalayas with not a patch of landscape beneath, no sign of a break in these endlessly impenetrable mountains. How would the pilot find his way to a landing place, wherever it was far below? I closed my eyes and waited, and the wait was very long.

At last we began to descend slowly, it seemed cautiously, slipping through a narrow pass, dropping to a single landing strip in the middle of nowhere. Nowhere at all. We were eighty miles from Lhasa at what was said to be the only airport in Tibet, and nobody was there to meet us. From the empty plane, the other passengers had disappeared into thin air. As we stood alone on the tarmac, surrounded by mountains, wondering what to do about it, a Chinese in a business suit approached us warily.

"Do you speak Spanish?" he asked.

"No!" we said in one voice.

He repeated the question. "No, no, not a word," we cried. Was one supposed to speak Spanish in Tibet?

He looked around impatient, bewildered, and his face fell. "Something's wrong," he said. "You weren't expected. I don't know what happened or who you are. Anyway, come along." He led us outside to a small Chinese bus (no foreign cars are allowed in Tibet) and with the driver's help got us and our luggage squeezed inside. Once more he attempted to set things straight by addressing us in Spanish. We shook our heads, he shook his head and sat down, defeated.

As the driver started the bus I stared about me. Tibet was heaven enough, I thought, however unwelcoming—a wondrous place startlingly beautiful of blinding blue sky, dazzling sun, crystal air. We were on a narrow sandy road, the road to Lhasa, usually blocked by snow this time of year. We were beside a wide river and to the left jagged, treeless mountains of brown polished rock almost near enough to touch. For the eighty miles to Lhasa, with only a few scattered huts in clearings along the way and a huge painted Buddha carved in the rockface, it became insistently a trip to the end of the world, leading to more unthinkable beauty like this. I breathed in the Tibetan air and wrote "yak" in my notebook after catching sight of a solitary one—a shaggy kind of ox with long carved upward horns, its tangled black hair hanging like a curtain to the ground. Seeing him put me in mind of Hillary in the Himalayas, land of yaks and abominable snowmen.

Lhasa, the city of sun, is in the Gyi Qu valley, on a plateau sky-encircled by mountains stretching beyond mountains, crowned by a glittering of white peaks. As we entered the one city in Tibet, a city without walls, before our eyes was the tremendous Potala Palace rising up red, white, and gold with sacrificial flags flying, like the kingdom of God hovering in its majesty above the town, like Buddha serene against the mountain.

One long straight street looked to be the whole of Lhasa, with few trees, no traffic, gray flat-roofed houses modestly low, the populace invisible. Just then it occurred to Señor, as by now we called him, to nod in passing at a handsome white hotel standing alone below the Potala, gleaming in the sun and palatial itself.

"Stop!" H. C. yelled. "Isn't that the new Hotel Lhasa? Hold everything! That's where we're supposed to stay."

"No, señor, impossible," said Señor, turning round to frown at him. "You can't stay there."

"Why not?"

"Because the hotel isn't open, señor. It's shut, no admittance. They finished building it last month and took in a few guests. At the end of one week they closed it. Reason, bad management. Total disaster."

"Is it closed for good?" H. C. asked.

"Might open some day. Might not." [A year later it opened as a Holiday Inn under Swiss management.]

We drove on. Where Señor was taking us we doubted he knew, though actually it was the only place in town where tourists could conveniently stay. About four miles beyond Lhasa, we turned down a wooded lane that led to a group of buildings forming a small compound. A few rows of tiny orange-colored adobe cottages, each consisting of one room, stood side by side on the stone pavement. After stopping to consult a couple of maids sunning themselves nearby, Señor led us from the bus to three of these attached cottages and, while we opened the door and looked uncertainly inside, disappeared from sight. Where he and the driver went so fast we never knew. We found our luggage dumped in the road. Señor had without ado abandoned us, and we never saw him again or any Spaniards either.

Shortly, a Tibetan boy of about fifteen who spoke a little English appeared and, pulling us by the arm, insisted we go and lie down on our beds. Since altitude sickness, accompanied by dizziness, nausea, violent headache, nosebleed, is a common ailment at this height of 12,000 feet, for which oxygen bags were kept constantly at hand, it wasn't an unreasonable request. But to Lois and me it was highly unacceptable. We didn't want to go to bed, we wanted to find out the meaning of this rude reception.

"Take us to the manager," I said to the boy. "You know, the one in charge, the manager?" To our relief he nodded and led Lois and me panting for breath up the hill to a building where in an office on the second floor we found him, the one in charge. At first Deng Ke-ping stared at us thoroughly puzzled. Who were we? Where had we come from? He had received no information about us or our expected arrival (the information arrived next day from the CITS, whose representative he was in Tibet). Anyway, he held out his hand and smiled. Deng Ke-ping was in his thirties, tall and slender, sloppily dressed in jeans and sweat shirt, a man with warm eyes, friendly ways, quick laughter. "Tell me, do you speak Spanish?" Lois asked, and gave him a vivid account of our dealings with Señor.

He apologized at once. "I don't know what happened but, believe me, I'll soon find out. Meanwhile, allow me to welcome you. I speak Tibetan, Chinese, and English, whichever you prefer."

I liked him very much. "What I prefer," I said, "what I really wish, is that you were going to be our guide."

"I'll see to it you get the best," he said laughing, and we shook hands on that. A half hour later he appeared at our rooms to tell us he was moving us to more suitable quarters across the road. He pointed out the dining room in a separate building, where we would be given lunch and have our meals in future (there are almost no places to eat in Lhasa). Finally he said, "If you don't mind, I'd like to be your guide during your stay and show you what I can of Tibet. I shouldn't take the time from my job, but anyway I want to do it."

Already I felt happy in Shangri-La.

That afternoon Ke-ping took us in his own bus into Lhasa, the beginning of many wonderful excursions with him. Because the hour was late, we stayed to the modern part of town where he showed us the new buildings owned by Chinese, the Chinese theater, the department store large as a barracks where you could buy Colgate toothpaste and American cigarettes. As we two walked together I said, "You must be Chinese, but you don't look Chinese"—not with his round eyes, his dark skin, his height.

"Born in Shanghai, raised in Shanghai," he said. He came to Tibet nine years ago, sent here during Mao's Cultural Revolution, a bad time for him faced with the fear, resentment, hatred of the Tibetans toward the Chinese invaders, suppressors of their religion, rulers of their lives. Eventually his wife left him to return with their little girl to Shanghai, where he goes once a year to see them. "But for me," he said, "I will stay. I love Tibet, I love these people. This is my home. I am building myself a house in the compound, here I want to be."

Ke-ping is not religious, he told me, though he has come to believe in the man Buddha if not the god. He wants not a faith, he said, but a philosophy, peace but not nirvana. He is not a member of the Communist Party; few Chinese are.

Back at the compound, Ke-ping moved us into a larger guest house that consisted of three unheated rooms, one opening into the other, with a bathroom at the farthest end. It was an intimate arrangement for H. C. to find himself in such close quarters with four females, two of whom were now ill. My room came first in line nearest the outside door, so that I had to traipse through the other two rooms even to wash my face, which was seldom, since there was no hot water or no water at all. Besides I hated to disturb Agnes and Nina, who occupied the third room. Both were suffering from chest colds and, especially Nina, from severe nausea and altitude sickness. Luckily, in each of our rooms there was a thermos jug filled with hot boiled water and beside it a jar of jasmine tea. I found I could take a sponge bath in the large teacup after emptying it of tea leaves, and that particular problem was solved. I grew fond of my simple room with its one chair, narrow bed, bare floor, a clothes hook but no closet space, often no light but candles, a view of gardens not in bloom, and a book on the table, *Chinese Literature, Fiction, Poetry, Art, Summer of 1985,* that must have been put there by Ke-ping. On the first night I read in bed a poem by Lu Li that I liked. It sounded Chinese:

Once I came home in a snowstorm with snow on my body and cap.
"Papa," asked my child, "what did you bring home for me?"
"Some snowflakes," I replied.

It wasn't snowing but it was cold. At night the temperature dropped close to zero and by midday in unfiltered sunlight zoomed up to seventy degrees. Sleeping under piles of blankets, by noon you could sit in the sun in danger of sunstroke. I had expected blizzards in these mountains, wading through ice storms and avalanches. None fell on us in the land of snows.

The real journey to Tibet and the Tibetans began that morning when Ke-ping came early to take us to old Lhasa, the Old Town, where a narrow circular street, the Barkhor which pilgrims circled on hands and knees, started and ended at the Jokhang, the holiest temple in Tibet and the oldest. Most of the life of the city was concentrated in front of this shrine, in a marketplace swarming with Tibetans, buyers and sellers, where the brightest clothing, the gaudiest jewelry were sold, along with rugs, knives, silver bowls, and the staples of Tibetan life— the barley flour, *tsamba,* that looks like sawdust, the potent barley beer, *chhang,* yak butter in huge wooden tubs, quantities of tea in bricks. At the door of the Jokhang, spreading out into Lhasa's main square, other Tibetans were engaged in worship, prostrating themselves eight times at body length, flinging themselves forward in a ritual so strenuous they wore straw sleeves to protect them from bleeding on the flagstone pavement. The prostrations might last for hours, even days. A few knelt fingering prayer beads, or twirling prayer wheels containing strips of paper on which were written mantras that would soar to the sky and be heard by the Buddha. "Om mani padme hum," they murmured, "hail to the jewel in the lotus" (who is the Buddha), to draw his benevolent attention to their love and their need, in particular the need to be reincarnated next time into a better life.

Inside the Jokhang, where foreigners are free to go and only nine monks remain, the immense temple was dark and airless, heavy with incense, full of shrines lit by flickering yak-butter votive lamps and smoky from their fumes. It was built 1,300 years ago to house a precious statue of the Buddha brought by Princess Wen Cheng from China—a solid gold Buddha with blue-lidded eyes, its body gleaming with turquoises and fine brocades, its gold face impassive as Buddha always is.

Ke-ping held me close and H. C. protected Lois with his arms while we pushed through the turbulence in the marketplace, smiling at the Tibetans who stopped in their tracks, held up their children to stare, then smiled, smiled their greeting and welcome. An old woman stuck out her tongue at me, which is a sign of high courtesy to salute those one wishes to honor. It happened too fast for me to stick out my tongue in return, as politeness required me to do.

When we stopped before a tub of yak butter, Ke-ping asked the owner in Tibetan if I might taste it, and while a merry crowd gathered round for the sideshow he cut a sizable triangle and with a bow handed it to me. As they watched I ate it, smacking my lips at its smoothness and mild cheese flavor. Ke-ping said they told him, roaring with laughter, he should buy me the whole tubful to put more butter on my bones. They laughed to call it yak butter, for as any Tibetan knows the yak is male. The word for the female is *dri*.

We could so easily have become friends and drunk hours away over buttered tea together. Harsh as their meager life is of poverty and ignorance, the childlike Tibetans seemed glad of any occasion for merriment. They were comely though unwashed—a sturdy people, red-cheeked, with straight black hair, black eyes, more Indian than Chinese. The men were smooth-faced, clad in yakhide boots, a yakskin coat and fur cap, the women weighed down with several layers of garments, long skirts, earrings, a headdress over their black braids. Tibetans are said to be great singers and dancers. Ke-ping spoke of them as both gentle and fierce, forbidden in their reverence for life to kill any living thing (not even the yak that provides their meat, dung for fuel, skin for tents, tail for fly swatters)—the most religious people on earth. To force Communism on them with atheism the state policy was tragic, attacking their faith and banishing their god. As he sadly sees, they wait in vain for the day when the Dalai Lama will return.

And this the Dalai Lama, now fifty years old, is trying to do. In a piece of special pleading in the *New York Times* last August 9, he made bitter accusations against the present government: "In this period, our religion and culture has been destroyed. At least 1.2 million have died as a direct result of the occupation. Virtually all of the 5,700 monasteries and 700 temples of which we have records have been destroyed." He said nothing of Tibet's medieval state before the occupation, its appalling poverty, its exploitation of women who had no rights, to whom all sins were ascribed. His autobiography, *My Land and My People,* tells of the sweetness of life when it was based on submission and faith.

[Two years later, October 1987, as the world knows, a bloody struggle erupted in Lhasa when the Chinese again brutally enforced their rule.

In a march for independence, thousands gathered outside the Jokhang temple and a riot followed when police with machine guns fired into the crowd. People were stoned to death, monks tortured, foreigners expelled. Tibet is again inaccessible, a closed country. How has Ke-ping weathered this return to terror and despair?

China accuses the Dalai Lama of inciting the people. Yet for the Tibetans more than their life is at stake. If the Dalai Lama in whom the Goddess of Mercy resides does not return, they believe the line of reincarnation will be broken, with it the hope of eternity.]

Ke-ping refused to let us visit the Potala Palace till we had adjusted to the high altitude. The exertion of climbing hundreds of steps up thirteen storeys was, he said, too great a strain on heart and lungs. Instead he took us to the famed Drepung Monastery, where we climbed so many hundreds of steps I laughed at his solicitude. The three chief monasteries of Tibet, each of which barely escaped being destroyed by Mao's Red Guards, are the Jokhang, the Potala where the Dalai Lama lived, and the Drepung, the largest monastery in the world. This white pile five miles outside Lhasa, perched in tiers on the side of a mountain, always trained the Buddhist monks. Before 1959 it had ten thousand celibate monks, some of whom became living buddhas or bodhisattvas (buddhas-to-be), though I never learned—and Ke-ping couldn't tell me—how one knows when he has become a buddha, liberated from suffering into a state of enlightenment. Buddhism has no saints, only "those who know."

Out in the courtyard we found a crowd of little boys with cropped heads, nine or ten years old. Lois, who carries candies and small gifts in her handbag to offer any child she meets, promptly drew out a bag of green balloons and, in spite of lack of breath after the climb, began to blow them up. The boys were enchanted, not having seen a balloon before. As we stood by admiring Lois's resourcefulness, they ran wildly about, laughing, yelling, tossing the balloons in the air.

So we left them and went inside the temple, where Ke-ping led us by the hand in darkness, past the inevitable rows of immense Buddhas hung with white silk scarfs, the *khata,* that the devout bring in reverence; past the hundreds of perpetually burning yak-butter lamps the young novices were busy tending and replenishing, all the while bobbing their green balloons above their heads. Suddenly a monk who, it happened, was the abbot, appeared out of the dark and spoke gently in Tibetan to Ke-ping, his tone so benign, his manner so composed, I thought he was making a welcoming address. On the contrary. What he was telling our guide was to get those balloons out of there fast! Ke-ping recognized the crisis and acted quickly, rounding up the children, hurrying them and the deflated balloons out the door. It had been, at the least, the desecration of a holy temple, the profaning of sanctity. And the beauty of it was, it was handled so quietly, so well.

I wonder why rulers and emperors must have their summer palaces—even the Kublai Khan had one in Xanadu. The summer palace of the Dalai Lama, the Norbulingka meaning "The Jewel Park," is set in wooded grounds at the base of the Potala, the winter palace. It is guarded by two ferocious stone lions with red tongues, a striking group of white buildings trimmed blue and black with gold decor, where he spent the months from March to October, returning to the Potala in a golden palaquin. Though the palace is empty save for a few monks as caretakers, the pilgrims come, nomadic herders pitching their yakskin tents beside the Lhasa River, whose bridge is hung with red and yellow prayer flags flapping like laundry in the breeze. Lhasa is the holy city for pilgrims. They arrive from mountain villages and go from shrine to shrine prostrating themselves, more numerous than the few tourists who, said Ke-ping, till last year were almost unknown.

After comparing the garish furnishings of the summer palace with the Empress Dowager's in Beijing, Ke-ping and I walked beside the river and talked of reincarnation and sky burial. Reincarnation is an abso-lute doctrine of Tibetan Buddhism, and the Dalai Lama himself is a being reborn from the spirit of his predecessor. The Buddha, they believe, accepted this concept of rebirth. On such a beautiful day in Tibet, I looked about and could imagine coming back to live again and again under the crystal blue sky. "Better than behaving yourself in heaven," I said.

"Right!" Ke-ping said, laughing at the idea, and told me about sky burial, the manner in which at death the soul is freed to hasten to its next reincarnation. Each day at dawn the bodies of the newly dead are gathered and taken to a secret burial place, a rock or ledge above the city, by *ragyabas* or corpse disposers who perform the ancient grue-some ceremony. Like an executioner they chop the body into small pieces, then expose the morsels on a ledge where they are quickly devoured by waiting vultures. Tibetans believe the vultures are sacred birds who will hurry the soul from the body to a better life, bringing it nearer to paradise. (Actually in Buddhist teaching it is the karma—the character of a person, the sum of his good and evil deeds—that determines his future existence.) For this reason the hunting or killing of vultures is prohibited; tourists are forbidden to seek out the hidden rocks or witness the ceremony for fear of frightening away the birds.

"Would you like to be given a sky burial?" I asked Ke-ping. He shrugged. "Perhaps. Would you?"

"Well," I said, "I don't think they did it that way in Shangri-La."

Next morning we climbed to the top of the Potala, after the bus had taken us by a back road partway up Red Hill, which rises a thousand feet above Lhasa, to avoid the long stone staircase at the front of the palace. Even so we had hundreds of steep steps to ascend and descend, up and down in a bewildering maze of passages. By now Agnes and Nina had joined us, though Nina, hugging an oxygen bag, found she was too sick to get out of the bus. She closed her eyes and wished to God she had never come to Tibet.

The Potala, rebuilt many times since the seventh century, visible from wherever you are, is simply tremendous in size and splendor, like nothing on earth. It has ten thousand chapels and altars filled with images of jeweled Buddhas—past Buddha, present Buddha, future or coming Buddha (who continues to be reborn through time), the Buddha meditating, the Buddha preaching his doctrine, the Buddha and his disciples. Some of its thousand rooms contain stupas or tombs of former Dalai Lamas—the Great Fifth, who moved from the monastic Drepung and became ruler of Tibet. His gold tomb covered with jewels is sixty feet high, the Thirteenth's (who died in 1934) seventy feet and gold from top to bottom. The title Dalai Lama was conferred on the First in 1576, and the dynasties persisted till 1959 when the Fourteenth fled to exile. Not all the reincarnations were successful. The Sixth Dalai Lama, whose name meant Melodious Purity, became a playboy and poet who brought women to the Potala and loved them to excess as he loved wine and song. He was removed and probably strangled. A few others died mysteriously in childhood.

The Potala is indescribable. Ke-ping did his best to make it visible, leading us with a flashlight through the darkness, pointing to the many gods: of Compassion, of Mercy, of Wisdom, all qualities of the Buddha. In the Great Hall stood the Lion Throne where the Dalai Lama had sat crosslegged in the lotus position, an incredibly ornate room with a silk ceiling, rich carpets and hangings, scroll paintings. There in the Red Palace, between the two white sections that were quarters for hundreds of monks—and, in the lowest part, dungeons for torture and a cave of scorpions, not shown to visitors—the Dalai Lama lived in isolation, unseen by his people. Most of his rooms at the summit of the Potala were now open to view, where we walked freely through his private apartments, his library, reception room, sitting room, dressing room, meditating room. We examined his tea set, his narrow couch and robe, even his toilet—a hole in the floor lined with pink velvet, with a pipe reaching all the way to the ground (the longest toilet, Ke-ping said, in the world). From the terrace roof we gazed down, as the Dalai Lama had done, on Lhasa below, on its gray flat-roofed houses that looked worshipful in the sunlight.

Late that afternoon Nina was definitely worse, fevered and gasping for breath. Though she had refused for days to have a doctor, we asked Ke-ping to get one for her, and in no time he returned with a Chinese woman doctor, obviously accustomed to this sort of emergency, who brought with her a nurse and two interpreters. We hadn't known how dangerous a cold is in the thin air of Tibet, where it may quickly become pneumonia. The small, silent woman by her skilled treatment may well have saved Nina's life, at the least a long stay in hospital. Throughout that night she never left her patient's side, and with oxygen, antibiotics, drugs, herb medicines, and expert care brought her through the crisis. All next day aided by the nurse she watched over Nina till she was out of danger, in fact remained with her till Nina was safely on a plane out of the country. For this extraordinary service her professional fee was thirty-five dollars.

On the last morning in Tibet, we were up at four o'clock to be driven to the airport eighty miles away for the one daily flight to Chengdu—daily, that is, if the pilot dared to take off in winter fog, windstorms, frequent blizzards in the mountains. Accompanying us on the bus, besides Nina's doctor, was Ke-ping, who needn't have come, though we cherished him by now and wanted his company. On the bus he fell promptly asleep, having stayed up most of the night—on other nights as well while acting as our guide—to handle his desk work at the office. Tonight he had been in bed two hours. As we rode along under a diamond spectacle of stars and an unreal moon too large for the sky, the dawn over the Lhasa River began to color the barren rocks every shade from brown to magenta to shining gold—Tibet's version of daybreak.

When the driver turned on the radio, Ke-ping woke and listened, humming a Tibetan song he said was sung in Lhasa these days. I asked him to write the words in my notebook and he did, frowning as he struggled to translate:

> Let's make our world beautiful.
> We, no matter which continent you and me stay,
> Let's help each other.
> He helps you or I help you this time,
> You will help the others in the time to come.

It seemed to agree with Ke-ping's philosophy.

At the airport after many embraces he was gone and we were gone, airborne for the return from Shangri-La. Beside the window I sat and wept at the certainty I would never come back to this world, this beauty, or, the chances were, this kind of paradise. Why call it paradise? Why not *paradis perdu?* (A French proverb: "Le vrai paradis est le paradis perdu.") The spirit of the Buddha was alive in Tibet, who rightly saw life as a time of grief, inseparable from suffering. But it was like this: you lived some moments that were entirely good. You found something close to paradisal, then being a tourist quickly discovered its impermanence. I loved Tibet and wept to go. I couldn't take it with me.

There must be other world's ends, I thought, before the end of everything.

On arrival in Chengdu we found little Mr. Shi at the plane to meet us, beaming his joy and anxiety to please. His triumphant news was that he had got us into the Jinjiang Hotel, where we were supposed to be in the first place. The sight of him made eloquent how long a lifetime we'd been away, far from the comforts of hot baths, flushing toilets, and Mr. Shi's undiminished zeal to enlighten and entertain. Now he was perplexed as to what there was left to do. He had knocked himself out earlier to show us Chengdur, its Buddhars and pandars. What else would we care to see? Doubtfully he suggested an excursion to "Du Fur's cottage."

"Who is Du Fur?" we asked.

"A dead poet." It sounded desperate.

"If you're quite sure there's nothing else," said Lois, adding "Helen likes poets."

We might have visited the Tibetan quarter in Chengdu or the Lamaist monastery, but Tibet was a lost world behind us. At the open market Mr. Shi stopped the bus to let us choose between poor old Du Fur or spending the afternoon "thererr with all the fresh vegetablerrs." H. C. waved his hand. "Carry on," he said, like patience on a monument.

I should have known how vowels and consonants will trip you up. Mr. Shi was taking us to the home of *Tu Fu,* the greatest of Chinese poets, for whom the city of Chengdu had given a park in his honor and rebuilt the thatched cottage, or a version of it, where he had lived and written his poems more than twelve centuries ago.

A long walk lined with bamboo led to the cottage that contained several portraits of Tu Fu, imaginary of course, of a man born in the Tang dynasty. It had, surprisingly, none of his books on display. Mr. Shi himself had never read the works of Tu Fu but took his immortality on faith. "A grreat poet!" he exclaimed.

Tu Fu wrote two hundred poems in this cottage, which he built among clumps of bamboo on the outskirts of Chengdu after years of wandering in poverty, after "difficulties have made me stupid at living." He had been a drinking companion of the poet Li Po, vainly passing his days till, shortly before Li Po drowned while reaching out to embrace the moon in the river, Tu Fu went to live in his empty hut, "mute, friendless, feeding the crumbling years." There the wind tore off his thatched roof and he wrote "One Hundred Worries,"

> I do not sleep for worry over war,
> Yet have no strength to right the world.

As we left the park, Lois created a sensation by buying from a poor street seller a dozen fragile homemade birds on the wing to decorate her Christmas tree. It was the old woman's entire stock. Speechless at this turn of fortune, she was queen for the day, treated with esteem by the crowd that gathered to witness her unheard-of luck.

Having presented a weary Mr. Shi with a large box of chocolates (tipping is forbidden in China), we attempted to leave Chengdu next morning, delayed five hours waiting for the fog to lift. Meanwhile, our woman guide to Kweilin sat fidgeting the day away in the Kweilin airport. When at last we appeared, without inquiring what state we were in (Nina, still recovering from Tibet, was near collapse), she swept us out to the waiting bus, crying, "Please hurry, or we shall be too late! The cave closes at 4:30."

Had H. C. and I known beforehand we would have to go sightseeing in a cave, we would never have left Chengdu. One thing I value in H. C. is that like me he is claustrophobic and avoids, as well as he can, getting into tight situations like elevators, clothes closets, and caves. But there we were, cornered. We walked into the Reed Flute Cave hand in hand, breathed deep, and kept on going. Though an immense cave, luckily it was circular and as a sight distracting from moment to moment—now a pure crystal palace or again a lurid emerald and scarlet cathedral with weirdly shaped pillars and monstrous stalagmite candles. H. C., whose disposition is cloudless, looked respectfully at the walls closing him in and said, "My Dixie cup runneth over."

Kweilin is a landscape painting of cassia trees surrounded by vast mountains totally unlike the Himalayas. They rise up singly, stark black rocks in fantastic shapes like monoliths. The Chinese give them names—Elephant Trunk Peak, Folded Brocade Peak, Piled Silk Hill— and Chinese artists paint them endlessly, their two subjects being bamboo with panda and the marvelous mountains of Kweilin.

Next day our guide Julia, who described herself as a serene wife and mother, took us for a cruise on the Li River that winds with many bends and turns beyond Kweilin. From the upper deck we had a view different from any on earth—green limestone hills and sheer black rocks looming like prehistoric beasts. Stephen Spender thinks Coleridge's "Kubla Khan" is really about Kweilin, "where Alph the sacred river ran." It looks like an opium dream.

Our last stop in mainland China was at Canton, a southern city that stretches along the banks of the Pearl River. It's called the Goat City from a legend that five celestial beings descended from the sky to found it, each astride a goat with its mouth full of rice. More aptly it's called a violent city, where revolutions start and pockets are picked. From Canton Dr. Sun Yat-sen brought to an end the Manchu dynasty. In the Martyr's Park is a tomb holding the remains of five thousand martyrs of the 1927 uprising against the Communists. It stands mockingly near a Pavilion of Blood-Cementing Friendship between the Chinese and Soviet Peoples. Since 1960 when Mao and Khrushchev split over ideological differences, China and Russia have abandoned the idea of friendship.

I stood at my window in the White Swan Hotel overlooking the river, thinking about food—Chinese food. We had just had a delicious lunch in this supercelestial hotel with an interior waterfall and a garden of tall ferns in the lobby. Each of us had ordered with sighs of anticipation a hamburger with all the trimmings. A hamburger in China? The reason wasn't so much that we were Americans as that, by this time, we were unbearably tired of Chinese food. It was strange, a puzzling question throughout our stay: what had happened to Chinese cooking, considered to be the best in the world? Was Mao to blame for this cultural revolution as well? For a month we had eaten the same monotonous fare, the inevitable sautéed bean sprouts, bean curd, greens with salted peanuts, fried fish, watery rice soup to *end* the meal—served usually at a table with a revolving center on which were bottles of warm orange pop.

It was sad to think about in Canton with the stellar reputation Cantonese cooking always had. As H. C. said, it was the single disappointment of the tour. Then tonight's dinner at the hotel was a perfect chicken soup followed by Cantonese shrimp and Cantonese duck, a sweet cream dessert, after which I ate my words.

The train ride of ninety miles took us across the border to Hong Kong, in an old-fashioned coach with white lace curtains at the windows. A friendly Japanese leader of a group of tourists sat down beside me, fed me rice cakes, and entertained me with nonstop talk of his world travels. He wrote his name, Nobuski Sugita, in my notebook along with his Tokyo telephone number, and on arrival in Hong Kong swept me in his arms and kissed me smack on the mouth. I lay it to the computer age and television. I can remember when American movies were censored and the love scenes removed because kissing was sternly prohibited in Japan.

So the circle was complete. At Hong Kong our unbending guide, David Wang, viewed us with disdain and conveyed us to the same Golden Mile Holiday Inn. We passed the next three days gadding in and out of the shops, an amusement that with Lois was like sightseeing in a gold mine.

On the last night H. C. gave a farewell party at Victoria Peak, as if it were the ultimate joy of his life to squire four vocal women about. The evening included a ferry ride to Hong Kong Island, cocktails at the elegant Mandarin Hotel, dinner at the glass-walled Peak Tower restaurant overlooking the harbor where the "million lights" of Hong Kong glistened in the water. Not least was the rattling trip on the cable car that lurched at a forty-five degree angle, while the high-rise buildings along the mountainside tilted crazily like the Tower of Pisa.

And yet the one inescapable sorrow and regret of travel is always there, in Tu Fu's words,

> Those whom I encounter on the road,
> How many times shall I see in my life?

1 9 8 6

"Ugh, said Helen, shuddering from complex causes."—*Howards End*

Thinking it over, the media concludes that 1985 was worse than we thought, a horrendous collection of headlines: hijackings, kidnappings on a world scale, South Africa torn apart by apartheid. Libya assumed a role with Colonel Gadhafi praising terrorist acts as "heroic undertakings," threatening to wage World War III against us.

It was sweet escape to see the film "Out of Africa." Beforehand I blamed it for setting up Meryl Streep and Robert Redford to make romantic nonsense of Isak Dinesen's life and love. They did, but it didn't matter. Giraffes are excellent actresses. I saw Kenya again and a multitude of elephants, as Dinesen said, pacing along as if they had an appointment at the end of the world. I was sick for love of Africa.

When I returned to aerobic dancing, the sign on the wall said, "Register here for treadmill." That means me.

On January 28, tragedy silenced us. We saw it happen the way you walk headlong into terror. An explosion blew apart the space shuttle Challenger a minute after liftoff. Seven died, six astronauts and schoolteacher Christa McAuliffe, the young civilian aboard. The shuttle rose flawlessly. Without warning the hydrogen fuel tank exploded into a fireball, the first deaths in space in 56 space flights. Christa, mother of two children, was selected from 11,146 applicants. Her children witnessed the disaster—everyone witnessed it, schoolchildren, parents, wives, all.

Pascal said, "Man's unhappiness arises from one thing only, that he cannot abide quietly in a room alone." At home by myself, I'm reminded of that poor guy Larry Hagman, the television star of *Dallas,* who has adopted this solitary means of sorting out his life that, in the villainous role of J. R. Ewing, consists of greed, corruption, murder, adultery, and alcohol. In his living room at Malibu Larry has a huge wicker box large enough to abide quietly in with a hole for his head. And there he sits and meditates, waiting for peace. When he dies The Box, equipped with headphones, pictures of his family, and himself, will be lowered into the grave. Asked what good this pursuit has done him, he says, "I guess I learned I shouldn't worry so much."

On February 14, Ray Bradbury sent me for a valentine his latest murder mystery, *Death Is a Lonely Business.* At the moment I was deep into the B's of Brewer's Dictionary of 1,175 pages, noting that Buffalo Bill killed 4,280 buffaloes in eighteen months—another piece of lonely business. I put it down to read Ray's book, after which I sent him my love by Federal Express.

Ray says, "I think it is important for one writer to tell another of their love." This needn't be confined to writers, who aren't necessarily tender, but Ray ought to know what a writer should do as the author of 400 published stories, 20 books, 30 one-act plays, a full-length play, 70 essays, and no telling how many poems. I respect a man who has become a corporate state, the "Ray Bradbury Enterprises," with enterprises including a cat that eats bumblebees.

Robert Penn Warren is America's first poet laureate. I don't know why we finally need one, too late to wear the crown that the Victorian poetizer Martin Tupper said was "a call from God to waken men." It claims against all reason poetry is awake itself. Warren is eighty years old with piles of poems behind him. Since a laureate is Poet to the Monarch, now he'll have to praise the reigning Reagans.

Last year England acquired another laureate, Ted Hughes, Number 20 in a line three centuries long of all-male poets, though I can't believe the Queen read "Death of a Pig" or "Song of a Rat" before appointing him. His view is bloody and murderous ("A mouthful of screeches like torn tin"), and I fear for the royal family if words can kill.

"There are hardly any poets, or ever have been," said Robert Graves, who died in December at ninety after writing 137 books. Graves despised Yeats as a poseur, Auden as a "detestable poetaster," Pound as clearly crazy, Dylan Thomas as a "demagogic masturbator," Eliot as sold out to Anglicanism. He had a good word to say for Martin Tupper and his Tupperisms, for whom no song fills the air, no ringing of belles lettres.

Someone asked, "Who else was born on your birthday?"

"Charlemagne," I said. He would be 1,244 years old this year.

This April I have my pick of celebratory events: Reagan attacking Gadhafi as "mad dog of the Middle East," the death of the Duchess of Windsor, or the nuclear explosion at Chernobyl (each of which shows, as Neil Simon said in *Chapter Two*, "There's a lesson to be learned from all this. I wonder what the hell it is"). On April 14 Reagan ordered an air attack on Tripoli that bombed Gadhafi's camp and reportedly killed his infant daughter. Two days later Gadhafi denounced Reagan as child killer, trivial actor, pig, and Hitler #2, promising to retaliate while the word went out "Kill Americans!" We used to say the air was full of gremlins that in World War II caused aircraft to fail. Now the air is full of terrorists, real ones.

The Duchess of Windsor died in her house of jewels in Paris at eighty-nine, mindless for years, and was buried beside the Duke at Windsor Castle, not as her Royal Highness. Churchill deemed the marriage "one of the greatest love stories of history." Mencken called it "the greatest love story since the Resurrection." The true story was sadly different, a life of exile and idleness, nightclubs and boredom—a dutiful playboy, a greedy woman who charged for their appearance at parties, a thousand dollars for ten minutes.

On April 25 the scarifying event at a nuclear power plant at Chernobyl, in the Ukraine north of Kiev, was a disaster like Hiroshima, Nagasaki, and Three Mile Island. A reactor burst into a radioactive fireball that spread radiation cloud round the planet. It appears 100,000 were evacuated from an area severely contaminated. We are given a shattering glimpse of what can happen in a nuclear war, caused as this accident was by "human error," which is the answer to everything.

Günter Grass, for one, believes in the Big Bang theory. To the astronomers it means the way the universe was created at the beginning of time, exploding into existence with a flash of light and a big bang. But to Günter Grass in his new novel *Die Rättin,* the Big Bang ("der Grosse Knall") means the cataclysmic clap devised by man that will destroy the world by nuclear fission and man will not survive but rats will. The same phrase neatly serves them both, the beginning and the end.

Eliot's "This is the way the world ends / Not with a bang but a whimper" no longer signifies. We'll go with a bang.

We Americans like to celebrate with a bang who we are, especially on the one-hundredth birthday of the Statue of Liberty. Let freedom ring, we say, and for four days the air rocked with the sound of music— "God Bless America," "America the Beautiful"—to remind us we are not only free but basking in the exclusive right to pursue happiness.

The Lady appeared in the New York harbor in 1886, after the Civil War. Before that it would have been awkward to account for the slaves. Even on this July 4, 1986, James Baldwin, speaking for the blacks, scratched his head for words and said, "The Statue is to us a bitter joke. It means nothing." Freedom is no easy thing to define unless there are freedoms enough for everybody.

She was a gift from France, one we didn't want, a heavily draped female holding a torch above her head. Her function was unclear: she wasn't a religious symbol or a memorial to the dead, a warrior, a national hero, or an American Indian. Some thought she was a pagan goddess. The sculptor Bartholdi had hand-built her on a quiet street in Paris, with ears three feet long and an ample figure modeled, it was said, on Bartholdi's mistress. When we had to give her a pedestal, there was such grumbling she nearly went to Boston or Philadelphia instead, both having bid for her. But at the unveiling a hundred years ago we responded with appropriate crowds and hurrahs, though in his speech President Grover Cleveland said nothing about her being there to welcome immigrants.

Ellis Island started six years later, in 1892, to receive them—the refugees—at first from Europe: England, Ireland, Russia, Italy. Often they came from ghettos to fill our ghettos, to escape hunger but remain hungry. They still come, the unwanted Asians, the Cambodians greeted by our enmity to foreigners, the Mexicans as illegal aliens in hiding. Their reason is always the same, "It's better than where we came from."

The spectacle was made for television: the Reagans and the Mitterrands sailing down the harbor on the battleship *Iowa* to twenty-one-gun salutes; President Reagan lighting Liberty's torch; little children reciting their freedom poems; the Poet Laureate reciting his; Frank Sinatra, Kenny Rogers, Willie Nelson each singing his own arrangement of "America, God shed his grace on thee"; and crooner Rudy Vallee dying of a heart attack while watching the rites on TV. Even the commercials were patriotic, reminding Americans to take Pepto-Bismol after too much rejoicing in their luck.

"We're throwing the world's biggest party," said Ed Koch, Mayor of New York City, jubilant in his shirtsleeves. "Occasionally I become saddened by the corruption," he said, and quickly added, "but I try to keep my sense of humor."

So do I this July 4. After all, my grandmother was born in Liberty, New York. While her ancestors made it to this side of the Atlantic before Ellis Island could process them, they came for the same reason— liberty.

There's been talk going around about men and women. Nobody treats it as a really fresh subject but one increasingly timely, in need of settling. The other night Phil Donahue spent an hour of prime time defining "Man and Woman," telling us we're born of different sex and display that difference steadily through life. Peter Jennings led a three-hour discussion on ABC called "After the Sexual Revolution," which asked "What do men want?" "What do women want?" and "Does anybody know?" The conclusion was nobody knows, hence the predicament. Though women make up half the work force, they face discrimination, lower wages, and inferior status. Recently eight women newscasters, among them Washington correspondent Lesley Stahl, Joan Lunden of ABC, Maria Shriver of CBS, met on a panel to consider their uneasy role in the marketplace. They clamored so much, as shrill and voiceful as the girls in Clare Luce's 1937 play *The Women* (wives who said "What do you expect me to do, stay home and darn your socks?") that you couldn't tell what they were exercised about—discrimination, I guess, the domination of the male.

A book just published, *How Men Feel: Their Responses to Women's*

Demands for Equality and Power, by Anthony Astrachan, sounds the warning, men can't accept women as equal; frustrated by the threat to their world, the majority of men still think women belong in the home, their function is to have children, and anyway they're incompetent and inferior.

I was brought up a girl and told to be ladylike. Because my mother was divorced, she earned our living in a town where no woman with a child worked except the washerwoman who had ten to raise. By the terms of the settlement my father was ordered to pay fifteen dollars a month toward my support, an obligation he loudly resented as exorbitant, unfair, unreasonable, and would put him in the poorhouse. From Lizzie I learned financial independence. She taught me by word and stern example to look out for myself and pay my way.

The first test was at the University of Chicago when I had to choose between sticking to principles or becoming a golddigger. Since fifty cents a day was all I could afford for food, I was sometimes hungry enough to let the corner druggist, bald and forty, take me out for a meal, paid for by the favor of a goodnight kiss. With Bob, a student my age, the single standard prevailed; each bought his own ticket to a movie and the kiss was not given, it was exchanged.

In graduate school at Columbia I met my match and fortunately married him, a man who believed in equality for women. Early in our dealings when I suggested a fifty-fifty arrangement, he laughed. "Why not? Or you can be the breadwinner if you like and support me for the rest of my life."

With marriage came what women complain of as the present dilemma. I continued in graduate school, taught fulltime in a private school, and became a housewife in a New York apartment. B. held down two jobs, by day and by night while working for his Ph.D., washed the dishes, baked an occasional pie, protected me from lightning, and fought my battles with the plumber. It was fifty-fifty all right, though if you glanced up at Jove's golden scales suspended in the sky you would find the balance tipped in my favor. I had it both ways, the love and the freedom.

When we decided to have children, I took five years off to try my hand at bringing them up, the most humbling job I ever had. B. gave me Monday afternoons to myself, but I scarcely knew how to spend the time. When the boys were three and five we enrolled them in the Barnard School and I went back to work.

This, of course, is a personal not a panoramic view of the problem. I was aware of discrimination because it was an obstacle, fierce against working wives, pregnant working wives, working mothers, and women in general taking jobs from men. I also had doubts about my competitive role—was I worth my salt? Before he died, Lionel Trilling, a professor at Columbia, denounced the pressures to hire women in certain jobs, expressing his wary opinion that women ask too much before they're ready. "Some groups," he wrote, meaning women and blacks, "have not yet produced a large number of persons trained for the academic profession." Later several professors at Harvard told me their reluctance to admit women in the graduate school, not for the frailty of their minds. "Women want everything," they said, "marriage, children, career. They want a college job with tenure in the same school where their husband teaches. What can we do with them?"

I became a professor at Duke where B. was a professor. When Newman White as chairman asked me to join the English faculty as instructor I accepted, whereupon one member told Newman, "Either she goes or I go." Newman, unstirred by threats (a man of singular courage) replied "Go ahead." The resentment was understandable. Together B. and I had two salaries, two votes in departmental affairs. Until my retirement, the meetings would begin, "Gentlemen . . . and Mrs. Bevington." I may have set the cause of women's rights back thirty years.

Matters are more relaxed now toward both women and blacks, but academe is slow. For what it's worth, my advice to any working woman is, above all, find a man as indispensable to happiness. After that, my dear, do the best you can.

And bear in mind how much worse off women used to be:

Voltaire, asked why no woman had ever written a good tragedy, said, "The composition of a tragedy requires testicles."

Robert Southey replied to Charlotte Brontë when she sent him a few of her poems: "Literature cannot be the business of a woman's life, and it ought not to be. The more she is engaged in her proper duties, the less leisure she will have for it, even as an accomplishment and a recreation."

Lord Brougham: "Harriet Martineau! I hate her! I hate a woman who has opinions."

Edward Fitzgerald, when Mrs. Browning died in 1861: "No more Aurora Leighs, thank God!"

Tennyson:

> God made the woman for the man,
> And for the good and increase of the world.

Effie Gray died ninety years ago, without having written a book to tell her story. Yet her name stays alive, appearing in print rather often. Twice this week I've read comments about her, in a book of essays by Anthony Burgess, in a volume of autobiography by Frances Partridge, both of whom bring up the scandal of Effie's disastrous marriage to John Ruskin. A wedding night that occurred in 1847 still fascinates, seeming to prove that interest in Ruskin's impotence never dies. Or perhaps I read the wrong books.

She was born Euphemia Gray in 1828 at Bowerswell, a country house in Perth that her father bought from his friend James Ruskin, John's father. James was a rich Scottish wine merchant living in London, whose cherished son he and his wife dominated and seldom let out of their sight. Young John Ruskin met Effie Gray when she was twelve, he twenty-one. Years later, remembering how pretty and amiable she was, he begged his mother to invite her to visit them in London. In the formal courtship that followed, Ruskin treated her with polite deference but wrote her long, passionate love letters that yearned for her head on his breast, extravagant in adoration of his beloved: "My own Effie—my kind Effie—my mistress—my friend—my queen—my darling—my only love." They were married in the drawing room at Bowerswell when she was nineteen; his parents made excuses not to attend the wedding.

The marriage lasted six years and was never consummated. On their honeymoon the outwardly happy couple toured the Highlands and the Lake District, then returned to live with the Ruskins, who for a while treated Effie well. She wrote her parents, "I am happier every day with John . . . he is so pleased with me." They went much into London society, where Effie with her beauty and intelligence was an immediate success and John a literary sensation as the author of *Modern Painters* and *Seven Lamps of Architecture*. When they acquired a house of their own in Grosvenor Square, the Ruskins feared Effie was taking John away from them. In 1849 he went to Switzerland with his parents, leaving Effie behind, though he wrote her with ardor, "I look forward to your *next* bridal night," and closed with "Goodnight, my dearest, dearest bride." After two years of marriage, Effie's health showed the strain of their unnatural relationship. She wrote John that she wanted a child, that her doctor had advised her to have a child. On his return from Switzerland, John changed his routine and spent every day with his parents, going home to dine with Effie at night. She knew they were trying to win him from her and she was losing the battle.

By now Ruskin had become the champion of the Pre-Raphaelites, of whom the painter John Millais, one of the founders of the brotherhood, was leader. The two men had grown to be such friends that Millais saw no impropriety in asking Effie to pose for his picture "The Order of Release." It depicted a wounded Scottish soldier reunited with his wife, their baby in her arms, and except that he made her auburn hair black was said to be a perfect likeness. Ruskin, eager to have his own portrait painted, invited Millais to accompany Effie and him on a trip to the Highlands, where they stayed four months at Glenfilas while Millais worked on Ruskin's portrait. Having fallen in love with Effie, he watched with incredulity and anger her husband's brutal treatment of her, his open dislike, his faultfinding and abuse, so "unmanly" and "debased" that Millais in distress wrote Effie's parents to urge them to protect her.

A few months later Effie wrote the most difficult letter of her life, to tell her parents the truth about her marriage, entreating them to rescue her. Six years after their wedding night, Ruskin had told her the reason for his impotence—that the sight of her person had filled him with physical disgust and "that he had imagined women were quite different to what he saw I was." As Anthony Burgess remarks, he was shocked to discover his wife had pubic hair. Though a famous art critic who must have looked countless times at artist's models in studios, Ruskin deplored that detail of her anatomy (unimaginable on, say, the lily maid of Astolat).

Had only he been kind, Effie wrote her parents, she might have remained silent and lived and died in this state, but now John could not endure her and "I cannot bear his presence." In alarm her mother hastened to London to take her back to Bowerswell, after which the marriage was annulled and Effie resumed her maiden name. Ruskin did not contest the charge of "incurable impotency" but took the matter calmly. His parents, however, raged and stormed, heaping all the blame on Effie, spreading malicious stories of her conduct.

A year passed before Effie had recovered enough from the trauma to see Millais again. They were married at Bowerswell, went to live in London, and eventually had eight children, four sons and four daughters. For forty-three years she was happily married to the tall, handsome Millais, who died in 1896; Effie died the next year. It was Effie's grandson, Sir William James, who in 1947 told the story in *John Ruskin and Effie Gray* from the unpublished letters found at Bowerswell and under the floorboards of Ruskin's study. Ruskin died in 1900 after a series of violent attacks of madness.

Like everyone else, I have a dream.

I remember in the spring of 1939 peering into a rosy future at the Futurama exhibit of New York's World Fair. My children and I stood on a moving platform that revealed a better world with forthcoming scenes from the World of Tomorrow and Democracity, of which I recall robots doing the housework, fluorescent lighting, chrome plumbing, cities built on multiple levels, and a hangar for dirigibles. But the real future failed to cooperate. Instead it presented us with the rewards of World War II and the nuclear age, such as concentration camps, Korea, Vietnam, global terrorism, the deadly disease AIDS, and a computerized mentality.

"I have a dream," Edward Bellamy said a hundred years ago when he wrote *Looking Backward* about the year 2000, his vision of a golden age that would achieve the ideal of universal brotherhood. In the novel Julian West, a snobbish young Bostonian, falls into a hypnotic sleep in 1887 and is revived 113 years later. He falls in love with Edith Leete, a descendant of his former fiancée, and through her wise old father learns what happened while he slept. The American people, faced with ever-mounting disaster, were saved through a benevolent Nationalist Party and taught the simple religion of brotherly love. That was all it took. Capitalism was abandoned, private enterprise disappeared with crime, poverty, greed, advertising, war, disease. Peace prevailed. Everyone loved his neighbor and said his prayers.

Julian, the narrator, ends on a high note of expectancy, kneeling before Edith with his face in the dust, confessing "how little was my worth to breathe the air of this golden century." Bellamy, who died in

1898, a meliorist certain the world would save itself, said in a post-script, "*Looking Backward* was written in the belief that the Golden Age lies before us and is not far away." It's a future only thirteen years ahead. That's what scares me.

For the time being, the dream is greatly postponed by the antics of President Reagan who is living in a dreamworld of his own. Late in November a bomb burst in air (called variously the Iran scandal, a colossal blunder, a criminal act) when it was revealed we had been making secret shipments of American weapons to aid Iran in its war with Iraq.

Confounding as a piece of news, there was further revelation that the money from the sale of arms was being funneled to Nicaragua to buy weapons for the Contras, whom Reagan supports—the rebels seeking to overthrow the government. Reagan tried to extricate himself by saying, "I didn't make any mistakes." The question is, how close is the resemblance of this monkey business to Watergate of 1972 and Nixon's attempt at cover-up? Nixon too denied knowledge, withheld evidence.

Washington correspondent David Broder comments, "No sadder tale could be spun in this holiday season than the unraveling of yet another presidency."

Season's greetings:

"God help us, every one," says Tiny Tim.
Oscar Wilde: "Have a meretricious and happy new year."

1 9 8 7

Our man Reagan, the unruffled optimist, disposes of 1986 and its blunders, saying with a wave of the hand, "It was a very good year." "What will 1987 be like?" he was asked. "Better than ever. We will enter the next century having achieved a level of excellence unsurpassed in history." Wow. He must forecast the future by consulting fortune cookies.

Washington waited six years to recognize Reagan's antipathy to facts, his isolation from reality. Now they say he wanders in circles: "He lives in another world. Some things he chooses to believe and some not to." As the Iran-Contra affair smolders, James Reston asks sadly of a befuddled president, "Is it possible he doesn't *remember* what happened?" Nancy alone claims to understand him: "I know my husband. I know what he knows." But does *he* know?

Resolution for 1987: to get me to a better world, preferably Lapland and the midnight sun, till then accept the Reaganantics along with the monotonies.

C. S. Lewis said, "I love the monotonies of life." To ensure full enjoyment he abolished the twentieth century by never reading a newspaper (so did Henry James and Rilke). His success in staying out of touch with the news of the world appears in Lewis's *The Problem of Pain*, where he asserts it is the benevolence of God that gives men the "enormous permission to torture their fellows." That isn't the way Buddha looked at it under the bo tree.

My friend Charles, who loves India, has brought me from his travels a leaf from a bo tree—which is the tree under which Gautama sat when he attained enlightenment and became the Buddha. (Plato sat under a plane tree and attained the meaning of platonic love.) The bo or bodhi tree is a large, majestic, long-lived fig or pipal that grows in India. Under it the Enlightened One stifled in himself desire and found peace of the heart and clarity of the mind.

Charles saw the tree in the Deer Park at Sarnath outside Benares on the banks of the Ganges. But as happens with shrines, the city of Gaya in Bihar State 130 miles from Benares makes a better claim to the original tree. That part of town called Buddh Gaya contains the great twelfth-century Mahabodhi Temple at the supposed site, beside which a tree now grows that is said to be the living descendant of Buddha's tree—the tree of knowledge, the tree of wisdom, the tree of peace. There the Compassionate One through the night under a full moon meditated the meaning of existence and of man's suffering.

Buddha came to Benares from Gaya in the sixth century B.C., and in the Deer Park revealed his awakening to the five who became his disciples, assuring them of the possibility of release from the wheel of life—the endless cycle of existence—simply by following the right path toward peace at the still center. From Benares he went on to Uruvela, where to a thousand bhikkhus or followers by now gathered round him, he preached the Fire Sermon on man's life that burns with the fires that destroy him: "Everything, O Bhikkhus, is burning. With what fire is it burning? I declare unto you that it is burning with the fire of lust, with the fire of anger, with the fire of ignorance; it is burning with the anxieties of birth, decay, death, grief, lamentation, suffering, dejection, and despair."

Buddha's Fire Sermon, Eliot said, corresponds in importance to the Sermon on the Mount. In the *Waste Land,* Eliot's own "Fire Sermon" echoes Buddha's words for the same fires of lust, greed, hate, anger, ignorance, for the "burning burning burning burning" in the world today. Eliot too sought escape from the turning wheel.

(On his trip around the world, Mark Twain also saw a bo tree in Benares, with a monkey living in it. He called it renowned as "the tree in whose shadow you cannot tell a lie.")

Freya Stark had a talent for travel. She calls herself a wanderer all her life. In 1935, while in Arabia riding on a donkey and accompanied only by native guides, she wrote, "I was now recognized as a traveler and met everywhere with kindness." According to her, there aren't many born travelers, though people generally assume they are. Freya Stark deserves the label. In her many books including ten of travel, she gives bountiful advice on how to become one like her, postnatally, that is.

An Englishwoman still alive in vigorous old age in Asolo, northern Italy, she began her solitary expeditions in Persia and Arabia about fifty years ago. Before a journey she would spend months studying the language and the history. After World War II she learned Turkish because it seemed "absolutely necessary" to travel in Asia Minor, and on her own followed the path of Alexander. She had no money; her health was so delicate that doctors advised her to lead a quiet life at home without trying to walk. Instead she climbed mountains, braved the trackless desert on a camel's back, and sickened on every trip, nearly dying several times from dysentery, malaria, typhoid, dengue fever, heart strain, and once measles. She was a small dumpy person who loved dashing hats, party dresses, French face powder, and pink umbrellas—feminine by nature yet amazingly bold, terrified yet daring. It was timidity, she writes, that made her seek out dangerous places. Her hard-won accomplishment—in Iraq, say, where she traveled alone among bandits and murderers—was *not to be afraid*. An Arab proverb that inspired her was "Travel is victory." Some say she is the greatest woman traveler of this century.

After years of wandering where she pleased over the world, Freya Stark made a list of seven inestimable and needful attributes for the traveler to possess:

1. To accept values not one's own (which is tolerance)
2. To learn to make use of stupid men and inadequate tools (which is ingenuity)
3. To dissociate oneself from bodily sensations (which is endurance)
4. To take rest and nourishment when and whatever available (which is accommodation)
5. To love nature and human nature
6. To be unselfish (which is courtesy)
7. To be good-tempered at the end of the day as at the beginning (which is impossible)

These rules she drew up after traveling briefly with a couple of women who had none of the above qualifications. Women she found irritating as travelers, inclined to complain, make difficulties, exhibit little curiosity and no willingness to adjust to unfamiliar conditions. If she had to have a companion, let it be a man. Yet her best piece of advice, the secret of her success, appears in a letter to a friend: "Dear Christopher, I always wonder why it should be derogatory to behave like a woman when one is one."

Travel is of infinite worth to me. Its value that nontravelers fail to recognize is you never know which of the available images you'll bring home. I don't mean memories, I mean graven images. Like these:

> Saint Peter's right foot in Rome worn shapeless by the kisses of the faithful (some kiss it to cure the toothache)
> Twenty million bottles of champagne at Épernay
> Saint Ursula's eleven thousand virgins at Cologne
> Vichyssoise at Vichy
> Michelangelo's three *David*s in Florence
> Kangaroos in Australia eating potato chips
> Looking a lion in the face at Kenya
> Swimming in Walden Pond and climbing the Eddystone Light
> Yak butter in Tibet and the moon over the Himalayas
> The belly button of the world at Delphi
> Alpine meadows
> Annette Kellerman making a high dive at New York's Hippodrome (I was four years old)
> John Donne in his winding sheet at St. Paul's. Karl Marx at Highgate Cemetery. Napoleon under the dome of the Invalides

Tomorrow I'm going on a journey in search of the midnight sun, the Arctic Circle, reindeer, lemmings, Lapps, and cloudberries.

JOURNEY TO THE MIDNIGHT SUN   On a morning in June, we landed in Copenhagen after an overnight flight—twelve Carolinians, nine women and three men, which left the kind of sexual imbalance you have to expect these days. We were under way with the Cranfords, Lois and H. C., and the weather in Copenhagen was threatening rain.

After a hasty look at our stately little hotel, the Kong Arthur, my roommate Mozette and I, she in her Burberry and I in my London Fog, followed the advice E. M. Forster gave himself when he arrived in Alexandria, Egypt: "The best way to see this city is to wander aimlessly about." Since Forster had more time to wander about Alexandria (he stayed three years) than we to be aimless in Copenhagen, we went to the corner and took bus #16 to the Town Hall and Town Square. There we walked along Stroget, a mile-long "walking street" full of pedestrians and lined with a fetching array of Royal Porcelain for sale, an astonishing number of sweaters adorned with reindeer. We had tea and a Danish, a natural choice in Denmark, which tasted like the Danish I had for breakfast yesterday in North Carolina.

I give this account for the pleasure of saying what happened on bus #16 on our return. When I boarded the bus ahead of Mozette and handed the driver my round-trip ticket, he scowled at me, muttering, "Don't you know this is no good? The time is up, it's out of date." As I reached for my purse, he burst into laughter. "But you're welcome to ride," he shouted, "if you promise to give me a kiss for Christmas." The carful of passengers, all of whom seemed to understand English, were convulsed at the joke. One lady reached out and patted my hand to assure me he didn't mean it.

For dinner tonight we went by taxi in pouring rain to St. Gertruds Kloster, a seven-hundred-year-old monastery that in the Middle Ages was a sanctuary for the starving and the leprous in a wretched part of Copenhagen. Time passed, and in 1974 St. Gertruds opened as an elegant restaurant, to which we wayfarers came and were fed in the cellar whose vaults held 20,000 bottles of wine. The feast was extraordinary, the wine special, and the Bourbon $16 a shot, Denmark's way of discouraging public drunkenness.

Afterward I slept the sleep of a happy Dane under a *dyne*, the eiderdown comforter made from the accommodating local eider ducks.

Next morning Hazel took us in tow. Our defender and guide was an English redhead who had moved to Denmark as a girl, married a Dane, and grown passionately Danish, loyal enough to come to blows with any detractor of her country, especially a Swede. "We've been fighting the bloody Swedes for centuries," she said. "On a clear day you can see them under our nose just across the Sound." As we rode along Hans Christian Andersen Boulevard, the chestnut trees and lilacs were in bloom, there was flowering hawthorn and such tidiness. Copenhagen, once a Viking village, is a storybook town of Renaissance houses and copper roofs. The sculptor Thorvaldsen left behind so many monuments that to the children of Denmark a hero must be a man of stone with a seagull on his head.

At Nyhavn, the quarter where a canal runs down to the harbor, fine old merchant houses stood in a tight row along the quay. In a yellow one, No. 20, Hans Christian Andersen lived and wrote his fairytales. Born in 1805 the son of a shoemaker, a charity child, he came to Copenhagen at fourteen to make his fortune as an opera singer. For years he roamed the streets an object of ridicule, taken for a lunatic, till through his storytelling Hans's great height and ugliness turned into a striking dignity, the mockery turned to love. (The nearest he got to an operatic career was to fall in love with Jenny Lind.) At the end of the Langelinie, a promenade leading to the sea, Andersen's Little Mermaid gazes over the water. Seventy-five years ago Edvard Eriksen, founder of the Carlsberg brewery, placed her there—a tiny bronze mermaid the height of a woman if she were to stand with more than a tail to stand on—*den Lille Havfrue,* the pet and pride of Denmark.

A traveler to this city, the fastidious Sacheverell Sitwell, who complains they ought to give H. C. Andersen a rest, says nothing on earth compares with spending a summer day up to midnight at the Tivoli Gardens. As an amusement park Tivoli is a work of art. We had dinner at one of the entrances, in the Nimb restaurant that led directly to the gardens, and it was unexpectedly beautiful, a place of roses and shade trees, a quiet place—no noisy crowds, no hawkers, no attempt to attract tourists. Tivoli is for the Danes, beloved by them since it was opened in 1843. At the main gate a statue of old Andersen beamed down on a fun fair for children with carousels and roller coasters. To please the grown-ups there were open-air theaters, a Tivoli symphony orchestra, a Tivoli band, a discotheque, twenty-eight restaurants and cafés. And so many trees. When the lights went on at ten o'clock, the fountains played and the night dazzled as we strolled up and down.

On a windy day we set off for Elsinore, thirty miles from Copenhagen in North Zealand. Out in the suburbs beside the sea, Hazel pointed to a Pilsner beer bottle about the size of the Statue of Liberty, formerly a popular attraction at Tivoli, where people used to climb the inside stair to the cork, where during World War II Jewish refugees were hidden in the bottle and escaped capture. Out here was a deer park, a skyful of magpies, a sea with swans afloat on the salt water. Hazel said there were plenty of *nissen* around, Danish leprechauns wearing red caps, whom the trolls come down from Norway to devour. I asked if she remembered Ibsen's *Peer Gynt* and the motto of the Dovrë: "Troll, to thyself be enough." She frowned and shook her head. Hazel mingled only with Danish elves.

Elsinore is a small seaport town beside the Kattegat; its harbor, busy since the twelfth century, has a ferry crossing to Sweden only three miles away. Beyond the town rises the magnificent Gothic Kronborg Castle with green copper roofs, built by King Christian IV near the end of the sixteenth century—the castle that Shakespeare called Elsinore. It's a splendid setting for the play, with moat and dungeons, a great inner courtyard, a knights hall, a platform where the Ghost walked. Here through the years most Shakespearean actors have performed *Hamlet*—in our time Michael Redgrave, Richard Burton, John Gielgud, Laurence Olivier, who appeared here in 1937 with Vivien Leigh as Ophelia. In his book *On Acting,* Olivier said, "I think one of the best performances I was involved in was probably at Elsinore in Denmark." When a deluge of rain kept the cast from acting in the courtyard, they hastily improvised the play in the lounge of the Marienlyst Hotel. And in Elsinore that night, Olivier said, the actors were heroes. "I know—I was right in the middle of it."

For lunch at the Marienlyst, formerly a chateau where the royal family lived, the smorgasbord was sumptuous beyond a commoner's idea of Wednesday lunch—caviar, smoked salmon, shrimp, paté, pickled herring, salads, and so on, with second helpings. After that we were barely able to face another castle. Along the Danish Riviera, in the clean little village of the Palace of Peace stood Fredensborg Palace, Queen Margrethe's summer residence. Six miles further rose the turreted Frederiksborg Castle, majestic with painted ceilings, marble floors, porcelains, tapestries, and not a chair to sit on.

Two ships take turns making the overnight crossing from Copenhagen to Oslo: the *Dana Regina* and the *Dana Gloria*. Tonight was the *Dana Gloria*'s turn, no doubt to the captain's regret when a heavy winter storm worthy of the North Sea and highly inappropriate in June rocked, heaved, tossed the little steamer across the Skagerrak to Norway's coast. The seas ran so high those able to face dinner on the fifth-level deck were startled by waves crashing against the plate glass windows. The crew set up a counter in the corridor, silently handing two dramamine pills to anyone passing near. I've seen rougher seas, but this one wasted a perfectly good dance band, not a man in sight.

When we docked at Oslo this morning, our new courier and guide, Reidun Loose of Oslo, met us at the pier to accompany us through Norway. She was a lovable, durable woman of fifty, a world traveler who had lived in Indonesia, an accomplished skier, hiker, skater, who wore an attractive sweater and jeans, talked well and laughed often. She had postponed a trip to Tibet in order to lead us to the Northland and the midnight sun.

Oslo, at the end of the Oslo fjord, was founded in the eleventh century by Vikings and kept its name till, in 1624, the Danish king, Christian IV, became king of Norway and renamed it in his honor Christiania. In 1925 when Norway finally freed herself, it was again called Oslo.

All morning we rode about with Rei beside the white lilacs along Karl Johans' gate—the main shopping street at the end of which in democratic proximity is the palace of Olav V. We passed the Nobel Institute and looked in on Our Saviours Lutheran Church where Ibsen is buried. "Well now," said Rei, "there are two more sights that you'll never forgive me if I don't show you."

One was Frogner Park, which contains the work of Gustav Vigeland, a sculptor famed in his own country who died in 1943. After handing over the entire park to him to adorn as he pleased, Oslo was astonished if not overwhelmed when from forty years of steady labor Vigeland had filled it with more than two hundred naked lifesize figures—single or coupled or entwined, whole families clinging together, men, women, children, and many babies. On entering the park where a fountain was supported by six naked males, we crossed a bridge lined with bare white statues leading to a fifty-foot monolith covered with 121 inter-laced bodies wound about it—babies, youths, lovers, the middleaged, the aged, the dying—all humanity struggling to reach the top, all naked, all by Vigeland. He is said to be the most prolific sculptor of all time. And his single theme, endlessly repeated, was the life cycle and man's lifelong struggles within it.

Certainly it astonishes and certainly it is redundant and marvelously obsessive. It reminded me of the sensual Rodin whom Vigeland imi-tated, though Rodin had a wider range of subjects, some of them fully dressed. Just one figure clothed in thought like Dante at Rodin's *Gate of Hell* might have dimmed the glare.

On the Bygdoy peninsula is the world-famous collection of Viking ships, two of which were found buried near the Oslo fjord. In one, the *Oseberg*, a "long ship" perfectly preserved with thirty oars and (once) a single sail, an old queen and her woman servant were buried a thousand years ago, supplied with beds, blankets, sledges, a wagon, sixteen horses, four dogs, and an ox—the basic necessities for the life to come. In such a ship Leif the Lucky, about whom the old Norse eddas were sung, landed on the coast of America.

It's easy to believe the forefathers of these tall, strong, fair-haired northern people were Vikings—sea rovers and pirates who for more than 250 years, from the ninth to eleventh century, plundered and terrorized the Western world by sudden raids upon it, by rape, murder, conquest. Young men would go a-viking as part of their education, the Grand Tour of the Dark Ages. The Viking Canute, accompanying his father on an expedition to invade England, stayed to become England's king for eighteen years and in 1035 was buried in Winchester. Canute believed the Christian God loved him and the sea would halt at his bidding, which it failed to do.

In the other museum was the balsa raft, the *Kon-Tiki*, used by the Norwegian Thor Heyerdahl and his five companions to cross the Pacific in 1947 from Peru to the South Seas. In his book *Kon-Tiki*, Heyerdahl tells of the incredibly daring journey, outdistancing the Vikings' seafaring, in a raft made of nine balsa logs lashed together. Surviving this, in 1970 Heyerdahl crossed the Atlantic with seven men on a fragile raft made of papyrus, the *Ra II* (also displayed) on what he called the *Ra* expeditions because it took two trips and a lot of papyrus to reach the West Indies.

Luckily we picked up some sandwiches in the dining room at breakfast before boarding the Oslo-to-Bergen train for an eight-hour ride from coast to coast, across the highest range of mountains in Norway. The train carried us above the timber line and down to the sea, among fjords that made piercing blue cuts in the mountain wall. It went through two hundred tunnels, past Nyrdal a skiing resort, past Voss with its snow fences, till it dropped down in Bergen. And the more northerly we went the more grand, the more spacious was the view.

A friend asked me once, "You've never been to Bergen? Go at once!"

Bergen must be the most beautiful town in the world, touching the North Sea and climbing up the seven mountains among birch trees. Call it a trolls' town, a town made of flowers. When we walked from the Hotel Admiral next morning, the wharf was one huge flower garden, actually an immense flower market and beside it the fish market, a flower garden itself abloom with pink shrimp, silver herring, red salmon. The wharf is the most photographed spot in Norway.

Houses painted dark red and yellow with pointed gables stood in a solid row along the quay—the old Hanseatic quarters once owned by German merchants who used them for warehouses and allowed no woman to enter (lest an apprentice marry her and share profits with a Norwegian wife). From the fourteenth century for two hundred years the Hanseatic League, a federation of North German towns, ruled Bergen by controlling its trade while Bergen endured in shame its helplessness.

And from this harbor the Vikings set out on their raids.

Rei took us to Troldhaugen (trolls' hill) outside town where the composer Edvard Grieg and his wife Nina lived and are buried in the rock wall because he wanted to spend eternity there. The quaint little house, in which Grieg wrote the "Peer Gynt Suite" that is full of trolls, was built on a bluff above a fjord, enclosed by masses of foliage. His bronze statue showed a man five feet tall, delicately slim with a crown of blond hair. "He's exactly your size," said H. C. and told me to climb up and stand beside him shoulder to shoulder. "Twins," H. C. said, walking away and leaving me marooned.

On the way back we stopped at a stave church on a wooded hillside, a church found only in Norway (that once numbered eight hundred of them). The Fantoft stave church of the early twelfth century consisted of blackened upright wooden logs or staves arched into a series of pitched shingled roofs, each shaped like a pointed hat. The interior was dark and haunted, empty except for a crude crucifix and a bench along the wall for the old and sick. The Vikings used to leave their armor, pikes and battleaxes, on the porch and enter by the front door while the women slipped in through the side door and stood apart.

The flight north was along the coastal strip of Norway, of fjords and snow-streaked mountains to the region of the North Cape. It was the summer solstice, the longest day in the year, to which the Norsemen attached a mystical meaning of rebirth with the return of the sun. For us, we said, this sun will never set, the sun in the morning and the sun at night. Halfway there we crossed over the Arctic Circle.

"Happy Laplanding," someone yelled as we set down at Tromso, a town on a small mountainous island in the Bals fjord among rowan trees and silver birches. Tromso is a center for polar bear expeditions and excursions to the North Pole, whose citizens may be seal hunters or whale fishermen. Daffodils bloomed and people were eating lunch on their porches. The most extraordinary sight in town was the Arctic Cathedral with a ski lift behind it—a little Lutheran church triangular in shape, made of oddly corrugated white metal. Inside, the stained glass window covering the whole back wall behind the altar revealed an arresting figure of Christ, who appeared to be dressed for a polar expedition, his long body bundled and swathed from head to foot. I suppose the congregation, bundled to the ears themselves, wouldn't want to gaze upon a shivering naked Christ.

Not for a minute had it occurred to me in the land of the midnight sun that the sun at midnight would *not* be visible. Now Rei reluctantly warned us what to expect: it might well be hidden, obliterated, probably would be. For two months of summer, from the middle of May till the end of July, when it was meant to shine steadily on the just and the unjust, the sun was usually lost behind clouds, canceled by mists, rain, fog in this arctic world. In her many tours as a guide, Rei now admitted, she had never seen the midnight sun.

"Oh no, Rei!" I cried, as if it were her own fault. "It *has* to appear sometime, hasn't it, if we wait long enough? How else does it get its name?"

She laughed at my incredulity, which was outrage and deep disappointment. "Who knows? Maybe this time you will bring me luck."

Just before midnight we climbed with Rei into the ski lift that ran to the top of the tallest mountain behind Tromso. Up there in the snow on the high slope was a Lapland family ranged in front of their tent with a collection of furs and reindeer antlers for sale. The squat women stood beside their dark-skinned, sturdy men, the first Lapps I had ever seen.

Distracted by them I forgot to lift my head. Then suddenly we all turned at once and stared at the sky. *The sun!* There it was! There free of cloud was the sun at midnight, as radiant as if Turner had painted it, red-gold and luminous and blazing. Rei gave a shout of joy. She began to weep. Together we held hands and stared into the sun, till it was dangerous to look longer and we turned away, the sunlight reflected in our faces. After a while Rei and I started to talk in low tones about making journeys like this, to the tops of worlds, to world's ends, to midnight suns, as if it were a sensible errand and we were in search of something real that might be waiting—the peace, perhaps, that Rei herself was convinced was delusory and nowhere to be found. Here, I realized, was another skeptic on the lookout for paradise or thereabouts. Rei would soon be in Tibet, not expecting any miracles, though tonight glancing up at the burning sky she wasn't so sure.

I told her Hudson Strode's story of a man who was invited to climb a mountain one night to see the midnight sun and politely declined. "It's the same old sun, isn't it?" he said.

It wasn't the same. This sun was inconceivable, a sun beyond compare. And yet if it were winter instead, we would stand here in darkness and behold the aurora borealis, the moon and all the midnight stars.

After a few hours' sleep, we were up at six to start the journey in a motor coach round the North Cape and across Lapland. The day was well spent, a ten-hour trip blindingly scenic from Tromso to Hammerfest, more than two hundred miles above the Arctic Circle. Alone on a narrow road, we drove for hours beside the North Sea, beside a salmon river where the salmon come to breed this time of year, where a hundred seagulls hovered over a school of herring. Eventually we began to climb, higher and higher, and the mountains of Norway pine burst forth from clouds, and there were waterfalls.

Once we stopped at the little town of Alta to look at native wood carvings, and there I saw wild cloudberry blossoms found nowhere but in this polar region. Just outside town, in 1973 some little boys discovered carvings from the Stone Age, grotesque figures lightly etched on flat rocks, among which we walked trying to imagine an artist working there three thousand years ago. In Alta the houses had sod roofs in which thick rich grass and wildflowers grew, and Rei pointed out Alf's house—Alf the Norseman, our driver, a big smiling fellow whose northern speech Rei barely understood. But she liked him and they chatted on, old friends who had never met before. "Alf and I are talking about life in North Norway," Rei told us. "He says the summers are short, prices are terrible, so are taxes," while Alf who knew no English twisted round to smile in happy acknowledgment. Each time he helped us from the bus I said "Takk, Alf" to win another of his broad smiles.

We were in Lapland, not a country of course but a vast expanse within the Arctic Circle that includes northern Norway, Sweden, Finland, and the Kola peninsula of Russia. Norwegian Lapland, by far the most populous, is called Finnmark by the Norwegians because they dislike equally the Finns and the Laplanders. It is a wilderness of extensive forests and tundra—those treeless plains of rock, reindeer moss, and lichen.

More Lapps live in Norway than anywhere else, more reindeer than Lapps. Centuries ago the Lapps appeared, nobody knows when or from where, probably Asiatic in origin. They named themselves the Sami, never Lapps, their land Samiland. Some live in villages but more are nomads who in the spring with the sun's return drift about with their reindeer herds and pitch tents like wigwams of birch saplings covered with canvas. We passed several Lapp camps of twenty or more tents with reindeer skins spread out for sale and antlers in huge piles. (What would I do with a spreading antler?) There are some 170,000 reindeer in this area, of which you must never ask a man how many he owns. It would be like asking how rich he is.

By evening we reached Hammerfest in broad daylight, and in the little Hotel Hammerfest on the waterfront were served the most exquisite meal in memory, poached salmon flavored with dill and red cloudberries ripened by the midnight sun. When we left the dining room Rei stopped at the door of the sauna. "Don't you want to take a steam bath tonight, beat yourself with birches, and plunge into the North Sea?"

"That's for you Vikings," I said, "not for us Lapps."

Before I slept, I thought of what I had read about the spell of Lapland, how some feel it intensely and never want to leave. It has to do with the air, the cleanness, the beauty of the place, the endless summer light. As the month of May approaches each year, people watch for the sun, speak only of the sun, gazing at the hills for the first sign of light. When it comes they rejoice and plant gardens, forgetful that skies were ever dark.

Hammerfest is called the northernmost town in Europe, an Arctic village of snow-covered mountains and brightly painted houses with white lace curtains and potted begonias in the window. It is on the island of Kvaloy with an ice-free harbor where the sea never freezes over. Tourists look for polar bears in the street and sometimes see one.

In Norway they're generally known as the "ice bear," but in Hammerfest a "Royal and Ancient Polar Bear Society" exists and cordially invites you to join. You need only put in an appearance at Hammerfest City Hall and receive a diploma signed by the mayor that entitles you to mingle with bears. Ted promptly signed up.

The leaves on the rowan trees were in bud and reindeer grazed on the hills as we took a brisk walk around town with Rei. Considering what we had tackled for breakfast—smoked salmon, pickled herring, sausages, salami, ham, cheeses, boiled eggs, corn flakes, and oatmeal porridge—we were well fortified to hike to the North Pole not too far away.

Hammerfest, charming as a picture postcard, was destroyed in World War II when German troops retreating from Russia burned everything as they fled. The town has rebuilt itself to look as it did before it was ruthlessly consumed. The Nazis occupied Finnmark for five years.

On Midsummer Eve, we left to drive to Kaafjord and board a ferry to Honningsvag on the island of Mageroy, where people have lived since the Stone Age. Honningsvag, half the size of Hammerfest and like it leveled by the Germans, is a treeless village above the timber line, in a barren world of black rocks and tundra. At the Hotel Nordkapp just before midnight we bundled up in all available coats, caps, sweaters, scarves, gloves, for a drive to the North Cape about twenty miles away.

This time the midnight journey was really to the top of the world. The North Cape, the last outpost, an enormous mass of solid black rock, rises steeply a thousand feet above the Arctic Ocean. On a rough road built as late as 1956 (before that you climbed up the rock face), beside bare ledges and precipices, we made the ascent to the summit— to a mammoth flat slab of black rock so cold and windswept we seemed to arrive on a planet in outer space. It looked outlandish, as if a madman had painted the shiny black surface with fantastic patterns of white snow, whirled and twisted and streaked into crazy configurations. The cold was glacial, bitter cold in the high wind, and there was no midnight sun, only mist and cloud and freezing rain. A few figures moved about like ghosts blown by the gale, and we like ghosts moved among them. Stumbling across the plateau and inching toward the overhanging edge, expecting any moment to be swept to the ocean crashing beneath, I thought this was as close to world's end as I cared to go.

To continue through Lapland we recrossed the ferry and returned to the long straight roads of Finnmark. We were in an uncommonly amiable mood after only three or four hours' sleep, whether from the bracing air, the friendly reindeer, or our good luck so far. Rei said a Norwegian proverb, "Luck is better than wits," was handed down from Leif the Lucky, to whom luck was considered the most precious possession. You could have woman-luck or weapon-luck or weather-luck; everything depended on having it, and still does, Rei said.

She was in such good humor, laughing with Alf in Norwegian, laughing with us in English about being Norwegian, that Ted called out, "Do you know any Norwegian jokes?"

"We don't tell jokes about ourselves," Rei said. "Our jokes are about the Swedes."

"Tell us one."

"Well, let's see. How many Swedes does it take to milk a cow? The answer: four. Three Swedes to lift the cow and the fourth to milk it."

It sounded awfully funny.

Rei thought again. "How long can a Dane, a Swede, or a Norwegian stay inside a barn full of stinking goats? The answer: the Dane races out in a few seconds gasping for breath. The Swede stays a bit longer, then runs out faster than he went in. The Norwegian walks into the barn, the barn door bursts open, and out rush all the goats."

Near noon we reached Karasjok, accompanied much of the way by reindeer that wandered freely in the fields without a herdsman. Since many had lost their antlers for the summer, they looked like goats, small and grayish white, till here an antlered stag would pose among them, as noble as Landseer's *Stag at Eve*. Karasjok is considered the Sami capital, a Lapland community of two thousand inhabitants, all short, square, slant-eyed, given to wearing peaked hats with a bobble of red wool. The tight little houses were tidy and much alike. There was a school and a printing press for Norway's only Sami newspaper, which puts out a brochure to say of Karasjok, "The cultural activities are many as well as a chance to hunt and fish." In the tiny museum I saw a stuffed lemming, the size of a field mouse with yellow markings. Lemmings live in the arctic tundra and now and then make mass migrations to better feeding grounds, dashing down the coast of Norway and overcoming every obstacle, diving straight through a reindeer herd. Contrary to the myth, the one thing lemmings avoid is water, especially careful not to commit suicide by plunging into the sea. Why their reputation for willful self-destruction persists, something I wanted to find out, not even the Sami could say.

A hundred miles from Ivalo, which is across the border in Finnish Lapland, we came down from the arctic region to trees again, green meadows, field flowers, and tamer travels. Ivalo is where the airport is, but to our surprise Alf sped through it, keeping on for another thirty miles since Ivalo has no accommodations. For the night we stayed in the middle of nowhere at a sprawling compound called Saariselka. The Hotel Riekonkieppi consisted of a main building surrounded by woods and log cabins for skiers and dogsled explorers. As Alf deposited us at the door, he gave us the last of his tremendous smiles before turning back for the trip home to Alta. When he hugged me I saw how all those *taaks* I had said had paid off. We had achieved a friendship with a single word.

At breakfast Rei made her own forever farewells. She was leaving too, now we were in Finland, for an excursion alone. I grieved to lose her, everyone did; our only complaint was she should abandon us now. We spent the day with nowhere to go, temporarily stranded in these woods where, for once, there was no scenery and no blue sea. And while the Norwegian alphabet has 39 letters, it's a far easier language to live with than the Finnish, which is impenetrable.

The flight by Finnair on the one plane a day out of Ivalo carried us the length of Finland to Helsinki on the Gulf, "the white city of the north" even to its white lilacs. It was a pleasure to look at, a gracious city of chestnut trees and glistening white architecture, none of it medieval, for Helsinki has been fought over too often through the centuries, too punctually destroyed. If as they say Finland is a land of heroes, heroic it has had to be. At the time of the Vikings the Swedes made it a Swedish province, as it was till the eighteenth century when Peter the Great sent his armies across Finland and after ravaging half the country allowed Sweden what remained. During the Napoleonic Wars Finland was ceded back to Russia, from whom she gained her independence as late as 1917.

Herman Melville wrote of the bravery of the Finns against hopeless odds, a people who always expected to come out victorious and never did. Sibelius saluted this heroism in "Finlandia," which is practically the national anthem, and the Finlandia Concert Hall is an imposing, pure-white tribute to the composer. Helsinki looked positively dazzling along the Esplanade, about it a pervasive sense of space—a sea city encircled by the Baltic. But the authentic wonder was again a church, the Lutheran Taivallahi Church built inside solid rock on the side of a mountain. The eerie dark interior appeared subterranean, as if it were a hidden palace under the sea for the worship of strange gods. While this kind of thing seemed odd for sober Lutherans to be about, it's true their state churches tend to the extreme, ultra-modern or ornate like Catholic cathedrals. Nominally all Scandinavians are Lutheran, but these are secular times. The people pay church taxes and seldom attend a service except for the rituals of birth, marriage, death that Rei called "hatching, matching, and dispatching."

One country was left, only one. We crossed the Sea of Bothnia in an overnight steamer, the *Marietta* of the Viking Line, and docked at Stockholm fit as fiddles. In some ways it was the handsomest city, the most elegant, built on fourteen islands of the Baltic Sea. The Old City between two bridges had grown quiet and mellow with medieval houses and cobblestone streets. The red brick City Hall, a thing of rare beauty beside Lake Mälaren, said to be the most spectacular building since the Renaissance, was a creation of the architect Ostberg. Vast as a castle, it was completed in 1923, and each year the Nobel Prize ceremony is held in the Golden Room, when the king of Sweden awards all but the Peace Prize which is presented in Oslo, the gift of peaceloving Alfred Nobel who invented dynamite.

Volvos filled the streets of Stockholm, abundant with flowering parks, craft and furniture shops. Had we looked we might have found the PUB department store where Greta Garbo, born Greta Gustafsson, was a salesgirl before she left for America. In her film "Queen Christina" of 1933, she played the part of Sweden's notorious queen, the eccentric Christina, daughter of King Gustavus II Adolphus, who in the seventeenth century made Sweden a mighty power. Christina, a minor figure in Sweden's history and a decidedly peculiar one, was born in Stockholm. At eighteen she became queen, impressing everyone with her learning but proud, arrogant, headstrong, most of all queer. She likened herself to Alexander the Great and considered herself an emissary of God with homage her due. Her aversion to sex, marriage, and childbearing was so strong that, instead of marrying her cousin,

Charles Gustavus, she made him her successor and abdicated in 1654 at twenty-eight, leaving home on horseback in man's attire. In Rome where the pope received her warily as a converted Catholic, Christina continued to misbehave, chaste but mad. Twice she tried to recover her crown, at one time attempted to become queen of Naples and Poland, at another ordered her equerry murdered. She died in Rome, forgotten at sixty-three.

In her autobiography Christina thanked heaven for making her manly in body and spirit. Her voice was deep; she was short and hairy, pockmarked, bignosed. When Hollywood cast Greta Garbo as Christina, she wanted to wear an enormous nose and heavy eyebrows for an honest portrayal, but they obliged her to play herself, with John Gilbert as her ridiculous lover. Laurence Olivier was first assigned the role, but when he appeared on the set for a love scene, Garbo cold as marble dismissed him, saying "Life is a sad business."

We pleased ourselves on the last sunny days by taking a river cruise and, on the rocky wooded island of Lidingo, wandering about the home of Carl Milles, the Swedish sculptor who died in 1955. His villa stands on a promontory above the sea, with the Milles erotic sculptures of swooning lovers for some reason placed atop high thin pillars, where they look airborne. The mark of Rodin is upon them.

At a gala dinner to signal our departure, we had reindeer for an appetizer, now served in hotels and restaurants though, since Chernobyl, all reindeer must be checked for radiation. I found it unappetizing, strong like venison and rather tough, no worse I suppose than yak in Tibet or llama in the Andes.

Later, on our flight to New York we were put into the "business" class, which suited us very well, whatever business as homecoming tourists we might be presumed to represent. My own mission, which was accomplished, had been to see the midnight sun.

With lifted glass, "Skoal! to the Northland, skoal!" we cried, saluting that late Viking, Henry Wadsworth Longfellow, and his skeleton in armor. Thus the tale ended.

Back home the Congressional hearings on the Iran-Contra scandal were at last in production. The star performer, Colonel Oliver North, freely admitted to lying and destroying records to hide evidence of a cover-up. He defended lying to mislead and deceive as a virtue, wrapping himself in the flag for conduct "of which I assume the president was aware." Reagan has called him an American hero "who will be found innocent and won't need a pardon."

Admiral Poindexter, North's boss, testified he thought the president would have approved the operations if asked, merely tried to save him embarrassment by not asking. This provided Reagan with "plausible deniability," the tenable lie. Reagan believes he hasn't received a mortal wound; it is better to be called stupid than guilty.

Nancy Reagan has an "inflexible goal." She wants her husband to win the 1988 Nobel Peace Prize, and she wants him to belong to the ages with his head carved an Mount Rushmore. Her faith in the stars has unhinged her.

The news in Durham, North Carolina:

Headline, June 19: "Homosexuality Display Permitted at Public Library." According to the item, the library isn't promoting homosexuality or recruiting members, merely allowing a free expression of it in an exhibit during Lesbian and Gay Pride Week. How do you exhibit homosexuality?

Headline, June 21: "Chinese Have Fewer Sexual Dreams Than Americans." No reason given.

On a morning in July twenty-eight years ago, I made the first entry in my journal: "I'll begin with the gardenias," aware of a smell like Chanel #5 coming from the bush outside the open window. Then I sat at my typewriter wondering what to write about—a white house in the country, the cedar trees and magnolias, the petunias in the windowbox, the zinnias in the garden? Down in the meadow my neighbor's eight Herefords were lined up like Constable's cows, painted on the landscape, motionless in time. The scarlet tanager came and went looking for honeybees. This, I wrote, was the summer of a dormouse.

("You will have to live with these memories," said Eliot in the Four Quartets, "and make them into something new.")

Now in a much later July I sit in the same white house set about with cedar trees—but alone, by myself now. The meadow is empty of Mr. Easley's unassailable cows, and I've given up growing petunias. Heaven knows what happened to quiet the birdsong. The white gardenia bush just outside the window—yes, that is gone too.

After twenty-eight years I still keep a journal (not having reached the final stopping place) for the reason that a day unrecalled denies it ever happened, when the blur sets in. Gilbert White's journal of twenty-five years consists of ten thousand entries dealing tersely with harvest mice and serenely with the seasons ("Here and there a lamb," "One crocus blows"). He appears never to stop but to keep on recording the cycle of days long after his last entry, June 15, 1793: "Men wash their sheep."

Virginia Woolf's diary of twenty-six years, on the other hand, with its fulsome details of domestic life, stops abruptly on a Saturday, March 8, 1941, as she prepares to cook dinner: "I think it is true that one gains a certain hold on sausage and haddock by writing them down." Earlier she had noted, "I'd give a lot to turn over 30 pages or so, & find written down what happens to me." She would have found the last hurried postscript, "L. is doing the rhododendrons." Four days later she walked to her death in the Ouse River.

On October 28, 1837, Thoreau began the journal he kept for twenty-four years. Ninety years later, in the library of Columbia University I began to read the first of the fourteen volumes. A year and some two million words later, I came to the end, converted to an everlasting faith in Thoreau as a great simplifier who, while young enough, dropped out of the rat race and took up with muskrats.

Some journals are too much—Anaïs Nin's of 35,000 pages, Gladstone's, persisted in for forty volumes. My low opinion of André Gide comes from his prolonged concern with himself in the daily routine. Stephen Spender's journal of forty-four years (1939–1983) reads like an engagement book: "Lunch at the Savile Club," "Dined at the Astors'." Pauline de Rothschild asked him whether he was totally candid in his journal, "and I said I did not feel impelled to be (or rather I felt impelled not to be—that is what I meant)." Why then arrange for its publication?

This winter some unabandoned charitable hope put me at the mercy of Edmund Wilson's compulsive diaries from the twenties to the sixties, kept by a supremely vain man. Before he died in 1972, he asked Leon Edel to become editor of the prodigious outpourings that reveal Wilson's insensitivity to others, his appalling lack of humor. He considered the diaries of value as literary history and rejected Edel's suggestion he permit corrections and omit some passages; instead he inserted new material to make them "as readable as possible." They are intimate, gossipy entries about everything he did, everyone he knew. It was his custom to describe the occasions he had sex with each of his four wives, except Mary McCarthy with whom a stormy marriage was "absolutely nightmarish." The erotic scenes with one Anna in the twenties are, as Edel said, documented with zoological precision.

Call them diaries, journals, commonplace books—E. M. Forster kept a commonplace book from 1925 to 1968, forty-three years, in which he was as reticent as Wilson was confiding, strangely naive for a writer. (Katherine Mansfield, on *Howards End:* "E. M. Forster never gets any further than warming the teapot.") Yet one notation says something profound, perhaps even true, that the last word in human wisdom is *I simply don't mind.* It offers, he said, "an inviolable sanctuary." From people and circumstances.

"Finish, good lady, the bright day is done; and we are for the dark." The sun has set over the North Pole, the night has come on. But I'm not superstitious about it. There was once a midnight sun and it shone on me.

Noel Coward's only superstition was that it was bad luck to sleep thirteen in a bed.

Alone in my house, I've spent most of the day listening to Bertrand Russell's voice. In 1961, a few years before his death, he recorded for six hours details of his life, the people he knew, the opinions he held. He must have repeated himself often, for many are the same that he told B. and me during a day we spent with him in London. He was eighty then, a steady talker endlessly reminiscent over sherry, over lunch, during a long walk in Richmond Park, over tea.

I listen to him now saying in the same words, for instance, about people: Tennyson was a fraud, Browning an old ladies' darling, "I was terrified of Gladstone," "I couldn't do with Lloyd George." Einstein was a satisfactory great man, Shaw a vain and silly one, D. H. Lawrence "a bloodthirsty fascist with a profound contempt for mankind." About religion: "Nobody needs the consolation of things that are untrue." About sex: "I had a very powerful impulse to sexual freedom. One shouldn't be too hard on adultery." About the nuclear bomb: "We are all exposed to obliteration. I find it difficult not to be a little fanatical because the issue is so large." Russell predicted we wouldn't outlast the century.

Max Beerbohm said of him, "It is Bertrand Russell's saving grace that he isn't a woman. As a woman he would be intolerable." Because he talked so much.

I also played a recording of Edith Piaf's voice. Years ago to amuse the children, I used to set the speed from the old 33 rpm to 78 so that she chirped and twittered like a lunatic bird and they yelled with laughter. Now I hear Piaf at her own velocity wailing her love for fifty lovers who abandoned her: "I had so much love for a man who had too little for me." In 1950 on a holiday in the south of France, B. and I drove to Marseilles expressly to hear Edith Piaf. She came out on the stage of the music hall tiny in her black dress and black stockings, whitefaced, unsmiling—Piaf the sparrow. As she sang, her body tense with longing, I marveled that anyone that small, that frail, could endure the blight of so many catastrophic love affairs. To a man without ado they deserted her in spite of her constancy: "If our love dies you will always remain in my heart." And the audience went wild, knowing perfectly the hell of it themselves.

In real life, though, the opposite was true: Piaf was the one unfaithful to a vow. Margaret Crosland's new biography shows her fierce and demanding, a tough street singer who lived in Montmartre, drank too much, loved too many and left them for others, had a child who died, and existed in squalor till she was discovered by a homosexual cabaret owner in Place Pigalle. He heard her sing and named her *la môme Piaf* shortly before somebody murdered him. Piaf the waif became the songbird of Paris, till from excess of drugs and alcohol she died at forty-seven. One of her lovers, Eddie Constantine, told a journalist after her death, "Life with Edith was terrible . . . she was not attracted by physical love. Men had done her so much harm when she was young I think she was taking her revenge."

Beryl Markham was the astonishing girl who in September 1936 flew the Atlantic solo from Abington, England, facing dangerous headwinds, and landed headfirst in Nova Scotia as her plane dived into a mud swamp. Mayor LaGuardia gave her a hero's welcome when with a bump on her head she reached New York. I remember her well, since that summer I'd had my first flight in a plane, over London with a World War I ace, and dreamed some of becoming an aviatrix. I thought her courage less impressive than Amelia Earhart's (who was lost in the Pacific a few months later).

That was half a century ago. Beryl Markham told her story in a remarkably vivid book, *West with the Night,* published in 1942, after which she lived for forty years in poverty and oblivion in Kenya till her death last year at eighty-three. By chance rediscovered, her book a best-seller, she lives again in a biography by Mary Lovell.

I was wrong about Beryl Markham's courage. Born in England, abandoned by her mother and brought up by her father in Kenya, she was totally without fear. She ran free in bush country, learning from local tribesmen to hunt wild boar with rifle or spear, taught by her father to handle and train racehorses from his racing stable. At sixteen, tall, quite beautiful, she married a neighboring farmer Jock Purvis and, a few years later, the wealthy Mansfield Markham, unfaithful to them both. When as Mrs. Markham she became pregnant, everyone including her husband wondered who the father was. She and Markham separated when he found love letters from Prince Henry, the Duke of Gloucester, whom he suspected of fathering her son Gervase. On a visit to England, Beryl had been a frequent visitor to the royal apartments in Buckingham Palace, including once when Queen Mary walked in and Beryl hid in the cupboard. She received a small annuity from Prince Henry for the rest of her life.

In the 1930s Beryl took flying lessons and lived perilously by running an ambulance service in the jungle, carrying mail, and flying low over the African bush to scout for wild animals. Hemingway hired her to spot elephants from the air and declared her a "high-grade bitch" because she wouldn't sleep with him.

Beryl slept with everybody else, notably Denys Finch Hatton who was Karen Blixen's (Isak Dinesen's) lover, and Bror Blixen who was Karen's husband. A strange friendship existed between the two women; both were deeply in love with Africa and Denys. Karen had met Finch Hatton, a witty, elegant English aristocrat and big game hunter, while she was still married to Bror Blixen. At a dinner party Bror, slapping Denys fondly on the back, introduced him to a Swedish lady as "my good friend and my wife's lover." After her divorce, Denys moved his belongings, his rare books and Schubert records, to Karen's house, where he lived for six years between safaris, loving but determined to remain free. She was twice pregnant by him, unable to bear a child. None of this appeared in *Out of Africa,* where the idyll was kept.

At the same time Denys was intimate with Beryl and they hunted on safaris together. "Everyone knew how close we were," she said in old age; in her book she wrote of his courage and charm. When Denys acquired a plane, a two-seater Gypsy Moth, he flew Karen over the Ngong Hills, assuring her he had bought the plane for her. Yet soon after, as he was about to leave on safari and Karen begged to fly a short way with him, Denys flatly refused to take her. In a jealous rage she named her rival and they quarreled. Instead of making it up, he asked Beryl to go with him, saying he wanted to fly over the Voi reserve and scout for elephants, "and of course," Beryl wrote. "I said I would." At the last minute her friend Tom Black, who taught her to fly, had a premonition of danger and persuaded her not to go. On the takeoff from Voi, Denys's plane crashed to earth bursting into flames. With him was a little black Kikuyu boy.

September 30. On another subject, this is Saint Jerome's day, the greatest scholar of his age, patron saint of librarians. When in a dream Christ reproved him for caring more for Cicero than for God, Jerome sat down and compiled the Vulgate. He was not one of your saintly saints but argumentative, cross and abusive. I don't like him much because he preached the virtues of celibacy to a following of Roman matrons (like Paula, mother of five) and encouraged the perpetual virginity of virgins. His obsession with chastity roused antagonism and made so much trouble for him he left Rome for Palestine, accompanied by a loyal band of virgins. He died in Bethlehem in 420.

Though Saint Jerome denied that marriage was the equal in merit of virginity, "I praise marriage, but it is because they produce me virgins." Unfortunately he didn't come across Saint Ursula and her 11,000 virgins, who in the fourth or fifth century are said to have died in Cologne defending their virginity from an army of Huns.

El Greco painted Saint Jerome as a white-bearded holy man in a flaming red robe. I used to go to the Frick Museum and, in passing, scowl at him.

For true Christmas spirit, an editorial this morning says heaven is the place to look. Vincent van Gogh, presumably an occupant, finds the peace that eluded him on earth as he looks down on his belated fame and fortune. The starving, rejected van Gogh, who sold one painting in his lifetime and took his own life in a wheatfield at thirty-seven, can rejoice from on high that *Irises* was sold at Sotheby's for $53.9 million, the costliest picture in the world; van Gogh couldn't give it away.

This time of year heaven is obviously at hand, practically up in the attic. On television God is the one everybody lifts his eyes to appeal to, confer with, bargain with, rebuke, and (in a commercial) give thanks to for shredded wheat. The TV evangelists belabor God every night, who tells them to get busy and solicit funds.

In the *Times Literary Supplement* (that seldom makes jokes), a man goes to heaven and God says to him, "You're being reincarnated into a mayfly. Have a nice day."

Gorbachev and wife Raisa came for the holidays to celebrate peace on earth under the White House Christmas tree. Gorbachev and Reagan signed an agreement for arms reduction, a long way from total disarmament. Gorbachev spoke of the mounting risk of nuclear war.

The frosty wives, Nancy and Raisa, missing the point of peace talks, took an instant dislike to each other's clothes, manners, style, and person, and distinguished themselves by exchanging snubs. Raisa observed that Nancy lives in a museum.

"Who does that dame think she is?" Nancy is quoted as saying.

1 9 8 8

Everybody's worried about 1988, notes the *New York Times,* pointing to 1987 as the worst year since the Great Depression, ending not a minute too soon. "1988 will be a time to be cautious."

I ask myself, why write of something to be cautious about. To sound the alarm?

W. H. Auden: "I write because I like to, that's all."

E. B. White: "Tangling with a typewriter is sometimes the best therapy of all."

B. used to try to stop me. "Don't break your heart," he would say. Oddly enough, recently a stranger wrote to ask "Does it break your heart to write?" "Not so far," I answered.

But why not say what happened? And nothing to be gained by never saying.

January 22 was Byron's birthday, his two-hundredth. At the statue of him at Hyde Park Corner, the faithful celebrants gathered in wind, rain, and sleet, including Lady Elizabeth Longford, Byron's biographer, whose umbrella was blown inside out three times and the memorial wreath went whirling through the air, turbulent as the Romantic Movement.

Weep for him, he died young—young at thirty-six. But his hair was gray and he confessed he was tired of living and tired of loving.

They were wonderful teachers. There was Colette's mother, who cried out "Regarde!"

The novelist Janet Frame's mother, who stopped her children in their tracks. "Look!" she commanded. "Look!"

The actor Alec McCowan's father, who bellowed at him to stand still and take notice. "This is it!" he yelled. "*This is it!*"

Benvenuto Cellini's father, who looked into the fire and, seeing something move, beckoned to his son and gave him a box on the ear. "My dear child," he said, "I don't give you that blow for any fault you have committed, but that you may remember that the little lizard you see in the fire is a salamander."

By the same preceptorial method, teaching by the scruff of the neck, Look! they cried. Look!

I don't recall my parents taking me in hand. Charley's best advice was "Use your head!" Lizzie's was "Go chase yourself!"

In her autobiography, *Twice Over Lightly,* Helen Hayes says with some pride, "Helen Gould was my mother's idol. And that's how I came to be named Helen."

I, too. When I was born, nearly as long ago as Helen Hayes, I went nameless for a week because my mother was too ill to give me one and my father Charley, who wanted a boy, had nothing appropriate in mind. With God's help my grandfather, the Rev. I. J. Smith, picked and nearly baptized me Aftona Lily, in honor of the town of Afton, New York where I was born, and his daughter Lily. My mother, stunned when the news reached her, raised up and cried "Her name is Helen." Years later she told me that, in the panic of the moment, she remembered Helen Gould. "You were named for her," said my mother. "She was a good woman."

It shocks me that I never wondered till yesterday who Helen Gould was. Miss Hayes says she was the leading socialite of her day, "a model of elegance and tone to my mother." It appears she was born in 1870, eldest daughter of Jay Gould, the American financier who acquired millions by buying railroads and became known as the most hated man in New York, whose motto was "Take them before they take you." Of Jay Gould's six children who bickered over their inheritance and led generally unhappy lives, Helen alone was full of good works. In *The Goulds,* Edwin Hoyt says "her very goodness forbade the use of liquor in the house and successfully quashed any gaiety." She held daily prayer meetings and Bible readings, gave Bibles to all her friends, fluttered off to missionary conferences, supported the National Bible Society and the Salvation Army. She kept a series of snivelly little Pekineses each named Chinky, feeding them candies and cakes till they died of surfeit. She was a managerial busybody who tried to run her father's railroads after his death and keep her brothers from marrying actresses. Distrusting Vassar as liberal, she did her best to interfere and slow down female education. She tolerated no suitor for her hand in marriage but lived in unwavering virtue and constant fear of being assassinated for her money.

On the good side Helen Gould was charitable. She gave away millions with a free hand. In 1898, for example, she made a large gift to the United States government with the request just to spend the money any way it liked. Well advanced in spinsterhood she fell in love, age forty-four, with Finley Shepard, "an understanding man," who was assistant to the president of the Missouri Pacific railroad. They were married in 1913, retired to the Victorian mansion at 579 Fifth Avenue, attended church twice on Sunday, and adopted four children. A daughter-in-law, Celeste Andrews, wrote a book with the fascinating title *Helen Gould Was My Mother-in-Law*. It re-creates the pious home life of the Shepards, where in each of the guest bedrooms was a slim black volume titled "Bible Verses to Memorize, Selected by Helen Gould Shepard."

She died in 1938, and the papers referred to her as "the best loved woman in the country" for her good works—one of which was to give me her name, which I like better than Aftona Lily or Chinky.

When B. and I married and went to live in Greenwich Village, we used to walk of a Sunday the few blocks to Gramercy Park, which had a superior air unlike the dusty, careless look of the Village. It resembled a London square with stately houses and a green park, but because of the high fence and locked gate we only peered in at the flower beds and shade trees available to the residents. It never occurred to me to want to *live* there. I was happy in the Village.

A new book, *Gramercy Park*, by Carole Klein views the place as an American Bloomsbury. This was not my impression. Over the years B. and I often stayed at Bloomsbury Square in London, where anybody was free to sit in the park and smell the flowers; also, Gramercy Park seemed too stuffy and exclusive to attract a literary crowd. Albert Edward, Prince of Wales, visited there in 1860. Theodore Roosevelt was born in Gramercy Park.

Carole Klein's book doesn't say who lives there now. But she lists a surprising number of writers and other eccentrics who made it their sort of Bloomsbury. Herman Melville was a resident in 1863, already the author of *Moby-Dick,* forced to take an inglorious job as customs inspector because the world ignored him. He died there a recluse in 1891. Stephen Crane, another inmate, published his first book himself, *Maggie, a Girl of the Streets,* that no publisher would touch—a tale of an abused slum child who grew up to be a prostitute, finally a suicide. It sold two copies. One night Crane used a pile of *Maggies* to start a fire in his freezing room.

In 1904 O. Henry moved into Gramercy Park, wrote a story a week for the *New York World* and, a friend estimated, drank two quarts of whiskey a day, plus wine and beer at meals. His tales of Manhattan's "four million" would have the park for a setting.

Stanford White came to Gramercy Park in the 1880s, the famous architect who designed Madison Square Garden. All the town talked of his parties—where a naked girl sailed back and forth on a red velvet swing—and his scandalous affair with Evelyn Nesbit of the Floradora Girls. Stanford White with his red hair and mustache must have made a spectacular corpse the night he was murdered by Evelyn Nesbit's millionaire husband, Harry K. Thaw, when at Madison Square Garden Thaw leaped up and shot his wife's lover three times.

White's close friend and drinking companion, Augustus Saint-Gaudens, lived in Gramercy Park. He created a sensation with his sculpture of Clover, Henry Adams's wife, who one morning in 1885 went upstairs in their house in Washington, D.C., and swallowed potassium cyanide. Adams kept a grim silence about her; Saint-Gaudens portrayed her in marble as a hooded figure of grief.

But the indelible name to me in this history of a park is Carl Van Vechten's because he personally changed my life. Van Vechten came from Iowa to New York in 1906, an instant sophisticate and man about town, who wrote for the *New York Times* as America's first dance critic, rapturous in his praise of Pavlova and Isadora Duncan. He frequented Mabel Dodge's celebrated salon on Fifth Avenue and Gertrude Stein's apartment in Paris, adored by both ladies. With his second marriage to the actress Fania Marinoff, Van Vechten moved to Gramercy Park, where he gave riotous parties that lasted all night and throughout what he called the Splendid Drunken Twenties. As spokesman for the twenties he wrote seven novels, ending in 1929 when the

decade ended with the Depression. And the one that caught my innocent eye was *Peter Whiffle*. In the plotless novel, Van Vechten travels to
Paris where he meets Peter; in New York they attend Edith Dale's
(Mabel Dodge's) parties; and in Paris they meet again before Peter's
early death. Beyond that nothing happens. Peter merely talks all the
while, compendious on any subject.

It's the stylish talk that impressed me. At eighteen I believed everything I read, and the enlightenment this book provided filled pages of
my notebook. Such as,

"Peter had no principles and therefore he was reasonable."

"I have no respect for martyrs. Give me an intelligent hypocrite
every time."

"A man with a broad taste in food is inclined to be tolerant in
regard to everything."

The third aphorism changed my habits and my thinking. Assuming
tolerance to be one's chief aim in life, I stopped disliking any food or
drink, whatever edible or consummable came my way. It made me
popular with hostesses, and it has taken me years to admit a little
intolerance may be a good thing—at least for potato chips and second
martinis. I was touched, therefore, to reread Carl Van Vechten the other
day and catch a glimpse of my young self illumined by his nonsense. I
see now Peter Whiffle rhymes with piffle. Maybe it was meant to.

Those fearless explorers, the particle physicists, stir my mind more than
modern poetry does. They deal in the littleness of existence and the
bigness of existence on so prodigious a scale I seem to see the world
created anew through the inspiration of the atom.

Its littleness is such that the atom, of which the universe is made, is a
million times thinner than a human hair—so tiny, says Isaac Asimov,
that four trillion could dance on the head of a pin. The nucleus within it
is 10,000 times smaller than the atom. Protons and neutrons inside the
nucleus are ten times smaller than the nucleus. Quarks lurking within
the protons and neutrons are too minute to be measured, subatomic
particles so far unseen and theoretical. Some physicists believe the
quarks themselves, the basic building blocks of matter, can be broken
down and made to collide and split into parts or particles. Beyond that?
Perhaps nothing.

The bigness, as measured by Stephen Hawking, the theoretical physicist who is compared to Einstein, suggests that the limitless universe, which is infinity (composed of a hundred billion galaxies, each a universe itself with billions of stars) has no boundaries but goes on forever. It was not created and will never be destroyed. If then it has always existed without beginning or end, "What place, then," Hawking asks, "for a Creator?"

Steven Weinberg, another particle physicist, says the question to ask is Why? Why does the universe exist at all, why isn't there simply nothingness? It amazes him that we believe ourselves the center of a cosmos created with us in a central role—all this done for us in a grand scheme of things and a Great Chain of Being. Weinberg writes, "The more the universe seems comprehensible, the more it also seems pointless. The effort to understand the universe is one of the very first things that lift human life a little above the level of farce, and give it some of the grace of tragedy."

Lamentable facts (lately realized):

The latest edition of Webster's Dictionary omits the section on Rhymes. Poets no longer use rhyme and meter—too poetical.

Hell, defined anew by the physicists, is a black hole, a kind of infernal darkness that swallows light. Black holes, though theoretical (so is hell, isn't it?), are bottomless pits into which dead stars are swallowed up and vanish from the universe, as our sun will do. It's the best hell yet devised, better than Milton's "darkness visible."

"Eheu! Eheu! with what a weedy face / Black fact emerges from her swishing dreams."—Wallace Stevens, "The Naked Eye of My Aunt"

My farthest journey this summer was to visit the lemurs. Unfortunately they weren't in Madagascar, their native land, but in the primate center in the Duke forest. Duke is trying to save them from extinction, the world's rarest primate. (Man too is a threatened primate, under study at Duke.)

They look like monkeys except for the foxlike face, long furry tail, and enormous staring eyes. If you met a lemur in the night, God forbid, you might take it for one of the lemures, those spirits of the unburied dead that the Romans knew and feared, that Milton said "moan with midnight plaint." Very like the lemures are the lemurs called aye-ayes, who are completely nocturnal and appear to be all eyes staring nakedly at you like ghosts from a darkened cage. They say if one points his middle finger at you, you will die. The ancients drove away their lemures, who disturbed the peace, terrifying the good and haunting the wicked, by throwing black beans at them. The Duke center propitiates its aye-ayes with boxes of chirping crickets.

In daylight, swinging wildly from the tall trees or cuddling their young, the other lemurs are sociable airlings in spite of their bloodcurdling jungle racket and piercing screams. I'd still rather be looking at lemurs in the rain forests of Madagascar.

I never send postcards home from my travels. I don't keep postcards sent to me. Besides requiring no answer, the writer is obviously gloating: "Wish you were here" means "Don't you wish you were?" A card I received from the Gobi Desert contained the one word, "interesting."

Clive James has collected what he calls postcards in a volume with the appropriate title *Flying Visits*. They first appeared in the London *Observer* as the hasty notes of an unabashed tourist who sees what he can in a fly-by-night tour. The book jacket says James has invented a brilliant form of travel writing, and while I don't agree that postcards are really a new or brilliant way to communicate I'd vote him the best postcard writer in the business.

He uses the "blur of impressions" method to list the sights, like kangaroos in Australia or, on the freeway to Los Angeles, a billboard saying "I tried four mortuaries—Forest Lawn was lower." During the ten minutes he subsequently spent at Forest Lawn, James promised himself not to be seen dead there. Riding in a taxi in New York at what he clocked as 100 mph (traffic doesn't move *that* fast midtown), he thought he glimpsed Brooklyn Bridge and the Empire State Building before arriving at the Algonquin "vowing never to re-emerge until my week was up." In Japan he drank seaweed tea and watched the fat sumo wrestlers run into each other with the noise of colliding watermelons. Jerusalem provided a crowded view for his postcard, what with Christian, Islamic, and Judaic spectacles to tick off.

His best trip, to my mind, was one of perfect brevity when he flew around the world in three days, carrying a tote bag and a copy of Thomas Mann's *The Magic Mountain*. James left London for New York on the Concorde, pressed on to San Francisco, Hawaii, and Hong Kong, crossed mainland China to the Persian Gulf, and on to London by dawn Tuesday. He spent the three days in planes and airports, watched in-flight movies, ate too much, and found no time to read his book. It was the ultimate flying visit.

This was the miserable summer when temperatures soared and the weatherman kept saying "No relief in sight. Have a fantastic day," and I received five travel folders of a cruise in Antarctica among glaciers and penguins. Here is the journey to world's end and beyond I've been waiting for, with a stop in Patagonia where Paul Theroux made the discovery that *Nowhere is a place.* As he looked at the empty landscape, "I knew it was nowhere," he said. The last earthly paradise.

Theroux's experience was nothing new, though less rewarding than some ask of Eden. Long before him travelers went to a lot of trouble to get Nowhere, and returned home to tell of the signs and wonders. In 1515 one Raphael Hythloday, whom Sir Thomas More met on the street in Antwerp, claimed to have discovered the country of Utopia or "Nowhereland." On that remote island in an unknown ocean, Hythloday spent five happy years, where life was ideal and governed by reason, the arrangements for living being both simple and exemplary.

In the same century Rabelais recounted a journey Pantagruel and companions took to More's Utopia and added two or three Nowheres of his own, one the island of Medamothi from which Pantagruel sent his father a gift of three unicorns, lovely tame creatures that because of the horn on their forehead were fed by hand with apples and pears.

Nowhere was the land of El Dorado, a country of untold riches on the Amazon that Pizarro for one set out to find in his quest for gold. He found Peru instead, and the gold was radiant. Nowhere was the Seven Golden Cities Coronado sought in 1540 but discovered to be seven poor sunbaked pueblo villages.

In 1872 Samuel Butler came across a traveler named Higgs who by crossing a range of mountains in New Zealand arrived in Erewhon— Nowhere spelled backward. After being jailed in a land ruled by philosophers who worshiped the goddess Respectability, Higgs considered this no paradise and escaped in a balloon back to England. Twenty years later, as told in *Erewhon Revisited,* he returned for a second look and learned to his dismay that, following his miraculous ascent by balloon, the natives had made him into a god known as the Sunchild. In 1891 another Englishman, William Morris, wrote *News from No-*

where of a future time when London was transformed into a place where money was abolished, a miracle that didn't happen, said Morris, till 1972.

The kingdoms of the dead, however inaccessible in this life, count as Nowheres waiting to be explored—like Avalon, an earthly paradise in the Canary Islands, the abode of heroes of whom King Arthur was one. And the Fortunate Isles, described by Hesiod, Pindar, Horace, where the souls of the righteous dead live in bliss. These islands, also called the Elysian Fields, with rivers of milk and fountains of honey, were located by Homer at world's end, by Virgil made a part of Hades. In medieval lore, a land of plenty was Cockaigne, whose streets were paved with pastries and the rivers ran with wine.

A traveler could never hope to visit them all. My choice is Atlantis, an island in the Atlantic that in olden times was a powerful kingdom till, overwhelmed by the sea, it was swallowed up. Lost Atlantis, first mentioned by Plato in the *Timaeus* and the *Critias,* was a great empire near Gibraltar, said to be inhabited by descendants of the god Poseidon who slept with a mortal woman. Among temples and palaces, the people of Atlantis stayed happy and virtuous so long as the divinity of the god remained within them. Then came the earthquake that sank their world, and Atlantis has been sought for ever since. ("Only the Ship of Fools," wrote Auden, "is making the voyage this year.")

Someone asked Lou Holtz if the town of Fayetteville, Arkansas (where he was football coach at the time) was really Nowhere. Holtz replied, "No, but you can see it from there."

You can see the moon from there too, a Nowhere composed forevermore of rocks and nothingness. Mars may prove as empty when we land on it—no Martians in outer space, no moonpeople, no streams and green valleys, nothing.

What about Elsewhere?

First we had the nominating convention in August with the Democrats in Atlanta, where Michael Dukakis appeared unhappy but otherwise inconspicuous. Next we had the Republicans in New Orleans, where George Bush, addled by the heat, raised everybody's temperature by taking on Dan Quayle for his running mate. Quayle, announcing "I am the future," touted as a young, rich, ultraconservative senator from Indiana, more attractive than Robert Redford, became within hours the most unattractive man in America, labeled a draft dodger and follower of the golf cart. Why isn't he in the movies?

In September—the month and year announced by the fundamentalists as the date of The End, when millions of the faithful would be raptured to heaven to escape nuclear disaster, followed by Christ's Second Coming to start a new creation—nothing happened politically but a debate by the presidential candidates. Bush said not a word to explain the Iran-Contra arms deal, the towering deficit, Dan Quayle, Star Wars, or the homeless. Dukakis was attacked, remarkably enough, for his liberalism. Afterward Bush said he had "nailed" Dukakis, exposed and unmasked him as a liberal. Ample proof, said Bush, lay in Dukakis opposing the mandatory reciting of the Pledge of Allegiance by little children in the classroom. "Do we want this country to go that far *left?*" asked Bush. Jesse Helms of North Carolina called it incompatible with biblical morality. In derision Reagan referred to the Democratic Party as our *liberal* friends."

By the look of things, liberals may be facing the fate of the Liberal Party in England, at whose downfall and collapse that wise Greek scholar, Gilbert Murray, exclaimed, "How right they are and how extinct!"

"May all remaining events," wrote Sydney Smith in 1830, "be culinary, amorous, literary, or anything but political."

When I saw the play *You Can't Take It with You* in New York in 1937, I recognized it was a farce, a funny one at that. I also took it for a philosophy of life—which I meant to adopt—about being free to live your life in any manner you please. It made perfect sense to me.

Grandpa Vanderhof, the philosopher, knows full well you can't take it with you. Pretty shrewd, Grandpa is. One of the first titles George Kaufman and Moss Hart gave the play was *Foxy Grandpa*. Thirty-five years ago (that is, 1902) he quit his business by walking out the door and has been a happy man ever since, attending Columbia University commencement and hunting snakes in Westchester, refusing to pay a cent of income tax. "Well, I have had a lot of fun," he says. He tells God, "Remember, all we ask is just to go along and be happy in our own sort of way."

In Grandpa's permissive household that revolves around him, anything goes, the wackier the better. His daughter Penny writes plays because somebody delivered a typewriter to the house by mistake. Paul, her husband, makes fireworks in the cellar assisted by the ice man, who came one morning with the ice and has stayed on for eight years. The milkman stayed for five till he died; they never knew his name. Grandpa's married granddaughter, Essie, practices all over the house to be a ballerina, instructed by a mad Russian while her husband Ed plays the xylophone. His other granddaughter, Alice, a private secretary, the only normal member of the family and its only visible means of support, seems just a pretty girl too conventional to cut loose and enjoy herself. Nothing occurs to develop the theme except that a cheerful frenzy prevails: the skyrockets explode, Alice's staid fiancé and future in-laws are converted to Grandpa's relaxed ways, and after a near riot all thirteen of the cast spend the night in jail. Grandpa tells God, "Things seem to be going along fine."

The play was a Broadway hit (and a total disaster in London), superbly acted by Henry Travers as Grandpa. It won a Pulitzer Prize followed by popular revivals ever since, though the critic John Mason Brown took its measure when he described it as "pure and simple-minded, and admirable as such."

But what I fell for was the philosophy, which, as is clearer to me now, it has not got. Grandpa, a dotty old duffer, has missed the point: this isn't freedom, it's license. Totally lacking in Grandpa's view of the good life is selectivity. And that being an indispensable part of wisdom, his choices are silly, his judgment is weak, his tolerance is blind, and the results are terrible. To my relief I see I haven't tried to live like Grandpa Vanderhof after all.

1 9 8 9

I'd say 1988 was a middling sort of year—earthquakes, wars, hurricanes, drought, famine, airplane disasters—the world badly askew, the usual sort of thing.

Prince Charles, the uncrowned future king, turned forty in 1988. George Bush took over the Oval Office with Reagan still in it. Said he was fulfilling a posture. Our vocabulary was enriched by *couch potato, sleazeball,* and two new adjectives, *kinder* and *gentler,* that Bush proposed for the nation while lambasting Dukakis. The Tower of Pisa, on which I keep an eye, leaned a little nearer to its doom.

On January 1, in his farewell speech Reagan said in effect, "Don't blame me. Blame everyone else." He took credit for peace and prosperity, faulting Congress for the rest. Scholars say there are flaws in Reagan's version which borders on fantasy.

With January came the inauguration of President Bush, a five-day ritual, the most glorified and expensive in American history. Reagan's party in 1981 cost $15 million, Bush's cost $30 million; Reagan had ten inaugural balls, Bush had eleven. The "Presidential Inaugural Gala" again featured Frank Sinatra, in the new dispensation singing "Tonight I'll call you George." Bob Hope stood up in the audience yelling "George, it's great to see ya!" Loretta Lynn, the country singer whom George is stirred by, sang "Stand by Our Man," and Nell Carter howled "I mean that George is jumping!"

On January 20 Billy Graham was back to handle the prayers. Bush took the oath in the same thirty-five words said by George Washington two hundred years ago. Dan Quayle was sworn in, and for lunch quail wasn't served as it was four years ago. The parade included the Clydes-dale horses and Mormon Tabernacle Choir, the number of Bush rela-tives on hand was 240, and the security measures in the nation's capital, known as the murder capital of the world, were staggering.

It was, in George's words, "an outstanding job." The theme of "George to George" emphasized a span of history as if they were the first and last of the presidents. The tone, in contrast to the Reagans' sound effects, reflected a change to a comfortable reign with horseshoes in the rose garden, a homey White House filled with "caring" people and Millie the pregnant dog.

None too soon, Duke University is to become a center for the study of rights—our rights as members of the human race. You would think the unalienable rights Jefferson said were self-evident, followed by the Bill of Rights to protect our freedoms, would cover everything. Not so, not human rights or civil rights or equal rights. Human rights were adopted by the United Nations in 1948 to set forth on a world scale the basic rights and fundamental freedoms universally denied. Civil rights, guaranteed by the Thirteenth and Fourteenth Amendments, became a movement for racial equality with the Civil Rights Act of 1964. We're still evasive about that. Whites are even complaining they want their rights back. Equal rights (for women) died in 1982.

As for states' rights, rights of the unborn, squatter's rights, I just don't know. Have they got any?

THE ROAD TO MANDALAY "We're not tourists, we're travelers," said Vir-ginia at the end of the most strenuous journey so far. Tourists complain, travelers enjoy. We were travelers, uncomplaining, accepting, delight-ing in a month's journey to East Asia with Virginia, who heads the International Travel Club and refuses to send anyone anywhere with-out seeing the place first. A dozen of us (ten women and two men named Jim) led by the tireless Virginia, investigated Taiwan, Thailand, Singapore, Java, Bali, and—the spot foremost in our minds if they would let us in—Burma and the Road to Mandalay. Hereafter, Vir-ginia said, she would recommend the tour only to people like us, disposed by nature to endure.

On February 14 we arrived by Singapore Airlines in Taipei, capital of Taiwan. Before landing at the Chiang Kai-shek Airport, I caught a glimpse of a country green as Ireland and very mountainous. Had I lived so long knowing nothing of Taiwan except that for five hundred years it was Formosa? On the elegant Sun Yat-sen Freeway we sped the forty miles to Taipei, past bamboo groves and rice paddies, past a gleaming red-and-gold palatial Grand Hotel, built like a Chinese temple under the direction of Madame Chiang Kai-shek. Our hotel, the Asia-World Plaza, resembled a palace too, lavishly ornate.

Taipei, a prosperous city of motorbikes unlike the bicycles of Beijing, is not Communist despite China's attempts to take over Taiwan, and has no one-child-per-family law. Our guide, Albert Huang of the China Travel Service, born in Taipei and father of four, was proud to show off this modern, democratic city, of which the showiest sight was the Chiang Kai-shek memorial. Chiang died in 1975 in the land he reluctantly fled to in 1949 to escape the wrath of the Communists, and that under him became the National Republic of China. His soaring white marble monument with eighty-eight steps leading to it, which we promptly climbed, dominates forty acres that include the National Theater, National Concert Hall, and a great flowering park. Up there a placard ordered a respectful silence, but the Chinese on hand in great numbers as sightseers joked noisily and chased about, bursting with laughter as they snapped themselves instead of the exalted figure above their heads. At the grand arch below, a bride and groom were having their picture taken purposely with the leader in full view. So I never found out how far Chiang is revered as hero and lord, considering his reputation as virtual dictator, a convert to Christianity who renounced Buddhism and joined the Southern Methodist Church when he married Mei-ling—a man without scruple who carried off the priceless treasures of the Forbidden City in Beijing (now deposited in the National Palace Museum in Taipei). Loyal, discreet Albert was obviously not the man to ask.

In the splendid Lungshan Temple, where it was hard to breathe in the vast interior crowded with Chinese, each one holding five joss sticks to place at the altar of the Goddess of Mercy, Albert bowed with palms together before the great gold statue. As we walked about, he softly described his religion as one composed of a Trinity: Confucius, Buddha, and Lao-tzu, founder of Taoism. Confucius taught a way of life, a morality and ethic achieved through courtesy, justice, compassion for others. Buddha, contemporary of Confucius, taught the right way to live to escape suffering and attain virtue and enlightenment. Lao-tzu revealed through Tao ("the way") the right way to end striving and bring peace to the mind and freedom from desire. Taipei is a Confucian city, Albert said, Tao is the key to Chinese culture, and the true religion is Buddhist.

That night at our hotel, lit with festoons of lights like an amusement park, I discovered in my room a copy of the *Analects* of Confucius beside the New Testament. I fell asleep reading the collection of his sayings, notably "If a man in the morning hears the right way, he may die in the evening without regret."

In America there is the Grand Canyon, in Taiwan the Taroko Gorge, one of the wonders of the world. We flew next morning to the town of Hualien near the coast, and there on a highway graced by papaya trees and water buffalo we drove to the Central Mountain Range that leads to the Pacific. Through an arch at the start of it we entered the Taroko Gorge, a twelve-mile canyon carved and tunneled through solid marble, lined with gigantic white marble cliffs all but touching each other. It was a perilous journey within a ravine almost too narrow to squeeze through, where the mountain walls closed in and hid the sky. A river ran below over marble pebbles, and there were swallows in the grottoes, and it was so unbelievably stark-white and beautiful that even Albert, who has been there more than a hundred times, caught his breath.

I said to him, "I have seen the splendor of the world," and wondered aloud whom I was quoting or misquoting.

"Me," said Albert, as we came out into the daylight.

At Hualien, a village of the Ami tribe, once headhunters who live to themselves in the mountains, Albert took us to the ceremonial hall for a performance of tribal dances. The young Ami girls danced, our ticket said, "with passion and activeness." Actually they moved in a trance, twisting their hands and fingers, tilting their heads, endearingly sedate and deliberate, their Oriental faces impassive—till it was over and they ran laughing like children to pull one of the Jims and me from our seats to dance with them. That was the time I felt most like a tourist.

We stopped at a marble plant, where surprisingly nobody bought as a souvenir a marble table weighing a ton, and flew back to Taipei for the next bout with Albert. At a downtown restaurant each of us concocted a Mongolian barbecue dinner of chicken, beef, shrimp, rice, vegetables, pungent sauces, and took it to the cook who spent one minute over a hot grill cooking it. Some of us managed three trips. That night we walked together through the Night Market, where at a stall Albert reached into a sack and offered me a betel nut because I said I wanted to chew one. I had seen Buddhist monks with mouths smeared crimson from the betel nut, which was reputed to have the same euphoric effect as the coca leaf in Peru. But Albert told me it would stain my teeth permanently pink. Anyway, it was time to bring to an end the wonderful Confucian pleasures of Taiwan.

THAILAND The flight to Bangkok lasted to nearly midnight. At the airport Suzie impatiently waited, our guide in Thailand, a short, round-faced Thai woman given to hugging who beamed her joy to see us and hustled us off to the Airport Hotel, briskly directing us not to unpack our bags but be up at 5:00 for a flight north to Chiang Mai! *Why?* we asked wearily, *Why*, when we had scarcely set foot in Bangkok?

By mid-morning we were in Chiang Mai on the Ping River, five hundred miles from Bangkok, a town consisting entirely, it seemed, of Buddhist temples and shrines. On the main thoroughfare I did notice "Daddy's Pizza" and a place called "Banana Split," but these were mere anachronisms. Chiang Mai was a collection of three hundred ancient temples, and a center for woodcarving, handicrafts, and elephants.

Tireless Suzie, taking full charge, never let us stop. Her name was Suvanee Chongluckana, and she reminded me of the bumboat woman in *South Pacific*, her black hair drawn back tight from her face, black eyes snapping—a constant talker full of squeals and jokes, plump, bold, irrepressible. She was unmarried, she said, but for some time now ready and hopeful.

"Yah!" Suzie exclaimed at intervals. "O.K.!" Pushing us impatiently into the bus, she set off for factories in nearby villages, a silkweaving, a silvermaking, a woodcarving, an umbrella factory. At the village of Sankamphaeng we saw the silk looms where the marvelous Thai silk is woven into lustrous colors. At the silver factory, where I coveted a silver necklace, the clerk said "Ask Suzie," and Suzie came running with a loud cry, "Buy it!" In the umbrella village professional artists sat painting parasols; in the woodcarving shop they made delicate teak-wood figures of Leda and the Swan and the Virgin Mary. To please herself Suzie added a stop at a Thai nursery for a walk among the thousands of orchids she loves.

That night before leaving us at the hotel she yawned, saying dreamily oh dear, what a pity it was, she still had a heavy date with an old boyfriend, then shook with laughter because she was joking. "It's hard to go to heaven," Suzie said, "but you can go to hell any time."

A short drive next day took us to the most sacred temple of the north, the Wat Doi Suthep, and the last ten vertical miles of it were straight up the mountain, where at the top the gold-spired temple rose above the world as magnificently as the Potala Palace in Tibet. The site had been found by sending an elephant to climb the mountain till at the summit it trumpeted, turned around three times, and dropped to its knees.

Within the gorgeous temple the Buddha, benign and calm, brought to Suzie's devout mind the many ways he has been presented through the centuries, sometimes pink and fat, sometimes lean, sitting cross-legged under the bo tree with hands folded or outstretched to say "Fear not, all is well." A reclining Buddha signified his release to nirvana or, if the feet were relaxed, showed him resting. A standing Buddha taught the word, a crown or topknot on his head, earlobes long and dangling. However it was, the Buddha's face was always serene, he was at peace, freed from suffering—far different (I sadly thought) from the crucified Christ whose crown of thorns and anguished face speak his suffering and death by man's will. Different, too, was the living bo tree from the tree to which he was nailed and where he died.

Suzie gave each of us a long-stemmed lotus flower and three joss sticks to place on the altar, and to please her we tried to keep the incense burning. It was then I wandered out to the compound where chrysanthemums were in bloom, hibiscus like red roses, the golden flowering cassia tree. And there in the garden to my amazement and joy I found a bo tree, luminous green and thriving, probably grown from a slip of the tree in India, a descendant of Buddha's tree. With immense satisfaction I sat under it, for a while wholly at peace, then reached up and carefully picked a shining, heartshaped leaf for my collection of two.

From the gold riches of Wat Doi Suthep we went on to the poverty of a hill village, one of a dozen inhabited by the Meo Hill tribes, climbing on foot up a dusty road too steep for cars. Every child in the village came running, some lugging a baby brother on their back, while the populace of fifty turned out with broad smiles to greet us, singing "What a Friend We Have in Jesus."

That night at Chiang Mai's Cultural Center, after removing our shoes at the door we sat on the floor with bowls of Thai food and watched a performance of Thai dancing. It was exquisite—classical and hill-tribe—of incredible grace and skill: the fingernail dance, the silk-reeling dance, the lotus dance, each girl moving trancelike, slender and graceful, her fingers backbending, her head held rigid under the stately spire of her headdress.

North of Chiang Mai in the Mae Sa valley was an elephant work camp where Siamese elephants are trained to haul logs from the forest and haul tourists on elephant rides. The last time I rode an elephant was at the Bronx Zoo, age four, round a sawdust ring at an elephant's pace. The ride this morning with Virginia was more like a dive on a roller coaster or a simple suicide. We were lifted up to the howdah fastened to the elephant's back, high above the Thai boy who rode on its neck and directed its unsteady steps. With diminishing hope we went crashing through thick underbrush, stumbled along in tangled vines and jungle, plunged headfirst to a stream and struggled up the other side. Virginia and I held on for dear life, nearly yanked out of our seats, prepared at each step to land on the elephant boy and sail over the elephant's head. It was harrowing. Suzie watched us with quiet laughter, but never went near an elephant. "Suzie!" said Virginia afterward. "Can't help loving that woman."

Bangkok, the capital of Thailand (Siam till 1939) is the most splendid city of Indochina, its temples and palaces made of colored tiles in reds, greens, gold, its many-tiered roofs edged with tiny bells glittering in the sun. In 1782 King Rama I, Lord of the White Elephant, built the Grand Palace surrounded by shrines and pagodas, with a Royal Chapel to contain the Emerald Buddha—the wonder of the East. One Siamese king who lived in the Grand Palace with his wives and concubines and sat on a gold throne was King Mongkut, about whom Anna Leonowens wrote *Anna and the King of Siam.* She was the English widow who in the 1860s taught English to the royal children, then numbering 67. The musical made of it, *The King and I,* is banned throughout Thailand as disrespectful, with King Mongkut in the person of Yul Brynner a prancing foolish clown. Actually he was an able ruler who before his reign had been a Buddhist monk.

On her way to the palace, Anna daily passed Bangkok's oldest temple, Wat Po, the Temple of the Reclining Buddha, and Wat Phra Kaew, the Temple of the Emerald Buddha—the same two we were gazing at now. At Wat Po the colossal Reclining Buddha, 160 feet long, occupied a whole building. It looked like a mammoth whale lying on its side, overlaid with gold plate, a picture of repose fearful to behold on such a large scale. At Wat Phra Kaew two ferocious stone lions guarded the doors that no evil spirit might enter where the Emerald Buddha sat high on a gold altar, carved from a single piece of green jasper. There we stayed, awestruck among the many worshipers.

Next day was a different story, spent at the Floating Market on the Damnern Saduak canal, one of the long canals branching off from the river beside Bangkok. The market, overhung with palm and mango trees, was really afloat, and from dozens of tiny sampans clustered together the quiet farmers in peaked hats sold their flowers, tropical fruits, vegetables wrapped in palm leaves. It was a cloudless day, with lunch in the Rose Garden before returning to our hotel, the Shangri-La—so peaceful a day I found myself considering again how it was always Shangri-La I sought to find, and seemed to find, on these journeys. Bangkok called itself the City of Angels, the City of God—more accurately known throughout Asia as the sex capital of the world. In the lounge I picked up a copy of the *Bangkok Post,* brought down to earth by the headline news, the comic strips of Peanuts, Garfield, Blondie, the racy advertisements of massage parlors promising sex and every fleshly pleasure, "the finest feelings in a world of privacy," with a special body massage available to VIPs. For sale was a "prestigious Cadillac," 1979 model. A message from the Samaritans of Bangkok urged contact with them "if you're suicidal or depressed and need someone to talk to in English or Thai."

Suzie lives in Bangkok and loves it above and beyond all other worlds, content with her lot. When she heard we were determined to go to Burma, now that visas had at the last minute been granted, she begged us to change our minds. "Why do you go to Burma," she wailed, "when you are safe with me here in Bangkok?" Burma, she said, was a dangerous country (which she had never seen), where we would be shot down by the police or made sick from the greasy food, where the people would not love us.

"Bangkok is so beautiful," she said. "Stay in Bangkok and be happy."

BURMA We went anyway. And Suzie was wrong about Burma, far from sure though we were what the reception would be. A few months ago Burma was on the edge of anarchy. In an uprising last August thousands marched twenty abreast through Rangoon demanding a change to democracy. At first the repressive military government had given in, but a month later it savagely reasserted control. Again thousands filled the streets, and this time soldiers gunned them down in a mass slaughter. Till last month no foreigners were allowed to enter the country, which is under martial law. Arrests and bloodshed continue, the deaths of student leaders. Schools and theaters are closed. A dictator, General Ne Win, makes war against the Burmese people, while their hatred of the military grows.

So with visas limited to seven days, what were we doing in Burma? We were there, it appeared, to go barefoot in and out of Buddhist temples, smiling at the friendliest people on earth, and to ride on positively the worst roads. The military left us strictly alone, only asking that we wear "polite" dress. I doubt we did any harm, and nobody did us any.

Like Tibet, Burma calls itself the Land of the Religion. Like the Chinese who rule Tibet, the government discourages Buddhism. Yet virtually everyone is a Buddhist and lives, or is supposed to live, as Buddha did, seeking to gain merit by good deeds in this life and be reincarnated into a better one. Every male is required to become a novice in a monastery for a period of weeks, months, or years, as he chooses. There he is taught by the monks a form of Theravada Buddhism, an older form differing from the Mahayana Buddhism of Tibet that elevates Buddha to a god and is founded on faith. Theravada teaches that Buddha was not a creator or savior but a man, and like him everyone must work out his own salvation. Nirvana is not heaven, it is peace of mind, peace of the spirit, peace on earth. In this troubled, suffering world, "Be a refuge to yourself," Buddha said.

In the Rangoon airport it was Burmese bedlam, no foreigners but ourselves visible among them, both men and women dressed in a short jacket and long wraparound skirt tied at the waist. They looked nice, a small people with coppery skin and dark eyes. Some women wore on each cheek a concentric circle of white paste.

Rangoon, the capital and port city, seemed everywhere contradictory, very poor and fabulously rich, its Victorian buildings badly in need of paint, the magnificent Shwedagon Pagoda which dominates the city made of pure gold. Our hotel, the Strand, built in 1901 when Burma was an English colony, was shabby genteel, while our guide Pansy like the pagoda was pure, untarnished gold.

T. S. Eliot chose to meet Lucretia Borgia in heaven, but I would settle for Pansy. Not that Pansy believed in heaven. "Buddha is not a god," she started off this morning. "Buddhism is a philosophy, a way of life." (Scholars still argue whether this form of Buddhism is or is not a religion.) She was a slight, pretty woman about Suzie's age, as different from Suzie as yin and yang. Pansy had gone to the University of Rangoon to become a doctor, but finding she had to kill living things had withdrawn. Her father advised her to study mathematics; instead she chose moral philosophy and found her vocation in the Buddha. She would never marry, she said, but would meditate in a small house alone. "Breathe out, breathe in, think of nothing," said Pansy. "That is meditation."

Burma is a land of pagodas, so many you wonder what else matters to them. The celebrated Shwedagon Pagoda rose up on Singuttara Hill, a gold cone-shaped stupa narrowing to a spire crusted with diamonds, rubies, one gigantic emerald, hung with 1,500 tinkling gold and silver bells. Eight hairs of the Buddha were said to be imbedded in the stupa. Four stairs led to a circular platform for the faithful. Surrounding the temple were dozens of smaller pagodas, as if the great one had given birth, and many trees—one of them a bo tree (brought from Buddh Gaya by U Thant, former secretary of the United Nations). In downtown Rangoon—a quieter city than Bangkok, without traffic or night life—another pagoda, the immense Sule, stood like an inverted golden temple bell, the tallest structure in the city round which Rangoon was built.

Face alight at these spectacles, Pansy took us to other temples where we could enter and gaze at the figure whose face was becoming very familiar. At one crowded shrine a small Burmese boy stepped by mistake on my bare foot and burst into laughter. So did I. Later, on our way out of the temple, he turned round and seeing me laughed again and threw me kisses, and I threw them back to him. "You are learning Burmese ways," said Pansy.

Next day we left Rangoon for a flight to Pagan. If like the Burmese I believed that powerful *nat* spirits, good and evil, hover constantly over my life, I would thank them for sparing us. We had been warned by our State Department against flying anywhere in Burma in their old beat-up planes with a record of fatal crashes. But we made it safely this time to Pagan, and Pagan was *nothing* but temples. A village in Upper Burma on the Irrawaddy River, it was once known as "the city of a thousand temples," though actually there were 2,217 of them, now scattered and strewn in ruins for miles over the Pagan plain. In the distance they looked like the brown spiraling anthills of Africa, while those nearby glittered in a glory of white and gold. The old palace of Pagan was gone.

In this holy place our guide was a strange encounter. He asked us to call him Zala (his name was Zaw Lwin), a native of Pagan who had during the recent riots lost his home and all his possessions. He was an attractive man close to forty, wearing a skirt, a *longyi,* that fell to his ankles. With courtesy and a wide breadth of knowledge, he led us about Pagan absorbed in revealing the look of it—the great Bupaya Pagoda on the bank of the Irrawaddy; the Shwezigon Pagoda with shrines of the 37 *nat* spirits; the shining white Ananda Temple dark as a cave inside with four huge statues. As the other guides had done, Zala told us the story of the Buddha (in Italian cathedrals do guides ever recite the life of Christ?): how Gautama, an Indian prince, was born in a wood while his mother Maya stood clinging to a sal tree, lived in a palace among lotus ponds, was married at sixteen and had a son, finally chose to abandon his wealth, kingdom, family because of the suffering he saw, and wandered six years as an ascetic in search of understanding. At thirty-five he found under a bo tree the enlightenment and the peace he sought.

But Zala was different. He wasn't devout like the others, and his eyes were not serene. One day as we walked together he said ruefully, "You see, I am a bad Buddhist," and counted on his fingers the five precepts a good Buddhist must obey: not to kill, not to drink alcohol, not to commit adultery, not to steal, not to lie. I said, "What about me? I'm a Christian with ten commandments to obey and seven sins to avoid," and I ticked them off. "You're lucky with only five." Zala laughed and said in that case we both were sinners.

He said he would never marry because he refused to have children growing up in Burma. He said he was trying desperately to leave his unhappy country and go elsewhere to live—to Bangkok, to Japan—as soon as he could escape, if he could escape. He said, "Please forgive me, I am talking too much," and his face was tense. Zala was one of the thousands who had taken part in protesting Burma's police state. He said, "I am in serious trouble."

At last we were on the road to Mandalay, with Zala still accompanying us. From Rangoon to Mandalay the distance is about four hundred miles, but by flying to Pagan we had mercifully shortened the trip. It was a narrow, godforsaken road we traveled, so eroded and full of potholes we bounced and rattled around like chiclets in the rickety bus. It was worse than the elephant ride.

I sat looking out at drab, empty fields, thinking of Kipling inevitably since this was the road he made popular:

> On the road to Mandalay
> Where the flyin' fishes play
> An' the dawn comes up like thunder
> Outer China 'crost the bay.

Did Kipling, who never lived in Burma, consult a map? His flying fishes must be frolicking in the muddy Irrawaddy River in the dusty reaches of Upper Burma, while the dawn out of China across the Bay of Bengal comes thundering over Rangoon. His Burma girl, waiting for her British soldier beside the old Moulmein Pagoda, is waiting in Moulmein in Lower Burma, southeast of Rangoon at the mouth of the Salween River. Looking for him "eastward to the sea," the poor girl is staring at the border of Thailand! What ailed the man?

Later I found in *Something of Myself*, his autobiography, that Kipling had tried lamely to explain the confusion. He said he wrote a song called "Mandalay" about a soldier whose girl lived in Moulmein, which "is not on the road to anywhere" and doesn't command a view of any sunrise across the Bay of Bengal. His excuse was he should have begun the song "Oh Mandalay" instead of "On the road to Mandalay." But it wouldn't have helped. The whole thing was, as Kipling said, "a sort of general mix-up." Or mess.

Another Englishman, George Orwell, did live in Burma for five years when it was a British colony, and served in Moulmein with the police force that kept the Burmese captive. "I hated the imperialism I was serving with a bitterness I cannot make clear," Orwell said. He wrote a bitter novel, *Burmese Days*, after resigning in disgust and guilt from "the dirty work of Empire," seeking to escape imperialism and "every form of man's dominion over man."

Mandalay on the Irrawaddy is framed by hills covered with pagodas. But the Golden City is no longer golden; the Gold Palace, built they said at the very center of the universe, was destroyed in March 1945 during

World War II when the British shelled the city occupied by the Japanese. The area is now a military installation, Mandalay Fort, with high walls and moat to shut the people out.

Mandalay was a kingdom till 1885 when the British invaded it and took over. During their occupation they treated the Burmese as inferior beings and servants, though Buddha had taught them all men are equal. In 1942 the Japanese expelled the British and brought terror to Burma; in 1945 the British drove out the Japanese; in 1948 the British departed for good; in 1962 a military dictatorship under General Ne Win took command—the history of Burma.

Halfway up Mandalay Hill rose the great Shweyattaw Temple, where the 1,729 steps I doggedly climbed led to the immense gold Buddha with right arm outstretched and beyond it to the top of the mountain for a view of the Irrawaddy. On Mandalay Hill, too, was the famed Kuthodaw Pagoda surrounded by 729 marble slabs containing Buddha's teachings recorded in Pali, and the group of buildings known as the "730 Pagodas," in a place so sacred it's believed Buddha himself came centuries ago to visit Mandalay Hill.

The guide who joined us in Mandalay was Win, another gentle, unworldly person dedicated like Pansy to following the right way. He offered to take me to a meditation house, and I was sorry to admit I hadn't time to meditate. For three years Win had lived by choice in a monastery, leaving to marry and beget a child now a year old. Very soon, he said, he would return to the monastic life (and the celibacy of a monk), giving up all earthly attachments because the need to do so was overwhelming. "What does your wife think?" I asked. He replied, "She understands."

For the last three precious days in Burma, we went from Mandalay to mountain country and the old British hill stations. This morning we flew to the town of Heho in the mountainous Shan State and spent the afternoon on Inle Lake, described in the travel folder as "outrageously picturesque," where lake dwellers built their houses, even their pagodas, on the floating islands. For hours we sped up and down the largest lake in Burma, on the lookout for the local fishermen called leg-rowers, who are noted for the way they row their boats standing upright with one leg curled round an oar. But equally diverting was our boatboy, Tin Win Yaun Hwe, who sat beside me pointing out the sights, his shoulders shaking with laughter—a brown, merry boy of I guessed fifteen, convulsed when he caught a tiny fish with his hands and thrust it into mine. Since he knew a little English, I finally asked "How old are you anyway?" which set him off again, slapping his bare leg and sharing the joke with the boatman standing above us. When he could catch his breath, "Twenty-nine!" he gasped. Tin Win of Inle was a happily married man with two children. Each night he meditated, as he showed me, with eyes tightly closed and hands joined. By day he rode in this little boat as boatboy, and he laughed because life was good.

It was an hour's drive north to Taunggyi, a delightful summer resort of flowers and orchards on top a mountain where in bracing air we spent the night and next morning met Aye Aye Hnynn, our last guide in Burma, in some ways the incomparable best.

I loved Aye Aye (pronounced A-A) and in the end knew least about her life because I didn't ask, accepting her for what she was. She lived in Taunggyi, a young Buddhist who seemed to belong in a temple. Since this was market day she took us first to see the hill people, distinguishable from each other by their mode of dress. The women of the Pao tribe, for instance, wore a long black gown with leggings and a large turban. Most of the women had a white circle or leaf pasted on their cheek. As a people they were dirty, sullen, suspicious of strangers. Yet at their homes in the hill villages, they greeted us with smiles, angry as they were, Aye Aye said, that since the riots their children were not in school. In one village I counted fifty-five small dirty children, staring at us hungrily in hopes of being fed or smiled at.

Shrines were few in the hill country, but Aye Aye knew them all. "Remember, Buddha is not a god," she told us, and her devotion to him shone in her face. There was one temple with a large sign at the entrance, "Ladies must wear brassieres." In another, the Hsinhkaung Monastery, as we wandered about Aye Aye said suddenly with a glad cry, "I think the bishop is here today. I will ask if he will see you."

The next moment U Sasana was approaching us, a smiling bishop in a maroon robe like a toga, who held out his hands in welcome. As we gathered round him, he seemed so glad to know our names and our separate selves as Aye Aye introduced us, that Jim (one of the two Jims) launched into an account of his experiences in World War II when he was a fighter pilot over Burma. "That's the real reason I came on this trip," Jim told him. "The Japs shot me down and took me prisoner, so I never got a chance to see Burma at all."

To this story the bishop listened amazed. He stared into Jim's eyes and reached out to embrace him. "But so was I! So was I!" he cried. "I too was a fighter pilot in that war. I too was shot down over Burma by the Japanese who took me prisoner and tried to kill me. As you see, I didn't die, here I am." He smiled a little and went on soberly, "But from that experience I became what I am now, a Buddhist monk."

Jim was listening, shaken, close to tears. Later he said, "I know, I know. I thought some of becoming a priest myself."

That happened in Pindaya, a small town famous for its tremendous caves. According to legend, Aye Aye said, angels used to live in them, where now in the deep interior were thousands of Buddhas, thousands of years old, of various sizes and shapes, some of them statues in niches, some gilded, some carved into the rock. For the first time in my life I was unafraid to walk in a cave, partly because the Buddhas calmly accompanied us, partly because Aye Aye clutched my hand and never let go. We made the long dark circuit together, she and I, and came out laughing into the bright air.

After a night spent among pine-covered summits at the country hotel in Kalaw, another hill station near Pindaya, where Tudor houses and small English gardens still remained, next morning we got into the bus and went tearing down the mountain over steep, winding, dreadful roads with incredible depths of view. We drove on to the village of Heho to take the plane back to Rangoon, and in the small airport said a sorrowful goodbye to Aye Aye. At Rangoon we were met by Pansy, who saw us off on still another plane, this time out of Burma and once again to Bangkok.

As she left us at the boarding gate, Pansy put her soft cheek next to mine and whispered "Till we meet," and I whispered "Till we meet." But she meant in some future life, some haven, some nirvana. And, alas, I did not.

SINGAPORE The last time I saw Singapore there were wild monkeys swinging through the trees of the Botanic Gardens. Rickshaws filled the streets and junks and bumboats filled the Singapore River.

Now Singapore belongs to the Western world, a city like Hong Kong of international hotels and glorified skyscrapers, one of them 73 stories high that claims to be the tallest building in the world—a city of Chinese people but not of Confucian philosophers and Buddhist temples. Our hotel, the four-hundred-room Dynasty on Orchard Road, is Chinese in style with a pagoda on top but with huge crystal chandeliers in the lobby, a European cuisine, and what they call an American breakfast.

I was impressed by a sign downtown that said "Fortunes told by computer." How modern can you get?

The Raffles Hotel, soon to be closed for renovations to modernize it, takes one back a century ago to British colonial days. I'm glad I got here in time for the roast beef and Yorkshire pudding in the Elizabethan grill, and for the memories kept alive of Kipling who found the beds uncomfortable, Joseph Conrad who used to sit on the veranda, Somerset Maugham who wrote *The Moon and Sixpence* about Tahiti in a room upstairs. Raffles himself, Sir Thomas Stamford Raffles, came in 1819 and bought Singapore from the Sultan of Johore, changing it from a swampy fishing village to one of the world's busiest ports.

It's a garden city, clean and tree-shaded. An urbane Indian lady wearing gold chains showed us the sights: Little India, the jade collection in the National Museum, the view from Mount Faber. In Singapore, my guess is, time is best spent smelling the flowers and listening to the birds. Among the thousands of free-flying birds at the Jurong Bird Park were such sideshow oddities as the New Zealand kiwi that doesn't fly, a condor weighing eighteen pounds, a six-foot eagle taught to catch a mechanical rabbit.

A cruise in a Chinese junk took us round Singapore's spectacular harbor at sunset among the fifty-four islands, most of them uninhabited, two of them lost from sight during the rainy season. We had a Chinese buffet supper on board, and when we turned back the stars were out, in the harbor dozens of anchored ships glowed with courtesy lights, and the city of skyscrapers blazed like Manhattan.

BALI The flight to the island of Bali was five hours across the equator with a stop in Java to change planes. On arrival this afternoon at Denpasar, the capital, clogged with traffic, we hurried on by coach to Sanur Beach six miles beyond town and found lodging at the Hotel Bali Hyatt at the edge of the lagoon, whose slogan is "Life is yours at the Bali Hyatt."

Bali freely describes itself as an earthly paradise, the island of the gods, the jewel of Indonesia, heaven on earth, the navel of the world, and Shangri-La. I expected a sandy beach sloping to the sea with a chorus line of topless Balinese dancers. Instead Bali more nearly resembled the Hanging Gardens of Babylon, or an intensely cultivated tropical jungle, lush with exotic crimson flowers, tall ferns, coconut palms. And tourists.

From our balconied rooms, the sea was barely visible with all that foliage. But nobody could ask more of a hotel built on a former coconut plantation of two thousand trees, with five restaurants, open-air lounges, pools, and tropical gardens. Just don't drink the water.

Our guide Raka (whose card said "Raka Sudiarsa, Tour Guide, Flamboyant 2, Denpasar, Bali") was born in Bali and considers it the happy isle, the rainbow's end. Raka once made the mistake of moving to Java across Bali Strait to teach and work, but hastily returned to marry a hairdresser, live in a compound, and father four children.

The Balinese, he says, are very wise. They forget their birthdays and lose track of their age, hence of time itself. They are a deeply religious people of some 5,000 shrines in that small island, whose faith is a mixture of Buddhism, Hinduism, and worship of mountain gods. A cremation is a ceremonial to liberate the soul and appease the spirits of the dead who make a habit of returning to Bali, apparently their idea of paradise, and must be placated. They are a handsome people, a superstitious people, and probably a people with a high cholesterol level since their diet is mainly coconuts, from shredded coconut and coconut ice cream to food drenched and cooked in coconut oil.

Raka spent the day showing us, in outlying villages famous for their artistry, the goldsmiths of Celuk; the master woodcarvers of Mas who work in ebony, mahogany, and satinwood, and never repeat a pattern; the artists of Ubud, to whom Westerners have long been drawn, like the Mexican artist Covarrubias who lived there. At Ubud we stopped at a compound where the artists at work in the open pavilion were brothers. A compound in Bali consists of quarters for the generations of the same family, surrounded by a wall to keep out evil spirits. When a baby is born, the placenta is buried at the door of the compound to protect from harm the life of the child.

That night in Bali we sat in a theater to watch a group of Balinese dancers, agile as cats with arms waving, knees bent, legs turned outward in the movements of the trance dances. It looked highly accomplished but rather slick, a mannered performance staged especially to please the tourists. Bali had become a professional paradise.

JAVA Next day Raka was glad to be rid of us, for the reason it was his turn to entertain his relatives, numbering sixty, who gather once a month to exchange greetings and love. Half of our group was pleased to be left to lie on Bali's sunny beach. The rest, six with Virginia, jumped at the chance to cross Bali Strait for a look at Java. Raka arranged the trip, got us up at five Sunday morning, and took us to the airport, where my ticket was issued to Hellenoni Bevington—a name musical and Indonesian. In no time we were at the city of Jogjakarta, a lovely place dotted with temples. Instantly Madi appeared at our side to guide us—an old friend of Raka's, a Balinese and Hindu who has lived in Java the past eighteen years. Hindu or not, Madi defined Buddhism without prejudice. "Buddha said there is no god to be worshiped," he recited. "Buddha said all life is pain and suffering to be overcome by meditation." This, he added, was the "correct" way and led us on to Prambanan, the oldest Hindu temple in Jogjakarta.

The real reason we had come to Java was for the "wonder's wonder" that is Borobudur, the largest Buddhist temple in the world. It stands alone on a hill twenty-five miles west of the city, and from miles away looks like a brown pyramid mountain or a gigantic stupa.

The Borobudur was built early in the ninth century, no one knows why or who built it. For no discoverable reason, the temple was abandoned to jungle soon after completion and stayed deserted for centuries, left to time to whittle away its staircases and terraces. What purpose it was meant for or what the name means is in doubt since no record of it has been found. As a temple it has no altar, no relics of Buddha, only hundreds of statues and carved blocks of stone covering the outer walls to depict his life and enlightenment. Rediscovered after ten centuries, as late as 1973 the restoration was finally begun. It was completed in the 1980s.

In his book *Journey to Java*, Harold Nicolson took occasion to announce after his visit of six months that he totally rejected Buddhism as a way of life. In distrust of such "escape systems," he wrote, "the eight-fold path is not a path designed for my hurried footsteps. . . . I refuse to surrender my own personality to any doctrine." It was odd how empty his words sounded as I gazed at the magnificent Borobudur rising up like a "grand peut-être."

Our plane was late leaving Java tonight. While we waited at the airport, we were treated to a fashion show arranged by some enterprising concern, with several glamorous Javanese models parading about draped in rich Indonesian fabrics. In spite of this chic entertainment, we were glad to reach Bali in time for the farewell party we gave ourselves— friends and, as Virginia said, travelers to the end.

Then tomorrow came and we left Denpasar, flying home by way of Singapore, Hong Kong, and San Francisco. Twenty-some hours later when we reached Atlanta, blanketed in snow on a wintry night in March, I learned that a blizzard and ice storm had closed down the Raleigh-Durham Airport and completely paralyzed the city where I live and wanted to be.

Well, I told myself, the chances are.

As must be clear (and was clear to me), I liked best in East Asia being in the Buddhist countries, in Burma most of all with its shrines and pagodas—a poor backward country of infinite wealth from the past— in which a smiling, kind, gentle people live their faith in spite of the terrors around them and a future doubtful to predict. The anger and fear are constant there, but the peace is there too. I only hope that Zala in his great need has escaped to a new life with more freedom in it and the democracy he longed for.

Charles Kuralt put it mildly on the Sunday morning news: "This is a season of trouble."

At the end of April, 150,000 Chinese students in Beijing defied the government and marched fourteen hours in Tiananmen Square demanding democracy after forty years of Communist rule. A student banner echoed Patrick Henry: "Give me democracy or give me death."

(So the Burmese plead for democracy and die, the Chinese demand it and die, and nobody knows, precious though it is, exactly what to any of us it means.)

A few weeks later, thousands of Chinese soldiers put down the protest of a million people, firing machine guns into the crowds on the square and rolling over them with tanks in the bloodiest massacre in Communist history. "My government has gone insane," said a doctor as he walked among the dead. The People's Liberation Army was murdering the People. The new China had perished while Mao's Communism prevailed.

China's leader, Deng Xiaoping, credited with having restored China by his economic reforms since Mao's death, gave the order to use military force (Mao: "The Party must control the gun"). This criminal act of dictatorship was followed by the government's desperate lie that the unarmed students and others who were shot to death had never died at all; instead, rioters had attacked the soldiers with bombs and guns.

Deng, who hates democracy, has himself brought on another Cultural Revolution. This is the great leap backward in China.

The Eiffel Tower is one hundred years old, labeled a disgrace when built, though like other peaks it visibly unites heaven and earth. By now I've climbed so many peaks, pagodas, temples, shrines, stupas, mountains, monuments, walls, and towers—the Eiffel Tower, Leaning Tower of Pisa, Statue of Liberty, Empire State Building, Washington Monument, Pike's Peak—that I must be looking for something besides sunsets.

Mary Kingsley is one traveler with whom I wouldn't care to travel. She is too much like the daredevil Evel Knievel who jumps over Grand Canyon or the stunt men in the movies who dive from tall buildings and you wonder why they chose that line of work. Mary Kingsley's travels were hazardous in the extreme, such as going to live with cannibals and fighting off black leopards and crocodiles, especially for one so disaster prone with an exceptional talent for mishaps, close calls, narrow escapes, tight corners, and ill winds.

She was a spinster thirty-one years old when, in 1893, she made her first journey to West Africa. Up to then she had lived in seclusion in London, captive in a Victorian household where she cared for an invalid mother while her father roamed the world as a private doctor to aristocrats. When both parents suddenly died and her brother Charles set off without her for the Far East, Mary boarded a cargo boat out of Liverpool and, she wrote, "went down to West Africa to die."

Far from dying in the Africa she came to love, she thrived on hairbreadth rescues, bouts of malaria, threats by natives and beasts, invigorated by danger and ready for the next collision. In the eight years she had to spend between her parents' deaths and her own death, Mary Kingsley found her world and her calling among the black people she valued over missionaries and most of mankind.

She made a striking figure, tall, slender, quite beautiful, dressed wholly in black with long woolen skirts and heavy shawl, her pale blond hair drawn tightly back and topped with a small black hat. It's hard to picture her in that outfit tickling a hippopotamus with her umbrella, mingling with gorillas and naked savages, or up to her neck in the black slime of a mangrove swamp.

Her two books, *Travels in West Africa* and *West African Studies,* tell of the two journeys she made, omitting some of the worst adventures because she feared nobody would believe her. The first trip, lasting eleven months, took her from Sierra Leone and Freetown, a ramshackle British colony, to Liberia, on through unknown jungle country in the French Congo to the Cameroons and Calabar. As an excuse for traveling as a woman alone, she collected specimens from swamps and creeks for the London Zoo—strange fish and beetles, snakes and lizards. In 1894 on a second, longer journey to see Africans "at their wildest and worst," she went by canoe up the River Ogowé in the French Congo to territory inhabited by a cannibal tribe, the fearful Fangs. While preparing for this excursion, in Cameroon she fought a ten-foot leopard that had attacked a dog, at Calabar an eight-foot crocodile that got its forelegs over the end of her dugout canoe and tried to grab her. She encountered the Bubis who wore nothing but gaudy hats, a tribe so isolated they thought a white person was a fish washed up from the ocean.

At the Ogowé River that stretched for seven hundred miles, where only a canoe could shoot the foaming rapids, Mary assembled for the trip a crew of five Africans, naming them Gray Shirt, Singlet, Silent, Pagan, and Passenger, a hanger-on. It was considered a suicidal escapade by the many who made an effort to dissuade her. She carried with her trade goods, cloth and tobacco, for barter with the Fangs who lived in villages along the river. Hostile as they were, it was touch and go whether they would welcome her or eat her. The children were terrified and howled at the sight of her white face. Once she fell down a steep hillside through the roof of a Fang hut. Yet she managed to disarm a people whom she found brave, honest, free, however filthy their villages were with decomposed remains of crocodile and elephant they had consumed. They offered her smashed snails to eat, though human flesh was a preferred article of diet. In a Fang hut where she slept, she found hanging over her head a bag containing a shriveled hand, three big toes, four eyes, two ears. These she collected as specimens by scooping them into her hat.

Eventually, with her companions Mary left the canoe and pushed through dense forest, no longer fighting the rapids but crashing through jungle among snakes, centipedes, driver ants, huge spiders, and an occasional elephant. Walking ahead one day, she fell into a game pit fifteen feet deep lined with spikes, from which her heavy skirts saved her life. For several hours she struggled on, through a swamp up to her neck and over her head, emerging from the sickening stench and muck with a frill of leeches round her throat. At such times the interesting question occurred to her, "Why did I come to Africa?" The answer was Africa itself that compensated for every danger.

"I am no more a human being than a gust of wind is," Mary Kingsley wrote. "My people are mangrove swamps, rivers, and the sea." "I have never been in love," she confided in a letter to a friend, "nor has anyone ever been in love with me."

When the Boer War began in 1899, back in England Mary volunteered as a nurse, intending to return to West Africa as soon as she could. At Capetown she was sent to a foul camp to care for Boer prisoners of war. Two months later she came down with enteric fever and died. She was buried at sea off the Cape of Good Hope, and even there her skirts ballooned and she refused to go under.

Poetry, they say, is making a comeback. But I don't know. Perhaps it had better stay under wraps a while longer, though to mark its recovery Jimmy Stewart and Art Garfunkel come singing, both appearing on "Good Morning, America." Garfunkel recited his poems about love (his girl dumped him) and odes to Mother Nature. Jimmy Stewart, aged eighty-two, read in a quavering voice from his new book, *Jimmy Stewart and His Poems,* a best-seller. On the Johnny Carson show Jimmy said, "It took me twenty years to write these four poems," of which these lines from "The Aberdares!" refer, I guess, to the Aberdare Mountains in Kenya at the equator:

> The North Pole's rather chilly,
> Those who've been there all will tell.
> There's lots of snow and lots of ice
> And lots of wind as well.

This is called a new trend for retired actors.

Bill Moyers in his friendly quest for culture recently introduced six hours of readings by poets on PBS, which he justified by saying "There have been no known American poets since the death of Frost." Let's see, Eliot stayed alive till 1965, Sandburg till 1967, Ezra Pound and Marianne Moore 1972, Robert Lowell 1977, Robert Penn Warren 1989. No matter, the poets Moyers chose left the claim valid. Asked once what modern poets were up to, Philip Larkin said "Solving emptiness."

I was moved to cautious hope when I read in the *Times Literary Supplement* that the American Institute of Arts and Letters has presented a new award this year, one for light verse. "Light verse," said the *TLS,* "generally regarded as the poor sister of poetry was given a firm pat on the head." X. J. Kennedy, a sober poet who has written a book of nonsense rhymes, was the recipient of the award, notably for his epigram "To Someone Who Insisted I Look Up Someone,"

> I rang them up while touring Timbucktoo,
> Those bosom chums to whom you're known as "Who?"

That's not a pat on the head. It's a kick in the pants.

Quite a year, 1989. We had a parade of natural disasters unmatched from coast to coast, from Hurricane Hugo that tore into the Carolinas to the San Francisco earthquake that in fifteen seconds in October collapsed the Bay Bridge, hurled a freeway apart, capsized hotels, destroyed homes, made cracks in the earth up to seventeen feet. And this wasn't even the Big One, which is still to come.

In fulfilling his campaign promises of a year ago, George Bush was out to lunch—the President of Prudence, we said, a cautious man averse to taking risks. "I don't want to do anything dumb," he said, and went on talking about morality and "the vision thing," and honoring the flag, while we wondered about nuclear waste, the homeless in the streets, crime, drugs, a failing environment, abortion, AIDS, and the deficit. Cocaine and crack were available to schoolchildren. People couldn't die fast enough from drunk driving and airplane crashes. The hostages stayed captive. Meanwhile, we lowered our cholesterol, acquired more word processors and microwave ovens, played Trivial Pursuit, and gave up sex and feminism.

Samuel Beckett died in December, not the spokesman to define the present state of being but an interested commentator. "Our existence is hopeless," said Beckett. "We must invent a world in which to survive." Beckett found this world an absurd place and man not only absurd but trivial, a loser. In *Waiting for Godot,* the two tramps wait for deliverance but in vain; Godot will never come.

> Vladimir: "At least the waiting passed the time."
> Estragon: "It would have passed in any case."

Then came the good news—the revolution of 1989 with the sudden upheaval in Eastern Europe, where the people, sick of dictators and police states, demanded instead freedom and democracy. Poland was first to move, electing on August 19 a non-Communist government. Hungary followed, declaring itself no longer a People's Republic but an independent state. With a bang heard round the world the Berlin Wall collapsed when East Berlin opened its borders and East Berliners, imprisoned since 1961, poured into that part of the city it had been death to enter. By the thousand happy people danced on the Wall, climbed over it, used pickaxes to tear off chunks, attempting to hurl from sight the hated thing. An incredible event, one few believed would happen, was happening—the end of the Wall, end of the Iron Curtain.

"The revolution is proceeding much quicker than we expected," said a Czech citizen as a democratic form of government took over in Czechoslovakia. Bulgaria had already defied the absolute rule of the Party. Romania held out under a dictator who refused reform till in the bloodiest revolt of all Ceausescu was murdered with his wife. Little Albania alone was not heard from.

As the wind changed, 1989 brought to an end not a decade but an era of history. At the Malta Conference on December 4, Gorbachev and Bush declared a bright future ahead with a forty-five-year Cold War over, a World War III unlikely, a period of peace beginning. Loud and clear it came: Communism was no longer in danger of dominating the planet, dictators had gone out of style. Gorbachev, his vision intact, was named the Man of the Decade, who had brought us this far toward world stability even as he stoutly proclaimed, "I am a Communist, a convinced Communist. For some that may be a fantasy. But for me it is my main goal." He had encouraged reforms that could result in the abolition of his party and of himself, had called on the pope and promised religious freedom in Russia, had given his people a new look at their oppressors. By now, said the *New York Times,* Reagan seemed "curiously passé." He began the decade but Gorbachev ended it.

Yet the bad news still claimed major victories for the 1980s. As became increasingly true, the saddest word for our time—this year, this decade, this planet—was greed, the Age of Greed, our own national plague of ME-ism in the 1970s carried to the extreme of avarice and self-concern. "If anything," said the *Times*, "Americans in the 80's devoted themselves more singlemindedly than ever to self-enrichment and self-gratification." Worldwide symbols of greed appeared from Imelda Marcos's 2,700 pairs of shoes stored in her palace to Evangelists Jim and Tammy Fay Bakker's four Mercedes-Benzes, two Rolls-Royces, and air-conditioned doghouse; from hotelkeeper Leona Helmsley's attempt to prove that only the poor pay taxes to Ken Auletta's recent book *Greed and Glory on Wall Street*. The Berlin Wall itself was fair game at Christmas. A man offered $15 million for it; a company in St. Louis got hold of concrete slabs to chop up and package in gift boxes as stocking stuffers.

Six months after the massacre at Tiananmen Square, President Bush made friendly overtures to Communist China to restore former relations, winning a happy smile from Deng Xiaoping. To give him credit, on December 20 Bush took a great risk by sending 13,000 combat troops into Panama to bring Noriega—thug, criminal, dictator—to justice.

To improve further our chances in the 1990s, Bush promised to plant a billion trees in America next year and gave the impression he would plant them himself. I hope one of them is a bo tree. That is, if he wants to save the world.

Peace.

Helen Bevington has published many books, including *Doctor Johnson's Waterfall, Nineteen Million Elephants, A Change of Sky, When Found, Make A Verse Of, Charley Smith's Girl, A Book and a Love Affair, The House Was Quiet and the World Was Calm, Beautiful Lofty People, Along Came the Witch,* and *The Journey Is Everything.* She has written regularly for the *New York Times Book Review,* has published light verse in the *New Yorker,* and has contributed to *Atlantic Monthly* and *American Scholar,* among other periodicals. For many years she taught at Duke University, as did her late husband, Merle. She is now Professor Emeritus of English at Duke.

Library of Congress Cataloging-in-Publication Data
Bevington, Helen Smith
The world and the bo tree / Helen Bevington.
ISBN 0-8223-1153-4. — ISBN 0-8223-1165-8 (pbk.)
1. Bevington, Helen Smith—Biography. 2. Authors,
American—20th century—Biography. I. Title.
PS3503.E924Z477 1991
811'.54—dc20
[B]   91-7608 CIP